SSS: Social Skill Strategies (Book A)

A CURRICULUM FOR ADOLESCENTS

by

Nancy Gajewski

Patty Mayo

THINKING PUBLICATIONS® Eau Claire, WI

A Division of McKinley Companies, Inc.

01   00   99   98   11   10   9   8

ISBN 0-930599-51-9

Illustrations: Brad Krause and Linda Lofgren
Cover: James Christoffersen
Cover Design: Robert T. Baker

Printed in the United States of America

**THINKING
PUBLICATIONS**
A Division of McKinley Companies, Inc.

424 Galloway Street
Eau Claire, WI 54703
(800) 225-GROW • FAX (800) 828-8885
E-mail: custserv@ThinkingPublications.com
www.ThinkingPublications.com

DEDICATION

To our parents Gerald and Henrietta Wildman
and Everett and Barbara White for their love and
guidance, and to our husbands Luke and Mike
for their encouragement and support

ACKNOWLEDGEMENTS

The authors would like to express their appreciation to all those who have helped in the completion of this curriculum. We thank Barb Bialzik, Wendy Drew, Suzanne Gallagher, Arlene Craker, Mary Knapstein, and Kathie Martino for generously devoting their time in field testing units from **SSS** with their students, and Al Wheeler for his critique of Chapter Two. A very special thank you to Vicki Lord Larson, Sue Gruber, Walter Harris, Polly Hirn, Pattii Waldo, and Jill Wheeler for their many, many hours in reviewing **SSS** in its entirety. An additional thank you to Pattii Waldo, who allowed some of the activity pages she created to be included in **SSS**. We are grateful to Nancy McKinley for her technical and editorial advice and for making it possible for us to share this curriculum with you. Finally, we thank our husbands, Luke Gajewski and Mike Mayo, for their encouragement, support, and patience.

PREFACE

Social skill competence is critical for a person to function productively in the home, school, and community. Yet, many of the students in our educational systems, both in and out of special education programs, remain socially incompetent. The purpose of **SSS: Social Skill Strategies** is to provide a comprehensive curriculum which can be used with pre-adolescents and adolescents (grades 5-12). Adults with social skill deficits might also benefit from specific **SSS** activities if the activities are carefully chosen by professionals.

Special education teachers, speech-language clinicians, guidance counselors, school psychologists, reading specialists, and alternative or regular education teachers will find **SSS** to be an invaluable source for promoting social communication skill gains with their students.

Chapter One reviews the current literature in social skill training. Chapter Two describes 1) how to identify students with social skill needs; 2) how to structure a social skills class; 3) how to teach a social skill unit using a seven-step approach; and 4) how to promote transfer and generalization of social skills taught. The major portion of **SSS** offers social skill units which include several activity pages to be used with students to improve their comprehension and use of each social skill. The activity pages have been written at a third grade reading level according to the Fry (1977) readability formula and at a fifth grade reading level according to the Dale-Chall (1948) readability formula.

We feel that the social skills addressed within this program are universal across cultural and socio-economic groups, with the exception of a few skills (e.g., the rules for eye contact and proximity are different in the Oriental and Italian cultures.) The user of this curriculum, however, may choose to adapt some of the specific names or situations described within the units, to meet the needs of the students being taught.

This curriculum is a framework and does not take the place of a teacher's individual creativity or need for flexibility. We sincerely hope you find **SSS: Social Skill Strategies** to be a useful resource for improving the social communication skills within your students.

Nancy Gajewski
Teacher of the Emotionally Disturbed
D.C. Everest Jr. High School

Patty Mayo
Speech-Language Clinician
D.C. Everest Jr. High School

TABLE OF CONTENTS

PEER INTERACTION SKILLS (BOOK B)

Skill B-1.   Reputations

Skill B-2.   Starting A Friendship

Skill B-3.   Maintaining A Friendship

Skill B-4.   Giving Emotional Support

Skill B-5.   Giving Advice

Skill B-6.   Ignoring

Skill B-7.   Responding To Teasing

Skill B-8.   Peer Pressure

Skill B-9.   Joining In

Skill B-10.   Being Left Out

Skill B-11.   Tattling

MANAGEMENT SKILLS (BOOK B)

Skill B-12.   Being Assertive

Skill B-13.   Making A Complaint

Skill B-14.   Receiving A Complaint

Skill B-15.   Giving Constructive Criticism

Skill B-16.   Accepting Constructive Criticism

Skill B-17.   Making An Accusation

Skill B-18.   Dealing With A False Accusation

Skill B-19.   Compromising/Negotiating

Skill B-20.   Accepting Consequences

EMOTIONAL EXPRESSION SKILLS (BOOK B)

Skill B-21.   Expressing Feelings

Skill B-22.   Dealing With Anger

Skill B-23.   Dealing With Embarrassment

Skill B-24.   Coping With Fear

Skill B-25.   Dealing With Humor

Skill B-26.   Dealing With Failure

Skill B-27.   Expressing Affection

Skill B-28.   Dealing With Disappointment

Skill B-29.   Understanding The Feelings Of Others

Chapter One

A RESEARCH FOUNDATION

SOCIAL COMMUNICATION SKILLS: THE NEW WAVE

During the past decade, awareness of the need for teaching social skills to exceptional children has intensified. This heightened concern about the social competence of individuals with behavioral/emotional disturbances, learning disabilities, mental retardation, and speech/language disorders results from a plethora of research documenting the limited acceptance of handicapped students by their non-handicapped peers (Perlmutter, Crocker, Cordray, and Garstecki, 1983; Schloss, Schloss, Wood, and Kiehl, 1986; Schumaker and Hazel, 1984a).

Individuals With Emotional Disturbances/Behavioral Disorders

Schloss et al. (1986) state that "The main distinguishing characteristic of behaviorally disordered persons is deficits in social skill performance" (p. 1). Kauffman (1977) characterizes behaviorally disordered children as ". . . those who chronically and markedly respond to their environment in socially unacceptable and/or personally unsatisfying ways" (p. 23). Numerous studies have documented the correlation between social skill deficits and problems later in life: Juvenile delinquency (Roff, Sells, and Golden, 1972), psychiatric hospitalization (Goldsmith and McFall, 1975), bad conduct discharges from the military (Roff, 1961), and other problems have been associated with social skill deficits. Thus, it is essential for individuals with emotional/behavioral disorders to receive social skill instruction and to improve their social competence if they are to function adequately in society.

Individuals With Learning Disabilities

In an extensive review of research in the area of learning disabilities, Schumaker and Hazel (1984a) summarized empirical evidence indicating that learning disabled students have numerous problems with social skills. For example, learning disabled children are less liked than their non-learning disabled peers (Perlmutter et al., 1983), they perform similarly to juvenile delinquents on a role play test of social skills (Schumaker, Hazel, Sherman, and Sheldon, 1982), they participate with the lowest frequency among groups of low participators in school activities (Deshler and Schumaker, 1983), and their social problems continue into adulthood (Vetter, 1983). According to Schumaker and Hazel (1984b), the following weaknesses in interpersonal interactions were found in learning disabled children: 1) They tend to choose less socially acceptable behaviors in different situations; 2) They are inept at predicting consequences for behaviors; 3) They misunderstand different social cues; 4) They are less likely to adapt their behavior to meet the needs of their listener; 5) They exhibit a lower occurrence of appropriate verbal/nonverbal skills than their non-handicapped peers, and 6) They perform certain inappropriate skills at a significantly higher level of occurrence. Traditionally, learning disability programs have addressed academic weaknesses such as reading and spelling; however, weaknesses in social communication skill competence should also be remediated.

Individuals With Mental Retardation

Greenspan and Shoultz (1981) report that mentally retarded workers are significantly more likely to be terminated from employment for social skill deficits than for non-social reasons. If handicapped individuals are unable to compensate for their academic deficits through social competence, they are more likely to be underemployed and less likely to be satisfied than their non-handicapped peers (White, Schumaker, Warner, Alley, and Deshler, 1980). A comprehensive vocational training program for mentally retarded individuals must include a social communication skills component.

Individuals With Speech/Language Disorders

According to Wiig (1982a), social skill development is delayed in many exceptional students and has been found to develop as late as adolescence. Shames and Wiig (1982) document a need for social skill instruction with adolescents who have language disorders, developmental delays, severe hearing impairments, or who have been raised in a non-English speaking culture. Wiig (1982a) indicates additional needs for adults with acquired aphasia, for congenitally blind adolescents, and for shy children in regular classrooms. It is evident that social communication skills should be assessed and remediated within students who have speech/language disorders.

SOCIAL COMMUNICATION SKILLS: HOW ARE THESE SKILLS DEFINED?

Despite the recent upsurge in interest to improve social skills, confusion exists because of a lack of consensus among researchers regarding the specificity of definitions for social skills (Gresham, 1981a; Schumaker and Hazel, 1984a). According to Schloss et al. (1986), "Two approaches to the conceptualization of social skills are present in current literature. The first provides a general reference to the broad domain of social adjustment. The second identifies discrete behaviors recognized as contributing to social adjustment" (p. 2). Foster and Ritchey (1979) propose that social skills may be considered a part of a broader construct known as social competence. Hazel, Sherman, Schumaker, and Sheldon (1985) believe that social competence may be seen as a composite of skills:

1. Determining which social behaviors are appropriate in situations.
2. Determining which verbal and nonverbal social skills are appropriate.
3. Performing social skills fluently and in correct combinations.
4. Correctly perceiving verbal and nonverbal cues from another person(s).
5. Flexibly adjusting to feedback from another person(s).

The authors of this resource support the view proposed by Hazel et al. (1985), that being a socially appropriate individual requires more than correct execution of isolated social skills.

SOCIAL COMMUNICATION SKILLS: WHAT TYPES OF DEFICITS EXIST?

Gresham (1981b) has conceptualized social skill deficits along three dimensions: skill deficits, performance deficits, and self-control deficits. A **skill deficit** would indicate that the person has not acquired the necessary social skills (e.g., a child who accepts a compliment poorly because he was never taught to say "thank you"). This type of deficit would also include people with language disorders who have word-finding difficulties, or problems sequencing what they want to say.

A ***performance deficit*** describes the person who has the skills but does not perform them because of response-inhibiting anxiety or low motivation. For example, learning disabled individuals' feelings of incompetence might cause them not to use social skills even though the skills are present in their repertoires (Pearl, Donahue, and Bryan, 1983).

A ***self-control deficit*** labels the person who lacks adequate behavior controls to inhibit impulsive, disruptive, or aggressive social behavior (e.g., a child may possess the social skill of negotiating and may even use the skill at various times; however, his lack of self-control may sometimes get in the way of his performance of the skill). Schumaker and Hazel (1984a) suggest that any single child's deficits may be a combination of the three deficits (e.g., the absence of eye contact may represent a performance deficit, while the same child's inability to start a conversation may represent a skill deficit). Social skill instruction must address each of the three deficit types when they exist.

SOCIAL COMMUNICATION SKILLS: ASSESSMENT

Handicapped students are a heterogeneous group with respect to their social skill abilities, and an assessment system is needed to determine the individual needs for each student. Unfortunately, few acceptable assessment procedures have been developed (Arkowitz, 1981).

Gresham (1982) shares the concern that few, if any, well-standardized instruments have been developed to assess the social skill competence of handicapped children. He states that, "Generally speaking, advancements in the assessment of social skills have not kept pace with the advancements in social skill training techniques" (p. 128). Gresham also maintains that our lack of assessment procedures creates problems for our understanding of the "nature" of social skills, for our planning, and for our evaluation of training success (Gresham, 1981a).

Arkowitz (1981) suggests the following criteria for adequately measuring social skills:

1. Measure a person's behaviors as well as the consequences of those behaviors.
2. Identify overt behaviors and cognitive behaviors.
3. Look at quality and quantity of behaviors.
4. Determine if social skills are a part of the person's repertoire.
5. Look at the use of social skills in situations of interest.

Gresham (1981b) reminds us that a social skills assessment device should be psychometrically acceptable (i.e., have good reliability and validity, be sensitive to changes in the student, and give specific diagnostic information for instructional programming). Schumaker and Hazel (1984a) assert that in order to be useful to educators, a social skills assessment device should be quick and easy to administer and not require additional resources. While a number of social skill assessment devices exist (Goldstein, Sprafkin, Gershaw, and Klein, 1980; Jackson, Jackson, and Monroe, 1983; Wiig, 1982a; Wiig, 1982b), no single device meets all of the above criteria.

Social skill assessment devices can be categorized into six general types: 1) Naturalistic behavioral observation; 2) Analogue observation, which involves direct observation in contrived rather than naturalistic settings; 3) Behavioral rating scales; 4) Behavioral checklists; 5) Sociometric devices, which involve peer assessment; and 6) Assessments using hypothetical situations (Gresham, 1981b; Schumaker and Hazel, 1984a). After reviewing the advantages and disadvantages of the aforementioned assessment types, Schumaker and Hazel (1984a) recommend the use of behavioral rating scales for screening older individuals. They also state that "Behavioral checklists seem to be the most practical instruments for teachers to use for pinpointing target behaviors; preferably, they should be used in conjunction with contrived situations in the natural environment" (p. 429). **SSS: Social Skill Strategies** provides behavioral rating scales and checklists for the social skills taught within the curriculum. (See Appendices A, B, C, and D.)

SOCIAL COMMUNICATION SKILLS: HOW TO TEACH THESE SKILLS

Several procedures have been used to improve social skill competence, but procedures should be chosen according to which type of deficit the individual is thought to exhibit. For a skill deficit, procedures should focus on teaching the student how to perform different skills (Schumaker and Hazel, 1984b). Stephens (1978) presents evidence that for skill deficits, modeling and coaching are best used to teach new skills. Schumaker and Hazel (1984b) advocate the use of description, modeling, rehearsal, and feedback for teaching new skills.

Performance deficits are best remediated through manipulation of antecedents or consequences of behaviors (Gresham, 1981b). Schumaker and Hazel (1984b) recommend that for a performance deficit, procedures should focus on motivating individuals to increase their use of appropriate social skills.

For self-control deficits, procedures should focus on teaching strategies that decrease the use of inappropriate behaviors and that promote the use of more appropriate behaviors. Reports show that self-control deficits have been remediated through a variety of cognitive behavior modification techniques such as self-control training, self instruction, verbal mediation, relaxation, and self reinforcement (O'Leary and Dubey, 1979). **SSS: Social Skill Strategies** includes techniques and activities appropriate for the three social skill deficit types.

In addition, the educator should promote social skill acquisition and use through group interaction rather than through teacher-directed activities. The use of cooperative learning techniques is an effective way to encourage group interaction. When educators plan a lesson, they choose between structuring that lesson in these ways: 1) A competitive manner in which students participate in an activity to determine who is best; 2) An individual manner where students work alone and at their own pace, or 3) A cooperative manner where small groups of individuals work together to achieve an academic goal. Each of these three techniques has merit. Unfortunately, our current educational system utilizes competitive and individual methods the vast majority of the time.

The theory of cooperative learning is not new; however, it has been revived in the 1970s and 1980s by professionals such as David Johnson and Roger Johnson (1984), Robert Slavin (1974), and Elliot Aronson (1978). Currently, the research is filled with information about the academic and social benefits of cooperative learning. According to Johnson and Johnson (1986), there is ". . . a considerable difference between putting students physically into groups (merely rearranging desks) and structuring groups for cooperative learning (promoting positive interdependence and collaborative skills)" (p. 31). In order for a group experience to be truly cooperative, Johnson, Johnson, Holubec, and Roy (1984) state that the experience must incorporate the following four basic elements:

1) Positive Interdependence - Students must be dependent upon one another for task completion.

2) Face-to-Face Interaction - There must be verbal exchange among students.

3) Individual Accountability - Each student must be held accountable for learning the material so students can provide support and assistance to each other.

4) Appropriate Use of Interpersonal and Small Group Skills - Students must be taught the social skills needed for cooperative learning, and teachers must observe the groups to see that the skills are being used.

Johnson and Johnson (1984) outline the differences between cooperative learning groups and traditional learning groups in the following way:

Cooperative Learning Groups	Traditional Learning Groups
Positive interdependence	No interdependence
Individual accountability	No individual accountability
Heterogeneous	Homogeneous
Shared leadership	One appointed leader
Shared responsibility for each other	Responsibility only for self
Task and maintenance emphasized	Only task emphasized
Social skills directly taught	Social skills assumed and ignored
Teacher observes and intervenes	Teacher ignores group functioning
Groups process their effectiveness	No group processing

Reprinted with permission

Bohlmeyer and Burke (1987) cite the following benefits of cooperative learning: improved inter-personal relationships, improved cross-ethnic relationships, improved cross-sex relationships, increased self-esteem, improved role-taking abilities, and greater achievement. An effective social skills curriculum should incorporate cooperative learning techniques.

Current literature also addresses the importance of using "whole brain" learning strategies. Research indicates that both sides of the brain have different functions (Clark, 1986; Hatcher, 1983; McCarthy, 1983). The left brain is more responsible for linear, sequential, analytic, rational thinking while the right brain is more metaphoric, spatial, and holistic in nature (Clark, 1986; Gorovitz, 1982). It is important to be aware of the differences between the left and right brain and the way in which each person learns best. However, current research emphasizes the importance of teaching students to use both sides of the brain rather than relying solely on the dominant side. Learners who use both sides of the brain do best academically and socially (Webb, 1983) **SSS: Social Skill Strategies** provides a variety of "whole brain" learning activities.

SOCIAL COMMUNICATION SKILLS: GETTING THESE SKILLS TO TRANSFER AND GENERALIZE

Currently, discussion on social skills training is focused on whether the skills learned in the classroom are transferring to other settings and if the social skills are maintained over time. Previously, the assumption was made that use of skills would transfer to different settings automatically. An increasing body of research disproves this assumption (Stokes and Baer, 1977; Wahler, Berland, and Coe, 1979; Wehman, Abramson, and Norman, 1977). Stokes and Baer (1977) describe those training efforts which do not specifically plan for generalization as the "train and hope" type. Research on skill generalization (particularly in the area of social skill instruction) is limited.

"A behavioral change is generalized when it proves durable over time, when it appears in a wide variety of possible environments, or when it spreads to a wide variety of related behaviors" (Baer, Wolf, and Risley, 1968, p. 96). Educators have not developed a ". . . systematic, data-based technology for promoting transfer across . . . settings" (Anderson-Inman, 1986, p. 563).

Numerous variables have been identified that increase the probability that transfer will occur. Goldstein et al. (1980) describe the following:

1. Use of general principles which apply to training and real-life settings.
2. Overlearning (the higher the degree of original learning, the greater the probability for transfer).
3. Identical elements (the greater the number of identical elements in both the training and application settings, the greater the chance for transfer).

Current social skill research has gone beyond the fundamentals of teaching social skills and is emphasizing procedures for skill transfer. Teaching social skills is a relatively simple task. The challenge involves teaching the skills in a manner that will encourage students to use them in other settings. Teaching for transfer needs to be purposefully planned (Mayo and Gajewski, 1987). Schumaker and Hazel (1984b) urge that instructional strategies should enable instructors to teach skills and promote generalization and maintenance of those skills in natural settings. Walker (1979) summarized the problem in the following way: "The rule to remember is what you teach is what you get and where you teach it is where you get it" (p. 298).

Schumaker and Hazel (1984a) reported several studies which indicated that instructional procedures such as modeling, rehearsal, and feedback are not sufficient for producing generalized use of newly learned social skills. They conclude: 1) Criterion performance in role playing does not indicate how a child will do in the natural environment; 2) The final measure of the success of a social skill program must be taken in the natural environment, and 3) Students need generalization training in addition to traditional social skill instruction to promote transfer of skills. In addition, Adelman and Taylor (1982) propose that the lack of generalization of social skills may be caused by a lack of emphasis in social skill programs on the motivational aspect of social skill usage.

Self-regulated learning is a promising technique for promoting the transfer of social skills. Self-regulated learning encourages individuals to manage their cognitive abilities and motivational level, and thus attempt to improve their learning (Paris and Oka, 1986). A similar term, *metacognition,* is defined as having the student decide which strategy to use, decide when to use it, and finally, to monitor how effective the strategy was. For example, a student uses metacognition when he independently decides that apologizing is the appropriate skill to use, decides on the best time to make the apology, carries out his plan, and evaluates whether or not he made the apology correctly. Schumaker and Hazel (1984b) state that students must be prepared for problems that will arise, even when the student is using the social skill appropriately. Students must understand that there are people they will deal with who may be unreasonable because they are not socially skilled and, therefore, the students must be able to identify situations when the use of various skills is not feasible (e.g., when to negotiate and when it's useless to negotiate).

One curricular program which incorporates the idea of self-regulated learning in conjunction with social skill instruction is the **Making Better Choices Program** (Harris, 1984). The program includes two components for social skills instruction: 1) A metacognitive section, and 2) A social skill instruction section. In the first section, Harris teaches "cognitive planning strategies" which the students use for each social skill. Cognitive planning strategies teach students to go beyond simple usage of social skills. The strategies help students: 1) To control impulsiveness so they can make intelligent choices about social skills; 2) To decide on a plan (the skill steps); 3) To put the plan into action, and 4) To evaluate the results of using the social skill.

When teaching metacognitive strategies to students, it is essential that educators initially model the cognitive planning strategies for their students. "A characteristic of successful metacognition strategy instruction is the gradual transfer of control of the strategy from the teacher to the students" (Palincsar, 1986, pg. 122). In addition, the number of skill steps should be kept to a minimum and written as simply as possible. In a recent study, Gelzheiser, Shepherd, and Wozniak (1986) report that ". . . students, who have fewer rules (skill steps) to learn are better able to attain proficiency and to generalize" (pg. 127). **SSS: Social Skill Strategies** provides a list of specific transfer/generalization ideas (refer to page 21). In addition, this program incorporates ideas for transfer in every unit.

SOCIAL COMMUNICATION SKILLS: SUMMARY

Research documents a need for social skill education. Exceptional education professionals should be concerned with the social competence of the individuals they serve. Not only do many individuals with learning disabilities, mental retardation, behavioral/emotional disturbances, and speech/language disorders demonstrate social skill incompetence, but they can possess this weakness for different reasons. They may have skill deficits, performance deficits, and/or self-control deficits. A comprehensive social skills curriculum should be tailored for students with any or all of these three deficit types. Although a standardized social skill assessment device is long overdue, research indicates that the use of behavioral rating scales is currently the most effective for older students. Educators should work towards identifying which students need instruction and the priority skills for each student identified. Research documents acquisition of social skills after direct instruction, but it does not document generalization of those skills. Therefore, a professional interested in improving a student's social competence must directly plan for the transfer and generalization of each social skill taught. An effective way to do this is by pairing cognitive strategy training with social skill instruction so that students are able 1) To control impulsiveness so they can make intelligent choices about social skills; 2) To decide on a plan; 3) To execute the plan, and 4) To evaluate results of using the social skill.

SSS: Social Skill Strategies provides a seven-step approach for improving social communication skills that will be described in the next chapter. The seven-step approach incorporates the various techniques which were discussed within this chapter.

Chapter Two

RESOURCE GUIDELINES AND PROCEDURES

SSS: SOMETHING FOR EVERYBODY

The **SSS: Social Skill Strategies** program has been divided into two books: Book A and Book B include the same beginning chapters and the same appendices, but they include different social skill units. Book A includes social skill units A-1 to A-34 and Book B includes the social skill units B-1 to B-29. The titles of each unit are listed in the Table of Contents. The skills have been put into the five categories of: Introductory Skills (Book A), General Interaction Skills (Book A), Peer Interaction Skills (Book B), Management Skills (Book B), and Emotional Expression Skills (Book B). The books provide curriculum for a two-year social skills course when taught daily for a forty-five minute period.

SSS: Social Skill Strategies includes materials and a description of how to identify which students have social communication skill deficits and, therefore, need social skill instruction. The books explain the procedure for assessing and developing a hierarchical list of the social skills in need of instruction. This resource describes the procedure for establishing a social skills course, and a format for structuring a class period. It supplies a comprehensive description of a seven-step procedure for teaching each of the social communication skill units. This program provides suggestions for promoting transfer and generalization of the social skills mastered in a classroom situation.

Each unit in **SSS: Social Skill Strategies** focuses on a different social skill and includes structured activities which teach students about the skill and provide opportunities for practice. The number of activity pages within each unit varies depending on the complexity of the specific social skill. The units incorporate a wide variety of instructional techniques (e.g., group discussion, games, role plays, visualizations, cartoons, group projects, and guided practice pages).

Some of the activity pages within units are objective in nature; however, an answer key has *not* been generated. Numerous correct responses exist for many of the objective items and an answer key might stymie creative thought and discussion. Educators using this resource should focus on a student's rationales for answers as much as they do on the student's responses. As long as the student has a logical justification for a given response, it should be accepted as correct.

SSS: Social Skill Strategies is appropriate for students in grades five through twelve. Professionals (e.g., educators, counselors, psychologists) involved with special education students will find this resource invaluable for providing social skill instruction. In addition, **SSS** can be used when dealing with regular education students who may also be experiencing social skill difficulties. This resource includes materials and ideas that will be effective for teaching students with social skill deficits, performance deficits, and self-control deficits as described on pages 2-3 of Chapter One.

SSS contains letters which can be sent to parents and professionals who have contact with the students receiving social skill instruction (See Appendix E). The letters explain the rationale for teaching social skills and give suggestions to parents and professionals for promoting transfer of appropriate social skill use.

SSS: IDENTIFYING STUDENTS WITH SOCIAL SKILL DEFICITS

Schumaker and Hazel (1984a) advocate the use of behavioral rating scales and checklists for identifying older individuals with social skill deficits and for pinpointing target behaviors for those who do demonstrate weaknesses. Kazdin and Matson (1981) suggest using the strategy of subjective evaluation by obtaining information and feedback from "informed others" to establish training targets. Textbooks for educators emphasize the need for input from clients and their significant others as to which social skills to address. However, client interviews, self-monitoring, and self-ratings are seldom employed to identify training priorities (Schloss et al., 1986). The **SSS** program includes two rating scales: one which is a self-rating scale and one which is to be completed by significant others. The **SSS** program also advocates the use of client interviews, and self-monitoring by students.

Rating Scale - Adult Form

SSS: Social Skill Strategies provides a social communication skills rating scale to be completed by a parent, case manager, and any other adult who has observed the student's use of social skills in a natural setting (See Appendix A). The estimated readability for this rating scale is seventh grade, according to the Fry Readability Scale (Fry, 1977). The Social Communication Skills Rating Scale (Adult Form) asks the adult to rate the student on each of the 63 social skills contained in **SSS** based on his/her observation of the student. Each social skill is described on the rating scale to make it as explicit as possible. The rating scale has been broken into the five categories of: Introductory Skills, General Interaction Skills, Peer Interaction Skills, Management Skills, and Emotional Expression Skills. The adult may complete the entire rating scale or only certain sections, depending on the information desired. Use of this rating scale may be more effective if a knowledgeable educator is present when the adult completes it to explain items the adult does not understand.

Rating Scale - Summary Form

When the rating scales have been completed and returned to the educator, the scores may be compiled on the Student Social Skill Summary Form, which is partially shown below and is included in Appendix B.

STUDENT SOCIAL SKILL SUMMARY FORM

STUDENT'S NAME:	Identified as Being Problematic	Demonstrated Comprehension of Skill in Class	Demonstrated Correct Use of Skill in Class	Reported/Observed Use of Skill Outside of Class	GRADE:_____ YEAR: _____	Identified as Being Problematic	Demonstrated Comprehension of Skill in Class	Demonstrated Correct Use of Skill in Class	Reported/Observed Use of Skill Outside of Class
A-1. Eye Contact					B-1. Reputation				
A-2. Manners					B-2. Starting A Friendship				
A-3. Volume					B-3. Maintaining a Friendship				
A-4. Time And Place					B-4. Giving Emotional Support				
A-5. Tone Of Voice					B-5. Giving Advice				
A-6. Getting To The Point					B-6. Ignoring				
A-7. Staying On Topic And Switching Topics					B-7. Responding To Teasing				

This summary form lists all of the 63 social skills rated, with a place to indicate which skills were rated as being problematic. There are different ways for educators to record the data. One alternative is to place a checkmark next to the social skills which were rated as being either a *one* (never) or a *two* (seldom) and not to mark anything next to the social skills which were rated as being either a *three* (sometimes), a *four* (often), or a *five* (always). Another alternative is to place a checkmark next to only those rated as *one, two,* or *three.* A third alternative would be to write down the number assigned by the adult, instead of using a checkmark. The authors suggest using this form in a way that works best for the educator.

There are several possible uses of the Student Social Skill Summary Form once it has been completed. One use is for the student to include a copy of it in his journal so the student has an overview of the 63 social skills and a listing of those skills which are problematic for him (See *SSS:* JOURNAL DESCRIPTION, page 15). Another use is for a copy of it to be included with the student's IEP to record when social skill objectives have been met. This can be done by placing a checkmark next to those social skills for which the student demonstrated comprehension and use in the classroom, and another checkmark next to those social skills reported or observed used outside of the classroom.

Rating Scale - Student Form

SSS: Social Skill Strategies includes a social communication skills rating scale, to be completed by the students themselves, on all 63 social skills (See Appendix C). This form is written at a fourth grade reading level, according to the Fry Readability Scale (Fry, 1977). This form is similar to the adult form, except that it is written in first person, (e.g., EYE CONTACT - I am good at looking at a person during a conversation). Educators may have students who are referred for special education programs complete the scale during the evaluation process. If there are students in the social skills class who have not had the opportunity to complete the rating scale, they may complete it during the first two class sessions. Although a brief description of each social skill is included on the student rating scale, the authors advocate reading the rating scale aloud, while the students rate themselves, to provide explanation as needed and to avoid erroneous responses by disabled readers.

Student Conference

A conference should be held with each student individually, shortly after completion of the rating scales. During the conference, the educator and student should review the student's self assessment and the educator should ask the student to identify the skills which he/she feels are most problematic. By allowing the students to comment, they may be more motivated to improve their social skill deficits. The authors realize that some students will deny having any social skill problems and will complete the rating scale in an unrealistic manner.

Independent Activities

While the educator is conferencing with an individual student, the other students can be completing one of the ten independent activity pages included in **SSS** (See Appendix F). The independent activities discuss social communication skills in a general manner and may be completed with minimum supervision. Each activity page takes approximately one 45-minute class period for most students to complete. The authors realize that some of the independent activities (e.g., word searches) do not have the same educational value as the activities within the units; however, they were purposely designed so the students could complete them independently.

Class Summary Form

After completing the conferences and rating social skills for instruction, the educator may compile each student's data on the Class Summary Form, which is shown here (for Book B) and is included in Appendix D.

CLASS SUMMARY FORM
BOOK B (Mark the social skills which are problematic for each student.)

SOCIAL SKILLS

STUDENTS' NAMES

| B-1. Reputation | B-2. Starting A Friendship | B-3. Maintaining A Friendship | B-4. Giving Emotional Support | B-5. Giving Advice | B-6. Ignoring | B-7. Responding To Teasing | B-8. Peer Pressure | B-9. Joining In | B-10. Being Left Out | B-11. Tattling | B-12. Being Assertive | B-13. Making A Complaint | B-14. Receiving A Complaint | B-15. Giving Constructive Criticism | B-16. Accepting Constructive Criticism | B-17. Making An Accusation | B-18. Dealing With A False Accusation | B-19. Compromising/Negotiating | B-20. Accepting Consequences | B-21. Expressing Feelings | B-22. Dealing With Anger | B-23. Dealing With Embarrassment | B-24. Coping With Fear | B-25. Dealing With Humor | B-26. Dealing With Failure | B-27. Expressing Affection | B-28. Dealing With Disappointment | B-29. Understanding The Feelings Of Others |

SSS: SOCIAL SKILL STRATEGIES (Book A)

282

To complete the form, the name of each student who was identified as having a social skills need should be written down the left-hand column. Then, mark the social skills found to be problematic for each student. By doing this, you will have a profile of each of your student's needs. The Class Summary Form can help you identify the priority social skills and the sequence in which you will want to teach them in the class. It can also be useful for determining who should be grouped together for social skill instruction. If a certain social skill, for example - accepting a compliment, was not found to be problematic for any of the students, no instructional time should be spent developing that social skill. Suppose, conversely, a social skill is a problem for several of your students, but not for all. When you teach that social skill in class, the students who are not deficient in that area can be given the choice of participating with the class or working alone on one of the ten independent activity pages. Although some skills are prerequisites for others, there is no clear-cut hierarchy of skills. Therefore, the educator should teach the skills in order of need and not necessarily in the order presented in **SSS**. It is highly recommended, however, that the Introductory Skills be addressed first because they are prerequisites to other skills taught in the program.

SSS: PRE-GROUP SKILLS

Before instruction in social skills can begin, the educator must identify which students are capable of learning in a group and which are not. Many educators, because of the nature of their students (e.g., aggressive, acting-out) will find it impossible to hold any type of "group" instruction. A criterion for **SSS: Social Skill Strategies** is that the students be able to function in a group without causing major disruptions. Some students are not yet at this level. One excellent behavioral program, **Dubuque Management System** (Keystone Area Education Agency,

11

1990), provides a structured approach which enables students to work in a group. Inquiries can be directed to **Dubuque Management System**, Keystone Area Education Agency, 1473 Central Avenue, Dubuque, Iowa 52001.

SSS: STRUCTURING A SOCIAL SKILLS CLASS

Based on a review of current research and experience in teaching social skills to students, the authors feel it is ideal if educators can conduct a social skills class daily. In addition, they advocate a specific structure for each social skill class as depicted below.

Reinforcement Time:	Pair Practice Visualization Question Review	5 min.
Instruction Time:	Instruction of Social Skills	35 min. (approximately)
Personal Time:	Personal Page	5 min.

Reinforcement Time

The purpose of the reinforcement activities (i.e., pair practice, visualization, and/or question review) is to reinforce past social skills that students have learned. These activities should be completed during the first five minutes of every class period. The educator may wish to do only one or two of the activities each day, depending on how long the activities take with the particular students in the class.

Pair Practice

The first activity in the reinforcement section is pair practice. This activity involves having pairs of students do short, specified role plays. The pair practice activity should not be initiated until after a few social skills have been taught so students have more than one skill to practice. In addition, this activity should not be implemented until the students feel comfortable in role playing situations. When introducing the pair practice activity, the educator should explain that the students will be practicing the use of various social skills they have already learned. It is important for the educator to give the following rationale to their students:

Educator: Each of you will be role playing over and over again the skills that you need to work on. You will do this at the beginning of the class period. The reason you will practice them over and over is the more you do something, the easier it becomes for you. For example, the more you give speeches to audiences, the easier it becomes to give them.

Early in the year, when the students have learned a limited number of social skills, all the students will be role playing the same social skills during this activity. As soon as possible, the educator should individualize the social skills to be role played for each student by referring to the Class

Summary Form (See Appendix D). The priority social skills chosen for each student should be recorded on the Pair Practice Record sheet, which is shown below and included in Appendix G.

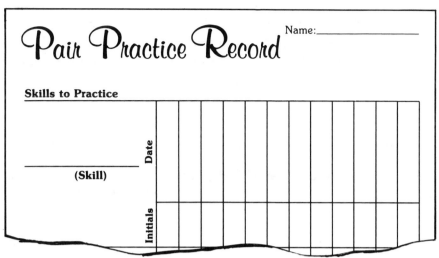

The Pair Practice Record sheet should be given to students to include in their journals. To complete this activity, have the students work in pairs. After both students have role played a social skill, they should initial each other's sheet to indicate which social skill was practiced. Eventually, the students should be able to complete this activity without receiving help from the educator.

Visualization

The second activity during the reinforcement section is visualization. This activity involves having students form a mental image of themselves. The students should imagine themselves performing one of their priority social skills. For example, a student who has difficulty with eye contact should form a mental image of himself using good eye contact. Explain to the students that many successful people use this strategy (e.g., athletes, salesclerks, actors). Remember that some students may not have much experience in forming mental images. Other students may be in the habit of forming only negative images in their minds. Therefore, initially the educator must verbally guide the students through this activity. The use of simple social skills (e.g., accepting a compliment) is suggested when first doing this. The following example illustrates how an educator could guide the students through a visualization activity:

> Educator: It's time for visualization. You may close your eyes if you'd like. Today, I'd like to have you receive a compliment in the correct way. When someone gives you a compliment, you say "Thank you." Picture this in your mind: Your teacher walks over to you and gives you a compliment about how well you did on your assignment. Picture yourself looking at your teacher, smiling, and saying, "Thank you."

After guiding several visualizations, the educator should fade the amount of verbal instructions provided until the students begin to do the visualization activities independently. After completion of the activity, the educator may want to ask individual students to describe the images they formed.

Question Review

The last activity during the reinforcement time is the question review. This activity involves the educator asking a few questions about previously taught social skills. A list is provided for the educator which includes several review questions for each social skill unit (See Appendix H). Question #1 for each unit always asks for the definition of the social skill. Question #2 asks for the skill steps or important tips to remember. The remaining questions pertain to application of the skill. The educator should ask the class a few questions from any previously taught social skill unit. The compiled list of questions makes it easy for the educator to choose questions quickly for the day. The purpose of this activity is to remind students continually of important aspects from past social skill units.

Instruction Time

This is the main portion of the class period during which direct instruction of social skills takes place. This portion of the class will be described later. (See *SSS: TEACHING A SOCIAL SKILL UNIT* on page 15).

Personal Time

The personal time should take place during the last five minutes of each class period. The purpose of this activity is to increase the students' positive feeling about their use of social skills. This activity was adapted from a self-concept curriculum entitled **Affective Skill Development for Adolescents** (Dembrowsky, 1983). The personal time activity involves having the students say the following statement aloud and in unison: "I am a good person. I am a friendly person. When I use my social skills, I get along better with people." This statement can be found on the top of the Personal Page, which follows and is included in Appendix I.

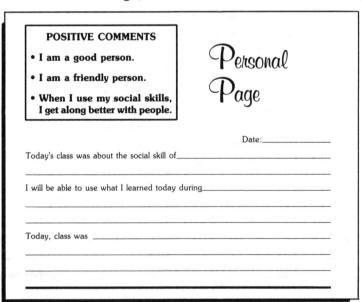

The purpose for the personal time activity should be explained to the students. The rationale is that the more often you say or think positive things about yourself, the more likely you are to incorporate those positive thoughts into your belief system (Dembrowsky, 1983). Educators must say the statement along with the students to acknowledge their belief in the benefits of the activity. Next, the students should complete the bottom of the Personal Page immediately after saying the positive statement aloud. The rationale for this activity is to make students continuously examine when they are using various social skills and when they will be using newly learned skills. The Personal Page may need to be adapted for use with low-functioning students. The students should keep an ample supply of Personal Pages in their journals for daily use (See SSS: JOURNAL DESCRIPTION below).

SSS: JOURNAL DESCRIPTION

The authors suggest that each student in the class have a three-ring binder to be used as a journal. The journal should contain the following: 1) the Pair Practice Record sheet (See description, page 13); 2) the Student Social Skill Summary Form (See description, page 9); 3) the Personal Page (See description, page 14). In addition, during each social skill unit, students may add completed activity pages to their journals. Students will use their journals at the beginning and end of each class period to complete the Pair Practice, Review Question, and Personal Page activities. They can easily refer to their journals when they wish to review for an upcoming test.

SSS: GRADING

The authors advocate using the "1/3 method" for grading student progress in a social skills class: one-third of the student's grade is determined by in-class and homework assignments, another one-third of the grade is determined by test/quiz scores, and the final one-third is determined by the student's participation in class. One method of recording participation involves use of the Daily Participation Point Sheet which is shown below and is included in Appendix J.

ATTENDANCE AND DAILY PARTICIPATION POINTS

Date:_____

Students' Names	Attendance (50%)	60%	70%	80%	90%	100%	Total Participation

If a student attends class but does not participate, he receives a daily participation grade of 50%. The student receives an additional 10% every time he appropriately participates in class. It is important that a positive classroom atmosphere be maintained and that students be positively reinforced often. Use of the Daily Participation Point Sheet will positively promote verbal participation. During classes when there is little opportunity for verbal discussion (e.g., students watching a videotaped program), students can be awarded participation points for positive behaviors other than verbal participation.

SSS: TEACHING A SOCIAL SKILL UNIT

After the educator and students have completed the reinforcement activities during the first five minutes of class (see Reinforcement Time on page 12), the instruction time may begin, which will be the major portion of the class period. The authors suggest using the following seven-step procedure for teaching each new social skill:

Step One: Social Skill Introduction

Step Two: Cognitive Planning Strategies

Step Three: Scripting

Step Four: Modeling

Step Five: Role Playing

Step Six: Homework And Concluding Activities

Step Seven: Transfer And Generalization Ideas

These seven steps have been separated and placed into a hierarchy for explanation purposes. In practice, however, the seven steps are integrated and do not have to be used in the exact sequence as shown above. The time required to address the seven steps will vary, depending on the complexity of the social skill being taught. Even the shortest units (e.g., eye contact) however, will take several class periods to complete. Each of the seven steps is described in detail below.

Step One: Social Skill Introduction

The educator must introduce each new social skill in a creative manner, using a method which will spark the students' interest. There are numerous ways to introduce a skill to enhance motivation for learning. A small sampling of ideas is provided below:

- The educator can role play the appropriate or inappropriate use of a social skill.
- The students can imagine a situation about the social skill.
- The students can listen to a short story about the social skill.
- The students can be shown a cartoon about the social skill.
- The educator can exaggerate the skill in a humorous and obvious manner.

Once educators have caught the students' interest, instruction of the social skill may begin. Each of the social skill units includes several activity pages which can be used during this skill introduction step, with the exception of the first and last pages of the unit, which are used at other times and will be described later. While a great deal of variability between the social skill units exists, some components remain constant. Each social skill unit includes:

1. The definition of the social skill. (Definitions can also be found in the Question Review pages in Appendix H.)

2. The skill steps or important "tips" about the social skill. Skill steps and important "tips" are also provided in the Question Review pages in Appendix H and on the Skill Homework Activity Page A at the beginning of every unit. The authors have identified the crucial skill steps for many of the social skills; however, some social skill units do not lend themselves to the development of ordered skill steps, so the essential points or "tips" to remember about the social skill are taught. The number of social skill steps have been limited because research indicates students are able to retain and transfer use of social skills better when there are fewer skill steps (Palincsar, 1986). In addition, mnemonic devices have been provided in some units to help the students memorize skill steps or tips.

3. Information which allows the students to understand why they need to learn the social skill and how it can be used at home, in school, and in the community.

Step Two: Cognitive Planning Strategies

Not only is it important to increase students' comprehension of social skills, but it is also essential to improve the cognitive planning strategies of learning how to identify which social skill to use and when to use it, and evaluating whether or not a social skill works appropriately. The need to incorporate cognitive planning strategies into social skill instruction was previously discussed (See SOCIAL COMMUNICATION SKILLS: GETTING THESE SKILLS TO TRANSFER AND GENERALIZE in Chapter One on page 6). Harris (1984) describes his **Making Better Choices Program**, which teaches a structured cognitive planning strategy during the first six lessons of his curriculum. Students learn the following sequence when planning the use of a social skill strategy:

STOP: Students monitor their tension level and take steps to calm down.
PLAN: Students decide which social skill to use and recall the skill steps.
DO: Students carry out their plan.
CHECK: Students evaluate how their plan worked and make necessary changes for the future.

This cognitive planning strategy is also incorporated into the remaining twenty social skill units of the **Making Better Choices Program**. Harris uses the following chart to depict his cognitive planning sequence:

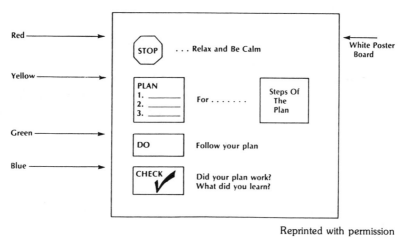

Reprinted with permission

FIGURE 1. The MBC Poster

To incorporate cognitive plannning strategies into a social skills curriculum, it is essential that the educator do the following:

1. Discuss cognitive planning strategies within every social skill unit.
2. Provide opportunities for students to consider different situations and identify which social skill would be appropriate to use and when to use it.
3. Discuss how to evaluate the success of each social skill used.

Step Three: Scripting

After providing the students with the essential information about the social skills, the educator is encouraged to have students read short scripts about the correct and incorrect use of social skills. The scripts should portray students using social skills in real-life situations, thereby providing relevancy for the students. The scripts will be helpful for those students who initially have difficulties role playing, and may clarify any confusion the students may have about the social skill after the initial instruction. The scripts are also useful with students who deny they have any social skill problems by allowing them to learn the proper use of social skills while not having to acknowledge their personal inadequacies.

Educators can write their own scripts for each social skill or use a commercially prepared program entitled **Scripting: Social Communication for Adolescents** (Waldo and Mayo, 1986). This resource provides scripts which demonstrate appropriate and inappropriate use of each social skill.

The scripting activity often increases students' participation. Students enjoy reading scripts because they are able to identify with many of the characters used in the scripts. In the authors' experiences with using social skill scripts, they have noticed that students with poor reading skills volunteer to read a part in a script just as often as average and above-average readers. The scripts may be used as the third step in teaching a unit or as an introduction to a new social skill unit. When doing the latter, the educator should ask the students to guess what social skill the script is depicting after it is read aloud.

Step Four: Modeling

It is essential that the educator model the social skill steps for the students. The authors suggest two methods of modeling:

1. Model the appropriate use of the social skill while simultaneously modeling the self-talk someone might say when using the social skill (e.g., "I wonder if these two people know one another? Maybe I should ask them if they know each other."). Self-talk is defined as the thoughts we have about ourselves and other people. In addition, the educator should model the cognitive planning self-talk that the students are taught to use for every social skill. (See description of **Making Better Choices Program** on page 17).
2. Model just the appropriate use of the social skill, phasing out the self-talk.

Research indicates that modeling is more effective when it is more realistic (Bandura, 1977). For example, the person modeling should act as though he is having a difficult time accepting NO from an authority figure, rather than just accepting the NO easily. In addition to modeling during Step Four, the educator should take every opportunity to model appropriate social skill usage throughout the school day.

Step Five: Role Playing

After modeling of the social skill has taken place, the students should practice and then role play situations where use of the social skill would be appropriate. Students should then be critiqued on how well they performed each social skill. Initially, a few students may be fearful of role playing; thus, the educator should take measures to help alleviate those fears (e.g., asking the class not to "make fun of" anyone who is role playing, letting the students initially role play without an audience). Some students will refuse to participate in the role play. Initially, these students can be given alternative assignments (e.g., writing role play situations, suggesting ideas for scripts), but every effort should be made to encourage them to participate as soon as possible.

Educators may develop their own role play situations for use with the class or may use already prepared role play situations found in social skill programs such as **Scripting: Social Communication for Adolescents** (Waldo and Mayo, 1986) or **Skillstreaming the Adolescent: A Structured Learning Approach to Teaching Prosocial Skills** (Goldstein et al., 1980). The role play situations must be relevant for the students. The educator might ask the class to brainstorm role play situations or ask for suggestions from individual students.

To begin this activity, educators are encouraged to give the students three role play situations. One should be a situation which could take place at school, one at home, and one in the community. Following are sample situations from the *Agreeing/Disagreeing* unit taken from **Scripting: Social Communication for Adolescents** (Waldo and Mayo, 1986).

(Home)   1. Your parents think you should not be involved in any after school activities so you can devote all your time to studies. Demonstrate how you would disagree with them in an appropriate way.

(School)   2. Your teacher gives you two days to complete a big homework assignment. Everyone in class, including you, thinks that will not be enough time. Show how you could express your disagreement in an appropriate way.

(Community) 3. You are shopping for your dad's birthday present. The salesclerk suggests that you buy him a shirt. Demonstrate how you could agree.

Reprinted with permission

The educator should read through and model all three situations with the students before asking them to work with a partner to practice role playing each one. While the partners are practicing, the educator should spend time with each group, making certain that everyone is staying on task and is correctly role playing each situation. When everyone is ready, the entire group should meet together. Partners should take turns coming to the front of the class to perform one or more of the situations they were given to practice.

Goldstein et al. (1980) advocate having the social skill steps (or tips) displayed at the front of the room during role plays for students who may forget the skill steps. This can be done by writing the skill steps on the chalkboard, putting the steps on a poster, or listing the steps on pages of a large sketch book. The sketch book allows educators to keep all social skill steps together in one place, and they can easily flip to each social skill when necessary. Students often refer to the skill steps (tips) before they do their role plays and during the role play if they get confused.

The educator should determine which students might have difficulty following the skill steps during the role play. Those students should role play using self-talk (aloud) to help display appropriate use of the social skill. Verbalized self-talk should be faded as soon as possible to ensure appropriate skill acquisition.

The partner for the role play should be carefully chosen. When practicing social skills that involve interactions with adults (e.g., accepting NO, accepting consequences), the role play situation should occur with an adult to promote transfer (See SOCIAL COMMUNICATION SKILLS: GETTING THESE SKILLS TO TRANSFER AND GENERALIZE in Chapter One on page 6). It is also suggested that other school staff members (e.g., school principal, regular educators) be involved in role plays to further promote transfer and generalization of skills. For social skills that involve the student interacting with peers (e.g., resisting peer pressure, starting a friendship), peers may be selected as partners. Educators are cautioned to choose only those students who take role playing seriously to be partners, because the person being critiqued must be serious.

Stokes and Baer (1977) recommend the *multiple exemplar strategy* which involves students role playing with several different people instead of with just one person. This will help to ensure transfer across settings. For additional strategies and research on role playing, refer to

Skillstreaming the Adolescent: A Structured Learning Approach to Teaching Pro-social Skills (Goldstein et al., 1980).

It is important that the educator and student review the student's performance during the role play. The educator should provide positive verbal feedback immediately after the student finishes the role play. The student may also receive feedback from the Role Play Critique Sheet (See Appendix K). This sheet may be completed by a variety of people. The educator may use it to grade the student, or other students in the class who acted as observers may use the sheet to critique the role play. Students who role play may conduct a self-evaluation if the role play is videotaped. The authors suggest using videotaping as often as possible because it gives the students a chance to see themselves actually performing the social skill. They can observe body language, volume, tone of voice, and the skill steps for the given social skill.

Step Six: Homework and Concluding Activities

Homework assignments are a means of reinforcing the skills the students have been taught. One type of homework assignment is the Skill Homework Activity Page A, which is the first page of every unit. After instruction of each social skill unit, students should complete the homework assignment with a parent. Page A contains the name of the social skill, the skill steps (or tips) for each social skill, and a role play situation. Parents are asked either to act out the role play situation with their child or to observe their son/daughter using the social skill in a real-life situation and describe that situation. Parents are then asked to evaluate their child's performance by circling *needs more help, good,* or *excellent* on the homework sheet and sign the sheet. The students should submit their papers to the teacher for a homework grade.

The educator must contact parents and explain the Skill Homework Activity pages before students take any sheets home. (See *Step Seven: Transfer and Generalization Ideas* on page 21.) There will still be a number of students who have difficulty getting their parents to complete the Skill Homework Activity. These students may complete the activity with some other adult (e.g., a teacher, a youth leader, a neighbor). Occasionally, the educator may want to allow all the students to choose the adult with whom they would like to complete the activity.

During the instruction of the social skill unit, various **SSS** activity pages may also be used as homework assignments. Educators should assess, through guided practice, whether the students have mastered the concepts before assigning an activity page or part of an activity page as homework.

The authors have developed an end-of-the-unit Student Evaluation Form (See Appendix L) for students to complete. Students should use this form to rate how much they learned from the social skill unit and give suggestions on ways to improve the unit. While this sheet helps promote student involvement, students do not need to complete this form after every unit.

Another concluding activity involves having the students play a board game called **Communicate** (Mayo and Waldo, 1986). This educational activity reinforces important concepts discussed during each social skill unit.

Concluding activities could also include giving students tests and quizzes. Evaluating student performance on a regular basis will 1) assess student progress; 2) promote transfer of skills, and 3) impress upon the students that social skills class is as important as academic classes. The authors have found that testing students after every four social skill units is effective. A short quiz is beneficial after every social skill unit.

A review guide has been included at the end of every unit. Each review guide contains one question written at each of the six levels of Bloom's taxonomy of educational objectives (Bloom, Engelhart, Furst, Hill, and Krathwohl, 1954). The taxonomy includes the following six levels: knowledge, comprehension, application, analysis, synthesis, and evaluation. Unfortunately, most of the questions asked by teachers are at the knowledge and comprehension levels only. The authors believe that every student, including those with special educational needs, should be taken through all six levels of the taxonomy in order to improve their upper level thinking skills and to promote transfer and generalization of the social skill.

Students should be encouraged to refer to their journals when completing the first few questions of the review guides. Educators may need to help the students with the questions written at the levels of application, analysis, synthesis, and evaluation. Educators can use the same review guide for the test or quiz, or develop their own by referring to the review guide, activity pages, and review questions (See Appendix H) for the unit.

The following section includes ideas for concluding activities that will help to promote transfer of social skills.

Step Seven: Transfer and Generalization Ideas

Getting students to transfer their skills is the most important step in the process of teaching a social skill unit. Sadly, it is a step that is often forgotten. Numerous authors have recently addressed the lack of specific planning to promote transfer (Adelman and Taylor, 1982; Mayo and Gajewski, 1987; McConnell, 1987; Schumaker and Hazel, 1984b; Simpson, 1987). Educators need to ensure that a plan for transfer of skills is included in every social skill unit. The authors have compiled a list of strategies that can be used to promote transfer of social skills to areas outside of the classroom. Educators should incorporate several of the following ideas into each social skill unit to ensure generalization of skills:

1. **Initial and Ending Class Activities** - The following activities, Pair Practice, Visualization, Review Questions, Positive Comments, and the Personal Page, are set up to help students transfer the social skills outside the classroom. They are designed to help students overlearn skills, transfer the use of skills to the home, school, and community; and to change their self - talk/mental imagery to be more positive. (See SSS: STRUCTURING A SOCIAL SKILLS CLASS on page 12).

2. **Cognitive Planning** - This strategy teaches the student to monitor personal performance by assessing 1) when he should use a specific social skill; 2) how others respond to his use of the social skill; 3) if he performed the skill correctly, and 4) if he should do something differently the next time. Cognitive planning also helps the student calm himself down enough so that he can actually perform the social skill. The **Making Better Choices Program** (Harris, 1987) is an example of a program which incorporates cognitive planning with the instruction of social skills. (See SSS: TEACHING A SOCIAL SKILL UNIT on page 15).

3. **Practice Day** - The students need to receive numerous opportunities to practice newly learned skills. One method involves using the first 15 minutes of class on Monday for a review session and setting aside one entire class session each month for a cumulative review (Good and Grouws, 1985). The students can review social skill steps and tips and practice all of the past social skills they have learned.

4. **Red Flag** - Educators must integrate social skill instruction throughout the entire school

day. McGinnis, Sauerbry, and Nichols (1985) describe a *Red Flag* strategy in which the educator tells a student that he will be "set up" later in the day (or the next day). Being "set up" means that the educator will purposely do something which will cause the child to demonstrate his use of a particular social skill. For example, the educator might tell the student that sometime later in the day, she will make a false accusation to the student. The student is expected to demonstrate the proper way to handle a false accusation. After the *Red Flag* situation has taken place, the educator and the student should discuss how the social skill situation was handled.

5. ***Similarity of Environment and People*** - Try to make the practice environment as similar as possible to where the students will actually be using the skill. For example, if a student is often disciplined for misbehaving in the hallways, have the student practice "accepting consequences" out in the hallway in addition to in the classroom. Try to involve people the student will actually be dealing with (e.g., mainstream teacher, principal) in the role play activities. This will help the student transfer the social skills when dealing with these people.

6. ***Make Others Aware*** - It is important to make other school professionals (e.g., regular education teachers, counselors, principals, secretaries) aware of the social skills you are teaching to your students. Hand out a list of each social skill taught to help them better understand how social skills are defined and broken into skill steps. Educators would benefit from an inservice which explains social skill instruction and gives helpful hints for them to use with all of their students. A weekly memo can be sent to school personnel, which discusses the social skill currently being taught in your class. Encourage the staff to praise students when they see them using social skills appropriately. For example, the school secretary might praise a student for interrupting appropriately (e.g., "Wendy, when you interrupted me just now, you did it very appropriately."). If you are using a certain strategy with a student (e.g., not becoming impulsive), make sure that other people know the exact words and steps you are using (e.g., "Wendel, tell yourself to calm down. Take a deep breath. Take another deep breath and count to five."). Then others will be able to use the same strategy with the student and, hopefully, help him to transfer his skills to areas outside the classroom.

7. ***Parental Involvement*** - Parents must understand and become involved in social skill instruction. The educator may want to meet with parents at the beginning of the school year and go through the Social Communication Skills Rating Scale - Adult Form (See Appendix A). It is important to get parental input as to which skills their child needs to work on. The educator can also explain the Skill Homework Activity pages to the parent (See description on page 20). The educator should give pointers to parents about role playing, and emphasize that parents should reinforce their children any time they see them using appropriate social skills.

8. ***Self-Reinforcement and Monitoring*** - Several authors have recently advocated the use of student-centered strategies (Anderson-Inman, 1986; Fowler, 1986). A self-monitoring checklist is a reminder to the students of skills learned and where they are expected to use those skills. The students could write a personal contract which tells when, where, and how often they plan to use the skill. The students can self-monitor by keeping a record of how often they use various social skills. Educators should initially model how to self-monitor. The students should also be taught to self-reinforce (reward) themselves for completing a task or having responsible behavior. ***Transfer Activities: Thinking Skill Vocabulary Development*** (Mayo and Gajewski, 1987) contains a unit on motivation which helps students move from extrinsic to intrinsic motivation.

9. ***Reward/Behavioral Programs*** - Many students have not reached the level in which they can self-monitor, and they need more external controls to help them use ap-

propriate behavior. Behavioral programs which provide rewards and consequences may be necessary. Educators should have a plan for helping students move from the external behavioral program to taking responsibility for their own behavior.

10. **Group Contingencies** - McConnell (1987) emphasizes that social interaction involves the interrelated behavior of two or more people. While a student may be able to perform a specified social skill (e.g., he can begin a conversation), others may not interact with the student, thus making it almost impossible for him to demonstrate skill competence. A socially isolated student such as this would not receive the natural reinforcement that comes from positive interaction with one's peers. It is often necessary to set up group contingencies (e.g., the class will receive a reward if John initiates conversation with three people) so that the other students will encourage the student to perform the skill, and interact with him so that he is able to perform the skill. Educators are cautioned to choose a reward criteria that is set at a level the given student is able to meet.

11. **Peer Reminders** - Students should be encouraged to remind fellow students about using social skills (e.g., "Come on, John. Remember how we learned to control our anger. You can do it."). In addition, students should praise each other for using appropriate social skills (e.g., "You really handled it well when the teacher was criticizing you.").

12. **A-U Sheets** - An A-U (Acceptable-Unacceptable) sheet is a system that helps the student use appropriate social skills in every class (See Appendix M). The sheet can be designed to meet the needs of any student. The student takes his A-U sheet to each of his classes and his teachers rate whether he was successful at the goals listed on the sheet. An "A" from the teacher means acceptable, while a "U" means unacceptable. There is also a section for teachers to comment and write down the next day's assignment. The student turns his A-U sheet in to his teacher at the end of the day. The teacher keeps a record of how successful the student has been with the goals listed on the A-U sheet. The student may earn points based on how many "A's" he received during the day. The student also takes the A-U sheet home each night to show his parents. Additional uses of the A-U can be found in **Transfer Activities: Thinking Skill Vocabulary Development** (Mayo and Gajewski, 1987).

13. **Student Mediators** - *Mediated Dispute Resolution* involves student conflicts being resolved by the students themselves with the help of a trained peer mediator (Koch and Miller, 1987). When a conflict arises, the students are asked if they would like to "get mediated." Students then put the disagreement "on hold" until a peer mediator is found. In a mediation session, the peer mediator first explains the ground rules Then each student takes turns telling "his side of the story." The students then come up with a list of solutions, decide upon a solution and sign a written agreement. This strategy, which can be used any time throughout the school day, teaches students to compromise and negotiate. Transfer of social skills occurs when students learn to solve problems on their own rather than needing to have adults intervene.

14. **Transfer Contest** - The educator can hold "transfer contests" to motivate the students to transfer their newly learned social skills. One type of contest would involve the students writing about different times when they used their newly learned social skills outside of class. Another type of contest would be to have "social skill coupons" printed and distributed to parents and regular educators. Whenever these people observe the students using a social skill appropriately, they give them a coupon. The child turns in his coupons to his social skills teacher. The student who has collected the most coupons in an agreed upon amount of time wins the contest.

15. **Real-Life Outings** - While it is necessary to isolate social skills for direct instruction in the skills, the educator must remember that in *real life*, students must identify when

and which social skills to use and must use a combination of social skills at all times. It is important to take students on community outings in which they have the chance to demonstrate success in being socially appropriate. Such outings might include tours of area attractions, trips to restaurants, and sports activities.

SSS: USE OF COOPERATIVE LEARNING TECHNIQUES

As stated in Chapter One, social skill acquisition and use should be promoted through group interaction rather than through teacher-directed activities. The use of cooperative learning techniques is an effective way to encourage group interaction. For further information about the definition and history of cooperative learning, refer to SOCIAL COMMUNICATION SKILLS: HOW TO TEACH THESE SKILLS in Chapter One on page 4. Johnson and Johnson (1984) state 18 aspects an educator should consider when structuring a cooperative learning lesson:

1. Specifying academic and collaborative objectives
2. Deciding on the size of the group
3. Assigning students to groups
4. Arranging the room
5. Planning materials
6. Assigning roles
7. Explaining the academic task
8. Structuring positive goal interdependence
9. Structuring individual accountability
10. Structuring intergroup cooperation
11. Explaining criteria for success
12. Specifying desired behaviors
13. Monitoring students' behavior
14. Providing task assistance
15. Intervening to teach collaborative skills
16. Providing closure to the lesson
17. Evaluating the quality and quantity of students' learning
18. Assessing how well the group functioned

For a brief description of each of these 18 aspects, refer to Appendix N.

SSS includes four units which are structured in a cooperative learning manner. (See units A-28, A-31, B-9, and B-24.) When using any of the four units, the educator must keep in mind that several of the 18 aspects listed above will still need to be considered and planned for. The educator is encouraged to learn more about cooperative learning by reading **Circles of Learning** (Johnson et al., 1984), **Cooperation in the Classroom** (Johnson and Johnson, 1984), or **Learning Together and Alone: Cooperative, Competitive, and Individualistic Learning** (Johnson and Johnson, 1987), or by contacting the Cooperative Learning Center, University of Minnesota , 202 Pattee Hall, Minneapolis, MN 55455, (612) 624-7031. The educator is also encouraged to teach other units from **SSS** using a cooperative learning approach.

REFERENCES

Adelman, H. and Taylor, L. Enhancing the motivation and skills needed to overcome interpersonal problems. *Learning Disability Quarterly,* 5: 438-446, 1982.

Anderson-Inman, L. Bridging the gap: Student-centered strategies for promoting the transfer of learning. *Exceptional Children,* 52(6): 562-572, 1986.

Arkowitz, H. Assessment of social skills. In M. Herson and A. Bellack (Eds.), *Behavioral assessment,* 296-327. New York: Pergamon Press, 1981.

Aronson, E., Blaney, N., Stephan, C., Sikes, J., and Snapp, M. *The jigsaw classroom.* Beverly Hills, CA: Sage, 1978.

Baer, D., Wolf, M., and Risley, T. Some current dimensions of applied behavior analysis. *Journal of Applied Behavior Analysis,* 1: 91-97, 1968.

Bandura, A. *Social learning theory.* Englewood Cliffs, NJ: Prentice-Hall, 1977.

Bloom, B., Engelhart, M., Furst, E., Hill, W., and Krathwohl, D. *Taxonomy of educational objectives: The classification of educational goals.* New York: David McKay Company, Inc., 1954.

Bohlmeyer, E. and Burke, J. Selecting cooperative learning techniques: A consultative strategy guide. *School Psychology Review,* 16(1): 36-49, 1987.

Clark, B. *Optimizing learning.* Columbus, OH: Merrill Publishing Co., 1986.

Dale, E. and Chall, J. A formula for predicting readability: Instructions. *Educational Research Bulletin,* 27: 11-20 and 37-54, 1948 (Jan. 21 and Feb. 17).

Dembrowsky, C. *Affective skill development for adolescents.* Jackson, WY: Self-published, 1983.

Deshler, D. and Schumaker, J. Social skills of learning disabled adolescents: Characteristics and intervention. *Topics in Learning and Learning Disabilities,* 3(2): 15-23, 1983.

Foster, S. and Ritchey, W. Issues in the assessment of social competence in children. *Journal of Applied Behavior Analysis,* 12: 625-638, 1979.

Fowler, S. Peer-monitoring and self-monitoring: Alternatives to traditional teacher management. *Exceptional Children,* 52(6): 573-582, 1986.

Fry, E. Fry's readability graph: Clarifications, validity, and extension to level 17. *Journal of Reading,* 21(3): 242-252, 1977.

Galyean, B. *Mind sight: Learning through imaging.* Santa Barbara, CA: Center for Integrative Learning, 1983.

Gelzheiser, L., Shepherd, M., and Wozniak, R. The development of instruction to induce skill transfer. *Exceptional Children,* 53(2): 125-129, 1986.

Goldsmith, J. and McFall, R. Development and evaluation of an interpersonal skill-training program for psychiatric inpatients. *Journal of Abnormal Psychology,* 19(2): 120-133, 1975.

Goldstein, A., Sprafkin, R., Gershaw, N., and Klein, P. *Skillstreaming the adolescent: A structured learning approach to teaching prosocial skills.* Champaign, IL: Research Press, 1980.

Good, T. and Grouws, D. Effective mathematics teaching in elementary grades. In D. Chambers (Ed.), *Effective teaching of mathematics, Bulletin No. 7447.* Madison, WI: Department of Public Instruction, 1985.

Gorovitz, E. The creative brain II; A revisit with Ned Herrmann. *Training and Development Journal,* 36(12): 74-77, 1982.

Greenspan, S. and Shoultz, B. Why mentally retarded adults lose their jobs: Social competence as a factor in work adjustments. *Applied Research in Mental Retardation,* 2: 23-31, 1981.

Gresham, F. Assessment of children's social skills. *Journal of School Psychology,* 19(2): 120-132, 1981a.

Gresham, F. Social skills training with handicapped children: A review. *Review of Educational Research,* 51(1): 139-175, 1981b.

Gresham, F. Misguided mainstreaming: The case for social skill training with handicapped children. *Exceptional Children,* 48(5): 422-431, 1982.

Hatcher, M. Whole brain learning. *The School Administrator,* 40(5): 8-11, 1983.

Harris, W. The making better choices program. *The Pointer,* 29(1): 16-19, 1984.

Harris, W. *Making better choices: A cognitive-behavioral approach for teaching social skills and cognitive planning.* Orono, ME: MBC Publications, 1987.

Hazel, J., Sherman, J., Schumaker, J., and Sheldon, J. Group social skills training with adolescents: A critical review. In D. Upper and S. Ross (Eds.), *Handbook of behavioral group therapy.* New York: Plenum Publishing, 1985.

Jackson, N., Jackson, D., and Monroe, C. *Getting along with others: Teaching social effectiveness to children.* Champaign, IL: Research Press, 1983.

Johnson, D. and Johnson, R. *Cooperation in the classroom.* Edina, MN: Interaction Book Company, 1984.

Johnson, D., Johnson, R., Holubec, E., and Roy, P. *Circles of learning.* Alexandria, VA: Association for Supervision and Curriculum Development, 1984.

Johnson D. and Johnson R. *Learning together and alone: Cooperative, competitive, and individualistic learning - Revised.* Englewood Cliffs, NJ: Prentice-Hall, 1987.

Johnson, R. and Johnson, D., Action research: Cooperative learning in the science classroom. *Science and Children,* 24(2): 31-32, 1986.

Kauffman, J. *Characteristics of children's behavior disorders.* Columbus, OH: Charles E. Merrill Publishing Co., 1977.

Kazdin, A. and Matson, J. Social validation in mental retardation. *Applied Research in Mental Retardation*, 2(1): 39-53, 1981.

Keystone Area Education Agency. *Dubuque management system*. Dubuque, IA: Dubuque Community Schools, 1990.

Koch, M. and Miller, S. Resolving student conflicts with student mediators. *Principal*, 66: 59-62, 1987.

Mayo, P. and Gajewski, N. *Transfer activities: Thinking skill vocabulary development*. Eau Claire, WI: Thinking Publications, 1987.

Mayo, P. and Waldo, P. *Communicate*. Eau Claire, WI: Thinking Publications, 1986.

McCarthy, B. *4Mat in action: Creative lesson plans for teaching to learning styles with right/left mode technique*. Oak Brook, IL: Excel., 1983.

McConnell, D. Entrapment effects and the generalization and maintenance of social skills training for elementary school students with behavioral disorders. *Behavioral Disorders*, 12(4): 252-263, 1987.

McGinnis, E., Sauerbry, L., and Nichols, P. Skill-streaming: Teaching social skills to children with behavioral disorders. *Teaching Exceptional Children*, 17: 160-167, 1985.

O' Leary, S. and Dubey, D. Applications of self-control procedures by children: A review. *Journal of Applied Behavior Analysis*, 12: 449-465, 1979.

Palincsar, A. Metacognitive strategy instruction. *Exceptional Children*, 53(2): 118-124, 1986.

Paris, S. and Oka, E. Self-regulated learning among exceptional children. *Exceptional Children*, 53(2): 103-108, 1986.

Pearl, R., Donahue, M., and Bryan, T. *The development of tact: Children's strategies for delivering bad news*. Unpublished manuscript, Chicago, IL: University of Illinois, 1983.

Perlmutter, B., Crocker, J., Cordray, D., and Garstecki, D. Sociometric status and related personality characteristics of mainstreamed learning disabled adolescents. *Learning Disability Quarterly*, 6: 20-30, 1983.

Roff, M. Childhood social interactions and young adult bad conduct. *Journal of Abnormal Psychology*, 63(2): 333-337, 1961.

Roff, M., Sells, S., and Golden, M. *Social adjustment and personality development in children*. Minneapolis, MN: University of Minnesota, 1972.

Schloss, P., Schloss, C., Wood, C., and Kiehl, W. A Critical review of social skills research with behaviorally disordered students. *Behavioral Disorders*, 12(1): 1-14, 1986.

Schumaker, J. and Hazel, J. Social skills assessment and training for the learning disabled: Who's on first and what's on second? Part I. *Journal of Learning Disabilities*, 17(7): 422-431, 1984a.

Schumaker, J. and Hazel, J. Social skills assessment and training for the learning disabled: Who's on first and what's on second? Part II. *Journal of Learning Disabilities,* 17(8): 492-499, 1984b.

Schumaker, J., Hazel, J., Sherman, J., and Sheldon, J. Social skill performances of learning disabled, non-learning disabled, and delinquent adolescents. *Learning Disability Quarterly,* 5: 388-397, 1982.

Shames, G. and Wiig, E. *Human communication disorders: An introduction.* Columbus, OH: Charles E. Merrill Publishing Co., 1982.

Simpson, R. Social interactions of behaviorally disordered children and youth: Where are we and where do we need to go? *Behavioral Disorders,* 12(4): 292-298, 1987.

Slavin, R. *The effects of teams in teams-games-tournament on the normative climates of classrooms.* John Hopkins University: Center for Social Organization of Schools, 1974.

Stephens, T. *Social skills in the classroom.* Columbus, OH: Cedars Press, 1978.

Stokes, T. and Baer, D. An implicit technology of generalization. *Journal of Applied Behavior Analysis,* 10: 349-369, 1977.

Vetter, A. *A comparison of the characteristics of learning disabled and non-learning disabled young adults.* Unpublished doctoral dissertation. Lawrence, KS: University of Kansas, 1983.

Wahler, R., Berland, R., and Coe, T. Generalization processes in child behavior change. In B. Lahey and A. Kazdin (Eds.), *Advances in clinical child psychology,* New York: Plenum Press, 1979.

Waldo, P. and Mayo, P. *Scripting: Social communication for adolescents.* Eau Claire, WI: Thinking Publications, 1986.

Walker, H. *The acting out child: Coping with classroom disruption.* Boston, MA: Allyn and Bacon, 1979.

Webb, G. Left/right brains, teammates in learning. *Exceptional Children,* 49(6): 508-515, 1983.

Wehman, P., Abramson, M., and Norman, C. Transfer of training in behavior modification programs: An evaluative review. *Journal of Special Education,* 11: 215-231, 1977.

Werner, E. *A study of communication time.* Unpublished master's thesis. College Park, MD: University of Maryland, 1975.

White, W., Schumaker, J., Warner, M., Alley, G., and Deshler, D. *The current status of young adults identified as learning disabled during their school career. (Research report No. 21).* Lawrence, KS: University of Kansas Institute for Research in Learning Disabilities, 1980.

Wiig, E. *Let's talk: Developing prosocial communication skills.* Columbus, OH: Charles E. Merrill Publishing Co., 1982a.

Wiig, E. *Let's talk inventory for adolescents.* Columbus, OH: Charles E. Merrill Publishing Co., 1982b.

INTRODUCTORY SKILLS

SKILL HOMEWORK ACTIVITY

_____
(Due Date)

Dear Parent or Guardian of: _____

This week we are learning about the social communication skill:

EYE CONTACT

This social skill is very important in interpersonal relationships.

The students have learned that they should have good eye contact when talking with someone. **_Having good eye contact_** means looking at a person most of the time during a conversation.

Before the due date, please complete one of the following activities with your son or daughter: (put a check mark by your choice)

_____ A. We acted out the role play situation listed below.

_____ B. I observed my son/daughter using this social skill in a real-life situation. (I have described the situation below.)

Description of real-life observation:

Role play situation:

YOU ARE TALKING WITH ONE OF YOUR PARENTS ABOUT GETTING A PET. USE GOOD EYE CONTACT DURING THIS CONVERSATION.

- -

Please circle the word below which best describes how your son or daughter did while using this social skill in either the role play or real-life situation.

NEEDS MORE HELP   GOOD   EXCELLENT

It is important for you to reinforce your child's use of this social skill at home in a positive way. Encourage and praise your child when you see the skill appropriately used. Remind him/her to use the social skill when necessary.

Thank you for your assistance.

Sincerely,

* *

PARENT/GUARDIAN SIGNATURE: _____

EYE CONTACT

Having **good eye contact** means *looking at the person you are talking with.* It is not necessary to stare at the person, but you should look at their face most of the time. People who have good eye contact give the impression that they are confident.

DIRECTIONS: Answer the questions.

1. Why is it important to have good *eye* contact?

2. Tell five instances when you could be talking with someone and you would want to have good *eye* contact (e.g., when I am asking my teacher about a homework assignment).

   a. _____

   b. _____

   c. _____

   d. _____

   e. _____

3. Tell two situations when you would *not* be able to have good *eye* contact with someone (e.g., when you're driving a car and talking to someone).

   a. _____

   b. _____

                                       SSS: Social Skill Strategies (Book A)

Name:_____

It's Those Eyes

DIRECTIONS: Look at each picture and read the paragraph next to it. Then answer the question at the end of each paragraph.

Ned Never Look

Ned Never Look doesn't have eye contact with anyone. He usually keeps his head down when he is talking to someone.

How do you feel when you talk with a person like Ned Never Look?

_____

_____

_____

_____

Sandy Stare

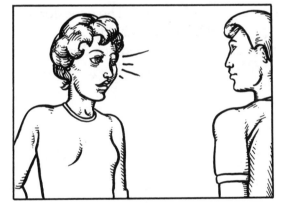

Sandy Stare never takes her eyes off you when she talks with you. Sandy stares at everyone she talks with.

How do you feel when you talk with a person like Sandy Stare?

_____

_____

_____

_____

Eddie Eye Contact

Eddie Eye Contact has good eye contact. He looks at you most of the time but doesn't stare at you.

How do you feel when you talk with a person like Eddie Eye Contact?

_____

_____

_____

_____

EDUCATOR PAGE: DO NOT DUPLICATE FOR STUDENTS

* *

DIRECTIONS: Complete the following activity with your students.

* *

Purpose: To show students that having *good eye contact* means looking at the person **most of the time.** This means not staring at the person or not having any *eye contact.*

Preparation: 1. Videotape one of the following:

- a short portion (approximately five minutes) of a television show. The videotape should show people engaged in a conversation using good *eye contact.* If at all possible, the educator should attempt to videotape a conversation when the television camera is on both people at the same time, rather than showing close-up shots of individual people.

- a short, educator-made role play in which a conversation takes place and the characters demonstrate good *eye contact.* The educator may also wish to videotape role plays in which the characters do not use appropriate *eye contact,* such as Ned Never Look or Sandy Stare (See *Eye Contact - C).*

2. Gather these materials:

- a videotape player
- the videotape (described above)
- several stop watches

Activity: 1. Tell half of the students to use the stop watches to time the **entire length** of the videotaped conversation.

2. Tell the other half of the students to choose one of the characters in the videotape. The students should turn the stop watches on whenever the character shows good *eye contact.* When the character does not have *eye contact,* the stop watches should be turned off and turned on again when there is good *eye contact.*

3. At the end of the videotape, compare the amount of time the person had *eye contact* to the total length of the conversation.

4. Discuss whether or not the character had *eye contact* a good percentage of the time.

EYE CONTACT - EYE CONTACT - EYE CONTACT - EYE CONTACT

1. Define the social skill of eye contact, and write an important tip to remember.

   _____

   _____

2. List two reasons why it is important to have good eye contact.

   (1) _____

   (2) _____

3. Describe a situation from the home, school, and community when you would want to use good eye contact.

   (home) _____

   (school) _____

   (community) _____

4. Tell one way that "Eddie Eye Contact" and "Sandy Stare" are the same, and one way that they are different.

   (same) _____

   (different) _____

5. Write or tell a short story about "Ned Never Look" going to a job interview, and tell what happens to him because of his bad eye contact.

   _____

   _____

   _____

   _____

   _____

   _____

6. Evaluate your own ability to have eye contact. Put an "X" on the line where you feel your eye contact is now and explain why you put it there.

   ●———————————————●———————————————●

   Ned Never   Eddie Eye   Sandy
   Look   Contact   Stare

   (reason)_____

   _____

   Put an "X" on the line where you want your eye contact to be, and explain why you put it there.

   ●———————————————●———————————————●

   Ned Never   Eddie Eye   Sandy
   Look   Contact   Stare

   (reason)_____

   _____

SKILL HOMEWORK ACTIVITY

_____
(Due Date)

Dear Parent or Guardian of: _____

This week we are learning about the social communication skill:

MANNERS

This social skill is very important in interpersonal relationships.

Some specific manners the students have discussed include saying _thank you_, saying _you're welcome_, saying _please_, saying _excuse me_, and using good table manners.

Before the due date, please complete one of the following activities with your son or daughter: (put a check mark by your choice)

_____ A. We acted out the role play situation listed below.

_____ B. I observed my son/daughter using this social skill in a real-life situation. (I have described the situation below.)

Description of real-life observation:

Role play situation:

YOU ARE SITTING AT THE TABLE EATING WITH YOUR FAMILY. USE GOOD TABLE MANNERS AND ASK YOUR BROTHER TO PASS THE CARROTS. REMEMBER TO SAY _PLEASE_ AND _THANK YOU_.

- -

Please circle the word below which best describes how your son or daughter did while using this social skill in either the role play or real-life situation.

NEEDS MORE HELP   GOOD   EXCELLENT

It is important for you to reinforce your child's use of this social skill at home in a positive way. Encourage and praise your child when you see the skill appropriately used. Remind him/her to use the social skill when necessary.

Thank you for your assistance.

Sincerely,

* *

PARENT/GUARDIAN SIGNATURE: _____

Manners...who needs them? WE DO!

Good manners are very important. People who have good manners are better liked than people who do not. Good manners should be used at all times. Some important good manners are listed below.

> Saying "Thank you"
> Saying "You're welcome"
> Saying "Please"
> Saying "Excuse me"
> Using good table manners

Some people have never been taught "good manners." They do not know any better. Other people know better but may want to get negative attention. An example of this might be someone burping on purpose and not saying "Excuse me." No matter what the reason, people who do not use good manners seem uncivilized. What do you think "uncivilized" means? Discuss your answer with others in class or write your answer on the back of this page.

You will impress people if you use good manners. Your friends will think you are polite. Adults will think more highly of you. You should not only use good manners once in awhile, but all the time. It is a good habit to get into.

Name:_____

Manners, Manners Everywhere

DIRECTIONS: Answer each question below.

1. Give two examples of when you would say "Thank you" to someone.

   a.

   b.

2. Give two examples of when you would say "Please" to someone.

   a.

   b.

3. Give two examples of when you would say "Excuse me."

   a.

   b.

4. List three good table manners.

   a.

   b.

   c.

5. Explain in your own words why you think it's important to have good manners. Write your answer in about 4-5 complete sentences.

EDUCATOR PAGE: DO NOT DUPLICATE FOR STUDENTS

DIRECTIONS: Complete the following activity with your students.

Discussion:
(Day 1)

1. Make a list of appropriate table manners and write them on a piece of poster board.
2. Discuss the reasons for using appropriate table manners. Also discuss that the manners we use when eating with family members may be more casual than those we use with other people.
3. Discuss appropriate topics of conversation for the table.

Activity:
(Day 2)

Allow your students to plan and make a meal. Place the poster with the list of table manners where the students can see it. Before you begin to eat, remind the students to practice the table manners they have learned.

Critique:
(Day 3)

Ask students to critique themselves on how well they used appropriate table manners. Be sure to emphasize the positive things they did. Have students write a short paragraph about all of the positive aspects of the meal and the manners people used.

MANNERS - MANNERS - MANNERS - MANNERS - MANNERS

1. Tell what *having good manners* means, and tell an important tip to remember.

   _____

   _____

   _____

2. What could be the consequences of having bad manners?

   _____

   _____

   _____

   _____

3. Pretend you are going to interview your father to find out how he feels about manners. Write three questions you could ask him.

   a. _____

   b. _____

   c. _____

4. Compare being with your good friends to being around adults in respected positions. Describe the similarities and differences in using manners in both situations.

   (same) _____

   _____

   (different) _____

   _____

5. Pretend you have an assignment to design a poster to hang in your school to help improve students' manners. What would your poster say?

   _____

   _____

6. Think of a person with whom you would like to start using better manners, and explain why. Then write two specific things you will do or say to improve your manners.

   (reason)_____

   _____

   a. _____

   _____

   b. _____

   _____

SKILL HOMEWORK ACTIVITY

_____
(Due Date)

Dear Parent or Guardian of: _____

This week we are learning about the social communication skill:

VOLUME

This social skill is very important in interpersonal relationships.

The students have learned about using the correct volume (loudness) when they talk. Most of the time we should talk with a normal volume. There are a few times when we need to talk louder than usual (e.g., when in a noisy room) and times when we need to talk softer than usual (e.g., when someone is sleeping).

Before the due date, please complete one of the following activities with your son or daughter: (put a check mark by your choice)

_____ A. We acted out the role play situation listed below.

_____ B. I observed my son/daughter using this social skill in a real-life situation. (I have described the situation below.)

Description of real-life observation:

Role play situation:

YOU DISAGREE WITH YOUR PARENTS ABOUT YOUR CURFEW. KEEP A NORMAL VOLUME AND CONTINUE YOUR DISCUSSION.

- -

Please circle the word below which best describes how your son or daughter did while using this social skill in either the role play or real-life situation.

NEEDS MORE HELP   GOOD   EXCELLENT

It is important for you to reinforce your child's use of this social skill at home in a positive way. Encourage and praise your child when you see the skill appropriately used. Remind him/her to use the social skill when necessary.

Thank you for your assistance.

Sincerely,

* *

PARENT/GUARDIAN SIGNATURE: _____

voLUME

Do either of these two people sound familiar to you? You know, the kid who's always yelling or the person who never speaks up in class. These types of people can really get on your nerves. They do not know how to use the correct volume (loudness) when they are talking. We need to use the correct volume when we talk to people. Why do you think it's important to use good volume? Discuss your answer with others in your group or write it on the back of this page.

Soft   Normal   **LOUD**

There are times when you need to speak louder or softer than you normally do. Some of those times are listed below.

Here are some places where you would speak softly:

- In the halls while classes are going on
- In the library
- When someone is sleeping

Can you think of any other times when you should talk softly? Write them below.

-
-
-

Here are some places where you would speak loudly:

- At a basketball game
- When you're talking to someone far away
- At a pep rally

Can you think of any other times when you should talk loudly? Write them below.

-
-
-

* *

DIRECTIONS: Circle the type of volume you would use in the situations below: loud, soft, or normal.

1. Your teacher is talking, and you need to borrow a pencil from the person next to you.   soft   normal   loud

2. Your father's boss is at your house.   soft   normal   loud

3. You are watching a movie in a movie theatre.   soft   normal   loud

4. You are at a football game and your team is winning.   soft   normal   loud

5. Your teacher calls on you to answer a question.   soft   normal   loud

6. You see your friend coming down the block.   soft   normal   loud

7. You are at a rock concert, and the lead singer wants everyone to sing along.   soft   normal   loud

8. You are out in the hall between classes.   soft   normal   loud

9. A teacher is disciplining you.   soft   normal   loud

10. You're talking with your group of friends at the park.   soft   normal   loud

VOLUME - VOLUME - VOLUME - VOLUME - VOLUME - Volume

1. Define the social skill of volume, and tell an important tip to remember.

   _____

   _____

2. Tell why it is important to use the correct volume when you talk to other people.

   _____

   _____

3. Describe a situation from the home, school, and community when you would need to use a quiet volume.

   (home) _____

   (school) _____

   (community) _____

4. Circle the type of volume you should use in the situations listed below.

   A. Your teacher is talking, and you need to borrow   soft   normal   loud
      a pencil from the person next to you.

   B. You are at a football game and your team   soft   normal   loud
      is winning.

   C. You are watching a movie in a movie theatre.   soft   normal   loud

   D. You are taking a walk with your best friend.   soft   normal   loud

   E. Your teacher is disciplining you for your   soft   normal   loud
      inappropriate behavior.

5. Pretend you are a teacher. You want to teach the social skill of volume to your students. Create a game you could play with them to help teach the difference between soft, normal, and loud volumes.

   _____

   _____

   _____

   _____

6. Write down the first name of one of your friends. Tell if that friend has a habit of talking too quietly, too loudly, or usually just right. Explain your answer.

   _____

   _____

SKILL HOMEWORK ACTIVITY

_____
(Due Date)

Dear Parent or Guardian of: _____

This week we are learning about the social communication skill:

TIME AND PLACE

This social skill is very important in interpersonal relationships.

It is important that students learn to choose the right time and place to talk to a person. They should ask themselves, "Is this a good time to talk to this person? Is this the right place?"

Before the due date, please complete one of the following activities with your son or daughter: (put a check mark by your choice)

_____ A. We acted out the role play situation listed below.

_____ B. I observed my son/daughter using this social skill in a real-life situation. (I have described the situation below.)

Description of real-life observation:

Role play situation:

YOU AND YOUR SISTER SHOULD DISCUSS WHAT WOULD BE THE BEST TIME AND PLACE TO ASK YOUR PARENTS IF YOU CAN GO ON A CAMPING TRIP WITH YOUR FRIENDS.

- -

Please circle the word below which best describes how your son or daughter did while using this social skill in either the role play or real-life situation.

NEEDS MORE HELP   GOOD   EXCELLENT

It is important for you to reinforce your child's use of this social skill at home in a positive way. Encourage and praise your child when you see the skill appropriately used. Remind him/her to use the social skill when necessary.

Thank you for your assistance.

Sincerely,

• •

PARENT/GUARDIAN SIGNATURE: _____

Name:_____

ASK YOURSELF

It is important to choose the right time and place to talk to someone. If you don't, the person you talk with may not have time to listen to you, or he may be in a bad mood and may get mad at you for talking to him then. Whenever you are going to talk to someone, ask yourself, "Is this the right time and place to talk to this person?"

Ask Yourself . . .

? Is this the

right time and

place to talk

to this person?

- **Is he busy?**
- **Is he in a hurry?**
- **Is he in a bad mood?**
- **Is this a bad place?**

SSS: Social Skill Strategies (Book A)

Name:_____

TIME and PLACE

DIRECTIONS: Tell why Ron chose the wrong time and place to ask the grocery store manager for an application.

Why was this the wrong time and place to ask for a job application?

Name:_____

THE RIGHT TIME AND PLACE?

DIRECTIONS: Read each situation below. Decide whether it is the right time and place to talk to someone or the wrong time and place. Write **RIGHT** or **WRONG** on the line. Tell **WHY** you wrote *right* or *wrong*.

EXAMPLE →

1. Jesse wants to find out which math assignments he missed when he was sick. It is the beginning of class. Mrs. Josky, the math teacher, hurries into the room. She is looking around on her desk for something. She tells a boy at the back of the room to calm down. Is this the right or wrong time and place to talk to her?

   _____*Wrong*_____ Why? *The teacher is in a hurry and has to start class. She probably doesn't have time to talk right now.*

2. Juan wants to ask his parents about staying overnight at a friend's house. He is with his parents at the table eating dinner. Is this the right or wrong time and place for Juan to talk to them?

   _____ Why?

3. Rebecca is really excited about the "A" she got on her science test. She wants to tell her best friend about it. When Rebecca finds Jennifer, she sees that Jennifer is crying because her boyfriend broke up with her. Is this the right or wrong time and place for Rebecca to tell her about the "A"?

   _____ Why?

4. Matt wants to ask his brother if he can borrow his new bike. Matt goes to his brother's room and sees that his brother is on the phone. Is this the right or wrong time and place for Matt to ask his brother about the bike?

   _____ Why?

5. Jackie wants to ask David about going to the school dance with her. David is in the gym with his friends watching a basketball game. Is this the right or wrong time and place for Jackie to ask David?

   _____ Why?

6. Adam wants to talk to his boss about working during the afternoon rather than at night. Adam's boss, Mr. Martinez, is sitting in his office. Mr. Martinez just got off the phone and looks like he's in a good mood. Is this the right or wrong time and place for Adam to talk with him?

_____ Why?

7. Molly wants to tease Luke about his new girlfriend. She sees him standing in the hallway. It looks like he's in an argument with someone. Is this the right or wrong time and place to tease Luke?

_____ Why?

8. Randy works as a short-order cook in a fast food restaurant. He isn't sure how late his boss wants him to work today. It's not too busy right now and his boss is in the back room. Is this the right or wrong time and place for Randy to talk with his boss?

_____ Why?

9. Mary wants to confront her brother about his using her tape player. When she walks in the house, she sees that her parents are yelling at her brother about not doing his chores. Is this the right or wrong time and place for Mary to confront her brother?

_____ Why?

10. Jim wants to talk to the assistant principal about the detention that he received from one of his teachers. The assistant principal is talking to two teachers. Is this the right or wrong time and place for Jim to talk to the assistant principal?

_____ Why?

Name:_____

Time and Place Log

DIRECTIONS: Complete the following log by filling in the information about people
you talked with or wanted to talk with.

_____

I talked with OR *I wanted to talk with:* _____
        (Circle one)

I talked about or wanted to talk about: _____

_____

Was it the right time and place to talk?   YES   NO

Why or why not?

_____

I talked with OR *I wanted to talk with:* _____
        (Circle one)

I talked about or wanted to talk about: _____

_____

Was it the right time and place to talk?   YES   NO

Why or why not?

_____

I talked with OR *I wanted to talk with:* _____
        (Circle one)

I talked about or wanted to talk about: _____

_____

Was it the right time and place to talk?   YES   NO

Why or why not?

_____

TIME AND PLACE - TIME AND PLACE - TIME AND PLACE

1. Define the social skill of time and place and tell an important tip to remember.

   _____

   _____

2. Explain, in your own words, why it is important to choose a good time and place to have a conversation.

   _____

   _____

   _____

3. Pretend that you want to break up with your boy/girl friend. Describe one bad time and place to do it and one good time and place to do it.

   (bad) _____

   (good) _____

4. Compare your mom with your dad: Tell what the best time and place to have a serious conversation with each of them *usually* is.

   (mom) _____

   _____

   (dad) _____

   _____

5. Pretend that you have a bad habit of choosing the wrong time and place to talk to people and you want to stop doing it. Think of two things you could do to help remind yourself of your goal.

   (strategy 1) _____

   _____

   (strategy 2) _____

   _____

6. Read the short story below. Decide if Molly chose a good time and place to talk to her mom or a bad time and place. Explain your answer.

   Molly wanted to get a part-time job to earn some extra spending money. She needed to ask her mom's permission. Her mom had just received a letter from one of Molly's teachers saying that she was failing the class. When Molly's mom talked to her about the letter, Molly decided to ask for permission to get a part-time job.

   Was this a good time and place to ask?   YES   NO

   (explanation) _____

   _____

   _____

SKILL HOMEWORK ACTIVITY

_____
(Due Date)

Dear Parent or Guardian of: _____

This week we are learning about the social communication skill:

TONE OF VOICE

This social skill is very important in interpersonal relationships.

The students have learned that how you say something can make a big difference. The students should use an appropriate tone of voice, especially when talking to authority figures (e.g., parents, teachers, principals).

Before the due date, please complete one of the following activities with your son or daughter: (put a check mark by your choice)

_____ A. We acted out the role play situation listed below.

_____ B. I observed my son/daughter using this social skill in a real-life situation. (I have described the situation below.)

Description of real-life observation:

Role play situation:

ONE OF YOUR PARENTS TELLS YOU THAT YOU NEED TO CLEAN YOUR ROOM BEFORE YOU CAN GO ANYWHERE. LET HIM/HER KNOW THAT YOU WILL CLEAN YOUR ROOM. MAKE SURE YOU USE AN APPROPRIATE TONE OF VOICE.

Please circle the word below which best describes how your son or daughter did while using this social skill in either the role play or real-life situation.

NEEDS MORE HELP   GOOD   EXCELLENT

It is important for you to reinforce your child's use of this social skill at home in a positive way. Encourage and praise your child when you see the skill appropriately used. Remind him/her to use the social skill when necessary.

Thank you for your assistance.

Sincerely,

* *

PARENT/GUARDIAN SIGNATURE: _____

Name:_____

IT'S THE TONE!

Your **tone of voice** *(how you sound when you say something)* is very important. HOW you say something is often more important than WHAT you say. A person can say the same words, but mean many different things. See the examples below.

"Yes, I'll do it." (cheerful)
"Yes, I'll do it." (angry)
"Yes, I'll do it." (teasing)
"Yes, I'll do it." (bored)
"Yes, I'll do it." (snotty)
"Yes, I'll do it." (sincere)

Practice saying "Yes, I'll do it," in all these different ways.

* *

DIRECTIONS: Read each situation below. Write what you would say to that person. Then write what tone of voice you SHOULD use. For some situations, there is more than one right answer. An example is done for you. Use the words at the bottom of the page.

EXAMPLE

➡ 1. Your teacher tells you to go to your seat and get started on your work.

____*Yes, I'm going.*_____(*Sincere*)

2. Your mother tells you that your good friend is at the front door.

_____(   )

3. Your father asks you to take out the garbage.

_____(   )

4. The principal tells you to come to the office after school for a detention.

_____(   )

5. Your friend tells you that the person you think is cute likes you.

_____(   )

6. Your teacher tells you that you're failing science.

_____(   )

helpful   worried   determined   happy

excited   embarrassed   sincere   apologetic

Tone of Voice

Educator Instructions: This activity may be done in several ways. The following scripts may be read/role played in class by the teacher and another person. The scripts may be recorded on a cassette tape by the educator, or the scripts may be role played and video taped. Questions follow each script.

Script #1

The scene takes place in a classroom. The teacher, Mr. Salinsky, is talking to the class. One of the students, Tori, is turning around and talking to the person behind her.

Mr. Salinsky: So, we see that Jupiter is the largest of all the planets. Can anyone tell me the name of the planet -- ahh, Tori, please turn around and face the front of the room. You need to stop talking.

Tori: (sarcastically) Yes, sir, Mr. Salinsky!

Mr. Salinsky: Tori, I'm going to ask you to stay after school tonight.

Tori: What? I didn't do anything! All I said was, "Yes, sir." Boy, that's not fair!

QUESTIONS

1. Circle the word that best describes Tori's tone of voice when she said "Yes, sir, Mr. Salinsky."

   cheerful   apologetic   sarcastic   nice   silly

2. Why did Mr. Salinsky ask Tori to stay after school?

3. Do you think Tori really didn't understand why Mr. Salinsky was angry?

   (circle one)   YES   NO

   Why?

Script #2

The scene takes place in a classroom. The teacher, Ms. Marks, is working individually with a child. She is trying to get the student interested in the assignment. The student, Jeff, seems very bored and tired.

Ms. Marks: Jeff, you've been assigned to work in the group that is doing a report on mammals.

Jeff: (bored) Oh boy, I'm really excited.

Ms. Marks: (trying to get Jeff excited) You're so good at doing reports and drawing pictures, Jeff.

Jeff: (bored) Yes, I can't wait to get started.

Ms. Marks: (annoyed) Jeff, you need to get over to your group and get started on the report.

QUESTIONS

1. Circle the word that best describes Jeff's tone of voice when Ms. Marks was talking to him.

> happy   angry   bored   funny   scared

2. Why do you think Ms. Marks started to get annoyed with Jeff?

3. How do you feel when you talk to a person like Jeff?

Name:_____

HOW YOU SAY IT

DIRECTIONS: Read the following script twice with a partner. The first time, read it with an angry tone of voice. The second time, read it with a calm tone of voice. Notice the difference you can make just by changing your tone of voice.

Terry: Have you finished your part of the report yet?

Chris: No, I didn't.

Terry: When do you think you'll be able to get it done?

Chris: Oh, who knows?

Terry: I hope it's soon.

• •

DIRECTIONS: Answer each of the following questions.

1. Tell a time when it would be appropriate to use an angry tone of voice.

2. Tell a time when it would not be appropriate to use an angry tone of voice.

3. Tell a time when it would be appropriate to use a cheerful tone of voice.

4. Tell a time when it would not be appropriate to use a cheerful tone of voice.

5. Tell a time when it would be appropriate to use a boring tone of voice.

6. Tell a time when it would not be appropriate to use a boring tone of voice.

TONE OF VOICE - TONE OF VOICE - TONE OF VOICE

1. Define the social skill **_tone of voice_** and tell an important tip to remember.

   _____

   _____

   _____

2. Tell three words that can describe someone's tone of voice.

   _____   _____   _____

3. Describe a situation when you would want to use a sincere tone of voice, an excited tone of voice, and an angry tone of voice.

   (sincere) _____

   (excited) _____

   (angry) _____

4. Compare the two situations described below, and decide which tone of voice you should use in each.

   (1) Your best friend just told you that he/she is moving to a new town.

        (tone of voice) _____

   (2) You just found out that you won an important award at school.

        (tone of voice) _____

5. Write a short story about Lisa, who used an insincere tone of voice when she apologized to her friend for being late.

   _____

   _____

   _____

   _____

6. Describe a time when you used the wrong tone of voice with someone and ended up getting in trouble because of it.

   _____

   _____

SKILL HOMEWORK ACTIVITY

_____
(Due Date)

Dear Parent or Guardian of: _____

This week we are learning about the social communication skill:

GETTING TO THE POINT

This social skill is very important in interpersonal relationships.

When a person is afraid to say something, he may avoid the subject by "beating around the bush." The person may be embarrassed about what he has to say, or is afraid the answer to his question will be _no_. The person may have bad news to deliver and is afraid to come right out and say it.

The students have learned that it is usually better to come straight to the point, instead of beating around the bush.

Before the due date, please complete one of the following activities with your son or daughter: (put a check mark by your choice)

_____ A. We acted out the role play situation listed below.

_____ B. I observed my son/daughter using this social skill in a real-life situation. (I have described the situation below.)

Description of real-life observation:

Role play situation:

PRETEND YOU RODE YOUR BIKE INTO THE GARAGE AND SCRATCHED YOUR PARENTS' CAR. DEMONSTRATE HOW YOU WOULD TELL THEM. GET STRAIGHT TO THE POINT.

- -

Please circle the word below which best describes how your son or daughter did while using this social skill in either the role play or real-life situation.

NEEDS MORE HELP   GOOD   EXCELLENT

It is important for you to reinforce your child's use of this social skill at home in a positive way. Encourage and praise your child when you see the skill appropriately used. Remind him/her to use the social skill when necessary.

Thank you for your assistance.

Sincerely,

. . . .

PARENT/GUARDIAN SIGNATURE: _____

Which Meaning?

The phrase **"getting to the point"** has two different meanings: One *literal* meaning (when you take the words for exactly what they say) and one *figurative* meaning (when the words mean something different than they usually do).

Below is an example of the **literal** meaning.

Here is an example of the **figurative** meaning.

The phrase **"beating around the bush"** also has two different meanings, one literal meaning and one figurative meaning. Below is an example of the **literal** meaning.

Here is an example of the **figurative** meaning.

There is a social communication rule that says, "DON'T BEAT AROUND THE BUSH WHEN YOU TALK TO SOMEONE. GET STRAIGHT TO THE POINT." To understand this rule, remember the **FIGURATIVE** meanings shown above.

Reasons Why

DIRECTIONS: Listed below are situations when you might beat around the bush. Add four new situations to the list.

1. You might beat around the bush because you got a detention at school and you are afraid to tell your parents.

2. You might not come straight to the point because you have a rip in your pants and you are embarrassed to ask permission to go to the sewing room to repair them.

3. You might beat around the bush because you want to break up with your boyfriend/ girlfriend and you are nervous about telling him/her.

4. You might have a hard time coming to the point because you have to tell your younger brother that your dog died and you are afraid he will be very upset.

5.

6.

7.

8.

DIRECTIONS: Below is a list of reasons why you want to avoid beating around the bush. Add two new reasons to the list.

1. Your listener might get bored.

2. You don't want to waste your listener's time.

3.

4.

(Sometimes, beating around the bush can be a good thing. For example, if you have to announce that someone/something died, you may want to do it gradually, to help ease your listener's shock.)

Name:_____

Practice Point

DIRECTIONS: For each of the situations below, write down the exact words you would say to the person. Make certain you get straight to the point.

1. You used your sister's portable radio without asking, and you damaged it. You are afraid to tell her, but you know you have to.

   _____

   _____

   _____

2. You're on your way to go bowling, and you realize you forgot socks. You are embarrassed, but you have to ask your friends to go back, so you can get some.

   _____

   _____

   _____

3. You want to ask your dad if you can get a cat. You are afraid to ask him, because you think he will probably say *no*.

   _____

   _____

   _____

4. You think you have been spending too much time with your boy/girlfriend. You would like to be able to spend some time with your other friends too. You are afraid he/she will be really mad, but you know you have to talk about it.

   _____

   _____

   _____

5. You helped count the votes for the student council election. You found out that your brother did not get elected. You know you'll have to tell him, because he knows that you counted the votes. You feel bad about having to deliver the news.

   _____

   _____

GETTING TO THE POINT - GETTING TO THE POINT

1. Explain what *getting to the point* means.

   _____

   Explain what *beating around the bush* means.

   _____

2. Explain why it is usually best to get straight to the point when you have something to say or ask.

   _____

   _____

3. Give an example of a time at home when you would talk to a parent and you would want to get to the point.

   _____

   _____

4. List three situations when you might be tempted to *beat around the bush*.

   (1) _____

   (2) _____

   (3) _____

5. Write a short story about Kris, who *beat around the bush* when she wanted to ask her teacher for extra time to work on her book report.

   _____

   _____

   _____

   _____

6. Read what Steve said to Theresa when he asked her out on a date. Decide if he got straight to the point or not and explain why.

   "Hi, Theresa. How is it going? There is a great comedy playing at the theater this weekend. Would you like to go see it with me on Friday night?"

   Did Steve get straight to the point?   YES   NO

   (why) _____

   _____

SKILL HOMEWORK ACTIVITY

_____
(Due Date)

Dear Parent or Guardian of: _____

This week we are learning about the social communication skill:

STAYING ON TOPIC AND SWITCHING TOPICS

This social skill is very important in interpersonal relationships.

The students have learned not to change to a different topic when they are talking to someone, unless they warn their listener of the topic shift first (e.g., "This is changing topics, but . . ." or "By the way . . .").

Before the due date, please complete one of the following activities with your son or daughter: (put a check mark by your choice)

_____ A. We acted out the role play situation listed below.

_____ B. I observed my son/daughter using this social skill in a real-life situation. (I have described the situation below.)

Description of real-life observation:

Role play situation:

YOU ARE TALKING TO YOUR MOM/DAD ABOUT WHAT YOU DID AT SCHOOL TODAY. YOU WANT TO SHIFT TOPICS AND ASK ABOUT SLEEPING OVER AT YOUR FRIEND'S HOUSE THIS WEEKEND. DEMONSTRATE HOW YOU COULD CHANGE TOPICS APPROPRIATELY.

- -

Please circle the word below which best describes how your son or daughter did while using this social skill in either the role play or real-life situation.

NEEDS MORE HELP   GOOD   EXCELLENT

It is important for you to reinforce your child's use of this social skill at home in a positive way. Encourage and praise your child when you see the skill appropriately used. Remind him/her to use the social skill when necessary.

Thank you for your assistance.

Sincerely,

• •

PARENT/GUARDIAN SIGNATURE: _____

About Topics . . .

A good rule to add to your "list" of social communication skills is this: **Stick to the topic** when you are having a conversation with someone.

A *topic* is *the main idea or subject of what you are talking about*. If you and a friend are talking about an upcoming school dance, you want to make certain that your comments deal with the topic of the school dance.

Below is a script between Jack and his friend Gary. Unfortunately, Jack has not learned the social communication rule of staying on topic.

Jack, The Topic Jumper

Situation: Jack is downtown picking up a part for his bike. He runs into Gary, one of his friends from school.

Jack: Hi, Gary!

Gary: Hey, Jack! How's it going? What are you doing down here?

Jack: Oh, I have to get a new part for my bike. Did I tell you what happened to it?

Gary: No, what?

Jack: Well, I was riding my bike down this big hill when I saw Jennifer. She's a new girl who moved into our neighborhood. Did I tell you about Jennifer? She's in our grade, and is she ever cute! She moved here from Clintonville. My grandma lives in Clintonville. We go there to visit her every Thanksgiving. Only we didn't go last year because I got my appendix taken out. Did I ever show you my stitches?

Gary: (Looking confused because Jack keeps switching topics) No, I don't think you have.

Jack: I had to stay in the hospital for three days. I was gone from home longer than that once, when I went to Boy Scout camp. That camp was great! We went fishing and hiking. The hiking wasn't quite as difficult as the hike I took with my dad last summer. We went on that hike right after my sister came home from college and was she ever mad at Dad for leaving right away. I better get going or the bike store might close. I'll see you later, Gary.

Gary: Bye, Jack.

        (Jack leaves. All Gary can do is shake his head and laugh at Jack for the way he jumps from one topic to the next, without warning his listener.)

* *

Tell how you would feel if you had a friend like Jack, the topic jumper.

More About the Topic Rule

When you have a nice long talk with your friend on the phone, it would get pretty boring if you talked about the same topic the entire time.

The social communication rule about staying on topic should have something added to it. The rule should go like this: **Stick to the topic, unless you give your listener advance warning that you are going to change it.**

Here is a list of things you could say, to go smoothly from one topic to the next:

1. "By the way . . ."

2. "This is changing the topic, but . . ."

3. "Speaking of that . . ."

4. "Oh, that reminds me . . ."

5. "This is off the topic, but . . ."

All the comments in the list above have something in common. They all give the listener warning that the topic is about to be changed.

DIRECTIONS: Read each of the situations below. If the person switched topics in a good way, write *good*. If the person switched topics in a bad way, write *bad*.

_____ 1. Eva and Luke are talking about last night's girls' basketball game. Eva says, "I thought the game was great. I love Tony's pizza. Let's go get some, I'm starving."

_____ 2. Melinda and Molly are trying to come up with an idea for their science project. Melinda says, "This is off the topic, Molly, but do you remember what our math assignment is for tomorrow?"

_____ 3. Nancy and Lou are discussing possible themes for their school dance. Nancy says, "This has absolutely nothing to do with the dance, but I need to ask if you've met that new guy named Mark yet."

_____ 4. Wayne and Lisa are trying to decide which video movie they should get at the store. Lisa says, "Steve said he saw a good movie. I need to go for a nice long run this weekend. I think I'm getting fat."

_____ 5. Judy and Abby are arguing about who is supposed to do the dishes tonight. Abby says, "I know it's your turn because I can remember doing them last night. Oh, and that reminds me, it's also your turn to clean the bathroom. I suggest you do it soon, because it looks like a pig pen."

What Could You Say?

DIRECTIONS: For each of the subjects listed below, write three different comments you could make that would stay on the topic.

1. School lunch

    • _____

    • _____

    • _____

2. Part-time jobs

    • _____

    • _____

    • _____

3. How parents should act

    • _____

    • _____

    • _____

DIRECTIONS: For each of the following situations, write what you would say next, to switch to a new topic appropriately.

1. You and your mom are talking about your grades. She says, "You're still doing really well in math. That always seems to be your best subject."

2. Your friend and you are talking about the food they serve in the hot lunch line. Your friend says, "I think the pizza is the best thing they serve here."

3. Your track coach is talking to you about how to improve your starts off the block. Your coach says, "Lean forward as far as you can, so when the gun goes off, you get a fast start."

Name:_____

Story Creation

DIRECTIONS: Write a script that includes two characters. Show that your characters know how to stay on topic. Your script should also include at least three good topic shifts. If you need more room, write on the back.

CHARACTERS: _____

_____

SCENE DESCRIPTION: _____

_____

_____

_____

Character's   Character's comment
name

_____: " _____

_____ "

_____: " _____

_____ "

_____: " _____

_____ "

_____: " _____

_____ "

_____: " _____

_____ "

_____: " _____

_____ "

                       SSS: Social Skill Strategies (Book A)

STAYING ON TOPIC AND SWITCHING TOPICS

1. Tell what the following two things mean.

   Staying on topic: _____

   Switching topics: _____

2. Explain why it is important to warn your listener before you switch topics.

   _____

   _____

3. Pretend you are talking to your boss about uniforms, and you want to switch topics so you can ask for next Saturday off. Write what you would say.

   _____

   _____

4. Write two topics you usually discuss with your friends and two topics you usually discuss with your parents.

   (friends)_____

   (parents) _____

5. Pretend that you have a bad habit of switching topics without warning your listeners and you want to stop doing it. Write down two strategies you could use to help yourself reach your goal.

   (Strategy 1) _____

   _____

   (Strategy 2) _____

   _____

6. Read the short script below. Decide if Paulette switched topics correctly or not. Explain your answer.

   Mark: I thought that test we took in science was pretty easy. What did you think about it?

   Paulette: It wasn't too bad, I guess. I hope I can make it to work without being late today.

   Did Paulette switch topics correctly? YES   NO

   Explain:_____

   _____

SKILL HOMEWORK ACTIVITY

_____
(Due Date)

Dear Parent or Guardian of: _____

This week we are learning about the social communication skill:

LISTENING

This social skill is very important in interpersonal relationships.

The students have learned that there are six good ways to show someone that they are listening:

1. Give the speaker good eye contact.
2. Lean forward slightly to show interest in what is being said.
3. Nod your head and give the speaker feedback to show you understand.
4. Ask questions that deal with the speaker's topic.
5. Give the speaker your full attention.
6. Let the speaker finish before you talk.

Before the due date, please complete one of the following activities with your son or daughter: (put a check mark by your choice)

_____ A. We acted out the role play situation listed below.

_____ B. I observed my son/daughter using this social skill in a real-life situation. (I have described the situation below.)

Description of real-life observation:

Role play situation:

YOUR DAD IS TALKING TO YOU ABOUT A PROBLEM AT WORK. DEMONSTRATE THE USE OF THE SIX STRATEGIES LISTED ABOVE WHILE YOU ARE LISTENING TO HIM.

Please circle the word below which best describes how your son or daughter did while using this social skill in either the role play or real-life situation.

NEEDS MORE HELP   GOOD   EXCELLENT

It is important for you to reinforce your child's use of this social skill at home in a positive way. Encourage and praise your child when you see the skill appropriately used. Remind him/her to use the social skill when necessary.

Thank you for your assistance.

Sincerely,

• •

PARENT/GUARDIAN SIGNATURE: _____

LISTENING FACTS

Fact #1: Of the four skills (listening, speaking, reading, and writing), listening is the communication skill you spend the greatest amount of time doing.

Below is a pie graph which shows how the average person's communication time is spent (Werner, 1975).

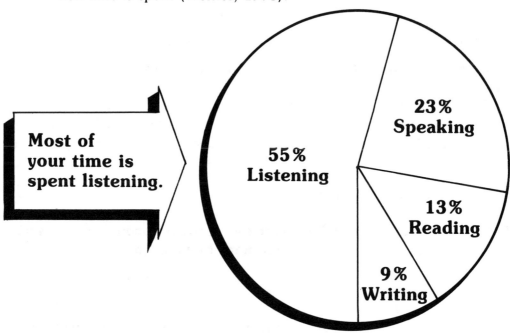

Fact #2: For a conversation to be a good one, the two people involved need to take turns being the speaker and the listener.

QUESTION: Tell what would happen in a conversation if two people were talking, and neither one was listening.

Listening Strategies

6 GOOD STRATEGIES

(TO LET SOMEONE KNOW YOU ARE LISTENING)

1 Give the speaker good eye contact.

2 Lean forward slightly to show interest in what is being said.

3 Nod your head and give the speaker feedback (e.g., say things like, "Oh yeah?" or "uh-huh!").

4 Ask questions that deal with the speaker's topic.

5 Give the speaker your full attention. (Try not to do two things at once.)

6 Let the speaker finish before you talk. (Don't interrupt.)

DIRECTIONS: Add three more examples to this list of times when you would want to be a good listener.

1. When your teacher is giving directions

2. When your friend is upset

3.

4.

5.

Name:_____

LISTENING in the CLASSROOM

"Attending" means *paying attention to the person you should be paying attention to.* It means watching and listening to that person. It means concentrating on what that person is saying.

DIRECTIONS: Pretend that you are teaching the four students pictured below. You are trying to teach the students an important lesson. When you look at the four students, which students seem to be paying attention?

Letters_____

DIRECTIONS: List five negative things that can happen when you do not attend and listen to the teacher when you are in class.

1._____

2._____

3._____

4._____

5._____

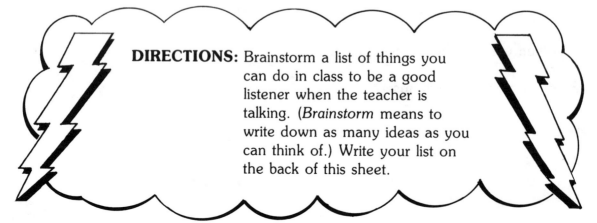

DIRECTIONS: Brainstorm a list of things you can do in class to be a good listener when the teacher is talking. (*Brainstorm* means to write down as many ideas as you can think of.) Write your list on the back of this sheet.

Name:_____

THINK ABOUT IT

Think of someone you know whom you consider to be a good listener.
(The person can be your age, older, or younger.)

Person's first name: _____

Explain what it is about that person that makes him or her such a good listener.

_____

_____

_____

Do you think you are usually a good listener or a poor listener? _____

Explain your answer:

_____

_____

_____

_____

Think of someone you know who you believe is a poor listener.
(The person can be your age, older, or younger.)

Person's first name: _____

Explain what it is about that person that makes him or her such a poor listener.

_____

_____

_____

Just Listen

Pretend that a good friend comes to you with a problem and asks you to help solve it. What happens if you don't feel comfortable giving your opinion, or you don't know how to solve the problem? Don't Panic!

SOMETIMES, ALL YOU NEED TO DO IS BE A GOOD LISTENER.

"I need to talk to you. It's really important. I had such a horrible night last night! I really need your help. Last night I was walking downtown and I saw my dad and this other lady walking out of some place. They were laughing. The lady looked like an old bag. Anyway, my dad actually kissed her! I thought I was going to scream! It was awful. How could he do that? I need you to help me decide whether or not I should tell my mom. She would go nuts if she knew. Boy, she'd feel really bad. But why should my dad get away with that? He can't do that to her! Of course, maybe I'm jumping to conclusions. Maybe there is a logical explanation. I'm going to talk to my dad about it and see what he says. Yeah, that's what I'll do. Gee, thanks so much for helping me out with my problem! You're such a great friend! What would I do without you? I'll call you later and tell you what I find out. Bye."

SSS: Social Skill Strategies (Book A)

Name:_____

What Went WRONG ?

Remember, there are six good strategies or "tips" to use when you want to show someone that you are listening:

1. Give the speaker good eye contact.

2. Lean forward slightly to show interest in what is being said.

3. Nod your head and give the speaker feedback to show you understand.

4. Ask questions that deal with the speaker's topic.

5. Give the speaker your full attention.

6. Let the speaker finish before you talk.

DIRECTIONS: In each of the situations below, Lester is a poor listener. After reading each of the situations, decide which of the six "tips" Lester should have used.

1. Lester's teacher was talking to him about correcting his assignment. He looked at the floor and then out the window. He did not look at the teacher.

    Lester should have used tip #_____

2. Lester's friend, Beth, was telling him about a movie she saw. Lester asked Beth if she got her hair cut.

    Lester should have used tip #_____

3. Lester's mom was talking to him about the importance of doing his house chores. Lester interrupted and asked, "Mom, what chores am I supposed to do?

    Lester should have used tip #_____

4. Lester's brother was talking to him about school. Lester tried to listen and watch TV at the same time.

    Lester should have used tip #_____

5. Lester's science class had a guest speaker. Lester slouched in his desk and yawned several times during the presentation.

    Lester should have used tip #_____

6. Lester's boss was telling him what he should do that day at work. Lester listened, but didn't move or say anything while his boss was talking to him.

    Lester should have used tip #_____

LISTENING - LISTENING - LISTENING - LISTENING - LISTENING

---

1. Define the social skill "listening" and list six ways to show someone you are being a good listener.

   (listening) _____

   (1) _____   (2) _____

   (3) _____   (4) _____

   (5) _____   (6) _____

2. Explain why it is important to be a good listener when your friend is talking to you.

   _____

   _____

3. Describe a situation from the home, school, and community when you would want to be a good listener.

   (home) _____

   (school) _____

   (community) _____

4. Contrast listening to a song on the radio with listening to your teacher giving directions. Describe how your listening skills would differ in each situation.

   (song) _____

   (directions) _____

5. Pretend you have an assignment to design and make a poster to hang in your school to help improve students' listening skills. What would your poster say?

   _____

   _____

6. During which class at school are you the best listener? Why?

   (class) _____

   (reason) _____

   During which class at school should you be a better listener? Why?

   (class) _____

   (reason) _____

SKILL HOMEWORK ACTIVITY

_____
(Due Date)

Dear Parent or Guardian of: _____

This week we are learning about the social communication skill:

STARTING, MAINTAINING, AND ENDING A CONVERSATION

This social skill is very important in interpersonal relationships.

The students have learned that many conversations begin with a greeting and name (e.g., "Hello, Mrs. Kiser." or "Hi, Shelby.") followed by small talk (e.g., "How have you been?" or "Sure is hot today, isn't it!")

The students have also learned that most conversations should end smoothly with some type of farewell (e.g., "Bye, David. See ya tomorrow." or "Good-bye, Mrs. Gajewski. Have a nice day.")

Before the due date, please complete one of the following activities with your son or daughter: (put a check mark by your choice)

_____ A. We acted out the role play situation listed below.

_____ B. I observed my son/daughter using this social skill in a real-life situation. (I have described the situation below.)

Description of real-life observation:

Role play situation:

PRETEND YOU ARE JUST GETTING HOME FROM THE SCHOOL DANCE AND YOU SEE YOUR MOM IN THE LIVING ROOM. DEMONSTRATE HOW YOU WOULD HAVE A CONVERSATION WITH HER. REMEMBER TO BEGIN AND END YOUR CONVERSATION SMOOTHLY, AND INCLUDE SOME SMALL TALK. (E.G., "HI, MOM. HOW'S IT GOING?" AND "WELL, I BETTER GET TO BED, I'M REALLY TIRED. SEE YOU IN THE MORNING.")

Please circle the word below which best describes how your son or daughter did while using this social skill in either the role play or real-life situation.

NEEDS MORE HELP   GOOD   EXCELLENT

It is important for you to reinforce your child's use of this social skill at home in a positive way. Encourage and praise your child when you see the skill appropriately used. Remind him/her to use the social skill when necessary.

Thank you for your assistance.

Sincerely,

* *

PARENT/GUARDIAN SIGNATURE: _____

Getting Started #1

Whenever you begin a conversation with a person, it is important to start with a greeting and a name. Saying "Hello, Mr. Welch" or "Hi, Pete" is a small thing, but it can make a big difference to the success of a conversation.

Below is an illustration of what could happen if a conversation is not started in the correct way. Notice the student does not greet the teacher.

Now, look at the difference in this situation, when the student remembers to say "Hello."

When you begin a conversation over the phone, you still need to greet and name the person you are calling, but you should also introduce yourself. (Even if you know someone very well, do not assume they will recognize you from your voice.)

Below is an illustration of what could happen if you begin a telephone conversation, and forget to introduce yourself.

Getting Started #2

Remember, it is very important to start a conversation with a greeting (a form of saying "hello" or "hi") and a name.

Pretend that two teens, Melissa and Carol, are interviewing for the same babysitting job. Based on what you read below, who do you think started the conversation in a better way — Melissa or Carol?

Melissa	**Carol**
Melissa: Are you the people who listed the babysitting job in the school paper?	Carol: Hello, Mrs. Simon. My name is Carol Theune. I read in the school newspaper that you are taking applications for a babysitter. I would like to apply.
Parent: Yes, we are. My name is Mrs. Simon.	
Melissa: Yes, I know. The office gave me your name.	Parent: Hello, Carol. Why don't you come in and you can tell me about your babysitting experience.
Parent: Oh!	

Carol did a better job of beginning the conversation, because she included a greeting and a name (e.g., "Hello, Mrs. Simon.").

DIRECTIONS: Write down the first words you would say to start the conversations listed below.

1. You come home from school and see your brother Ben. What would you say to start a conversation with him?

2. You call Marge, one of the other students in your science class, because you forgot when the project is due. Marge answers the phone and says, "Hello?" What would you say to start the conversation?

3. You go to the auto shop with your dad to get his car repaired. You see your teacher, Mr. Furst, is there also. You want to ask him what is wrong with his car. What would you say to begin the conversation?

4. You call your mother's office to see if you can talk to her. Her secretary, Ms. Johnston, answers the phone. What would you say to begin the conversation?

Small **Talk**

Listen to conversations that other people have. The first thing you will hear is the start of the conversation which includes a greeting. Next, you will probably hear what is called small talk. **Small talk** is *light/casual talk or chitchat*. It doesn't really mean anything important, but it helps people ease into the more important parts of their conversation.

DIRECTIONS: Below is a conversation between Mark and his father. Mark telephones his dad to ask for advice on what might be wrong with his car. Notice that the different parts of the conversation are labeled.

* *

Greeting
- Dad: Hello?
- Mark: Hi, Dad! This is Mark.
- Dad: Well hi, Mark!

Small Talk
- Mark: How's everything with you and Mom?
- Dad: Your mom and I have been feeling great. The weather has been beautiful. How is the weather out there?
- Mark: It has rained a lot in the last week, but it's starting to clear up.
- Dad: Well, it keeps everything green.

Main Point
- Mark: That's for sure. Say Dad, I'm having some trouble with my car. I wonder if you could give me any advice?
- Dad: Well, I can try. What seems to be the problem?
- Mark: Well . . .

(The conversation continues.)

* *

Notice that Mark made certain to chat with his dad for a while (small talk) before he jumped right in to the main reason he called. He wanted his dad to know that he was happy to talk to him. The small talk made the conversation go more smoothly. Sometimes, when people are in a hurry, there is not enough time for small talk. If you are not in a rush, however, including small talk is a good idea.

Below is a conversation between Paul and his mother. He gets home from school and finds her in the family room.

* *

Greeting
- Paul: Hi, Mom!
- Mom: Hi, Paul! How was school?

Main Point
- Paul: Mom, I need $5.00 to order a yearbook. Do you have any money?
- Mom: (sounding angry) You just get home from school and the first thing you do is ask for money?

(The conversation continues.)

* *

Notice that Paul left out the small talk. You can't be certain, but maybe if he had remembered, his mom wouldn't have been so upset when he asked for the money.

FIND THE PARTS

DIRECTIONS: For both scripts below:

    (1) Circle the section that starts the conversation with a greeting and name.

    (2) Underline the part you consider to be small talk.

    (3) Draw a rectangle around the part that starts the main point of the conversation.

Script #1: (Patty goes to her friend Laurie's house to borrow earrings.)

Patty: Hi, Laurie!

Laurie: Hi, I was hoping you'd come over. I'm bored out of my head!

Patty: How was English with that creepy Mr. Henry today?

Laurie: Great! He was sick. We had a sub.

Patty: Oh, yeah? Who did you have?

Laurie: Ms. Sorenson. She was pretty good. Have you ever had her before?

Patty: I don't think so.

Laurie: Do you have to study tonight, or can you stay?

Patty: I have to read my book for the report. Say Laurie, are you planning to wear your red hoop earrings this Friday?

(The conversation continues.)

* *

Script #2: (Aldo's dad just gets home from golfing. Aldo wants to ask if he can use the car to go pick up a new tape.)

Aldo: Hi, Dad!

Dad: Hi, Son. How was school today?

Aldo: Pretty good. How was your golf game?

Dad: Not bad. I shot a 43, but I missed a few short putts.

Aldo: Putting is a killer. Was it busy at the golf course?

Dad: No, actually. We had a pretty fast round.

Aldo: Say Dad, I was wondering if I could use the car to go pick up a tape?

Dad: Can you be home by 6:00? I have to go over and help Fred with his basement.

Aldo: No problem.

(The conversation continues.)

Questions

Pretend you are sitting in the waiting room at your dentist's office. Someone you know walks in and sits down beside you. You have been meaning to tell that person something for a couple of days. Now is a good time to tell the person, so getting a conversation going is easy.

But what if you don't have anything important to ask or say to the person? You say, "Hi! How are you?" and then can't think of anything else to say. The silence is uncomfortable and you feel like you should talk to the person. What should you say? How can you get the other person talking too?

Asking questions is an excellent way to get a conversation started and to keep a conversation going! Asking questions is also a good way to show that you are interested in the other person and not just interested in talking about yourself.

DIRECTIONS: Write down one question you could ask about each of the following topics.

1. A person's family -

2. A person's health -

3. A person's weekend -

4. A person's special interests -

5. A person's work or school experiences -

Pretend you decide to ask the person in the waiting room about his special interest in basketball. You ask, "How is basketball practice going?" and he says, "Good, but the coach has really been working us hard this past week."

Don't feel like your next question has to be about a different topic. Your next question can be a follow-up to what he just said. For example, you could ask, "Why has the coach been working you so hard?" By asking a follow-up question, you are showing the person that you heard what he said, and you are interested in finding out more.

How Does It All End?

Not only does a smooth conversation need a good start, but it also needs a good ending. Conversations should be ended with a farewell (e.g., "Good-bye, Ms. Smithson. Have a nice day." or "Bye, Luke. See ya around.").

Closing a conversation can be more difficult than getting one started, especially if the other person is interested in continuing to talk. Here is a strategy you can try:

Strategy: Before you say good-bye, make a comment that gives your listener a clue that you need to end the conversation.

Examples: "Well, I better get going here."

"Well, it's been nice talking to you!"

"The bell is just about ready to ring. We'd better go!"

"Oh, I almost forgot! I have to go . . ."

"I'll talk to you more later, I have to . . ."

DIRECTIONS: Write down what you could say to end the following conversations.

1. You are talking to your best friend between classes. You have to go up three floors for your next class.

2. Your mom is talking with you about the fishing trip your family is taking this weekend. You have to leave to go to basketball practice.

3. A boy/girl from school, who likes you, calls you on the phone. He/she won't quit talking, and you have to do some homework.

4. You are visiting your grandmother in the nursing home. She is very happy to have the company. You need to go home before it gets dark outside.

EDUCATOR PAGE: DO NOT DUPLICATE FOR STUDENTS

The following activity is most appropriate for use with students who are withdrawn and shy. The activity is relevant for students who feel uncomfortable starting and maintaining conversations.

DIRECTIONS:

1. Ask your students to brainstorm a list of questions that could be asked or comments that could be made during a conversation.

2. Divide your students into teams of two or three.

3. Tell the students that each team will be asked to have a conversation. During the conversation, each person on the team must talk, and pauses longer than 10 seconds will not be allowed. During the conversation, team members may refer to the list they brainstormed in step one. Let the students know that you will tell them when the conversation should be ended, so that the conversation can be ended smoothly and appropriately.

4. One at a time, give each team a chance to hold a conversation that lasts for 45 seconds. Each team that is successful should then be advanced to a 60-second conversation, then a 90-second conversation, a two-minute conversation, and so on.

5. Decide what length of a conversation you would like the teams to work up to, and then offer a reward when each team reaches that level.

6. This activity may be carried out during a part of several class periods.

7. You may need to remind your students to use follow-up questions.

8. After each conversation has ended, provide feedback to the team by pointing out strengths and making suggestions for improvement.

STARTING, MAINTAINING, AND ENDING A CONVERSATION

1. List two things you should include when you begin a conversation.

    (1) _____

    (2) _____

    List two things you should include when you end a conversation.

    (1) _____

    (2) _____

    Define *small talk*:_____

2. Explain why it is important to end a conversation smoothly.

    _____

    _____

    Explain the purpose of small talk.

    _____

    _____

3. Describe a situation at school when you would want to include small talk and a time when you would not want to.

    (small talk) _____

    (no small talk) _____

4. List two greeting and farewell words you would use with adults and two greeting and farewell words you would use with peers (people your age).

    (adult) _____

    (peer)_____

5. List five things you could ask or say that would be small talk.

    (1) _____

    (2) _____

    (3) _____

    (4) _____

    (5) _____

6. Decide if you are better at beginning conversations correctly or ending them correctly. Explain your answer.

    _____

    _____

    _____

SKILL HOMEWORK ACTIVITY

_____
(Due Date)

Dear Parent or Guardian of: _____

This week we are learning about the social communication skill:

PROXIMITY

This social skill is very important in interpersonal relationships.

Proximity means how far away to stand from someone. We use a very simple rule when talking about proximity: Usually stand an arm's length away from someone.

Before the due date, please complete one of the following activities with your son or daughter: (put a check mark by your choice)

_____ A. We acted out the role play situation listed below.

_____ B. I observed my son/daughter using this social skill in a real-life situation. (I have described the situation below.)

Description of real-life observation:

Role play situation:

YOUR MOTHER'S FRIEND IS VISITING FROM ANOTHER STATE. YOU ARE HAPPY TO SEE HER. GO UP TO HER AND START A CONVERSATION. REMEMBER TO STAND AN ARM'S LENGTH AWAY.

- -

Please circle the word below which best describes how your son or daughter did while using this social skill in either the role play or real-life situation.

NEEDS MORE HELP   GOOD   EXCELLENT

It is important for you to reinforce your child's use of this social skill at home in a positive way. Encourage and praise your child when you see the skill appropriately used. Remind him/her to use the social skill when necessary.

Thank you for your assistance.

Sincerely,

* *

PARENT/GUARDIAN SIGNATURE: _____

Name:_____

PROXIMITY

Proximity means *how close you stand to someone*. In our country, people usually stand about two to three feet away from someone when they are having a conversation with them. In some other countries, people stand closer together or farther apart when they talk. Proximity is easy to remember if you learn this simple rule:

STAND AN ARM'S LENGTH AWAY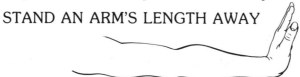

If you stand too close to people when you are talking to them, they may feel uncomfortable. If you stand too far away from people when you are talking to them, they may think that you don't like them. Look at the pictures below which show:
  1) people standing too far away.
  2) people standing too close.
  3) people standing just the right distance apart.

TOO FAR	TOOCLOSE	JUST RIGHT

1. How would you feel here?	2. How would you feel here?	3. How would you feel here?

DIRECTIONS: Write the proximity rule inside of the arm.

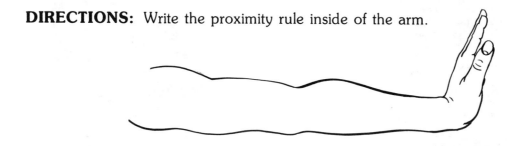

SSS: Social Skill Strategies (Book A)

Name:_____

S
T
A
N
D by Me

DIRECTIONS: Cut out the people below. Glue or tape them onto another white sheet. Place the people the right distance apart for having a conversation. Remember the rule:

STAND AN ARM'S LENGTH AWAY FROM SOMEONE

You may want to bring your people to "life" by adding a background to the picture. Ask your teacher to hold a contest to judge the best picture(s).

SSS: Social Skill Strategies (Book A)

PROXIMITY - PROXIMITY - PROXIMITY - PROXIMITY

1. Define the social skill of proximity and tell the rule to remember.

   _____

   _____

   _____

2. Explain why it's important to stand the right distance away from people.

   _____

   _____

   _____

3. Tell a time when it might be appropriate to stand farther than an arm's length away.

   _____

   Tell a time when it might be appropriate to stand closer than an arm's length away.

   _____

4. Describe how you feel when someone stands too close to you and when someone stands too far away from you.

   (too close)_____

   _____

   (too far away) _____

   _____

5. Write a short story about a boy who stood too close to people when he talked with them. Tell how the people felt when he stood too close. (Use the back of this page if you need more space.)

   _____

   _____

   _____

   _____

6. Evaluate yourself on the social skill of proximity. Circle the statement that best describes you:

   I usually stand too close.

   I usually stand an arm's length away.

   I usually stand too far away.

   Explain:_____

   _____

SKILL HOMEWORK ACTIVITY

_____
(Due Date)

Dear Parent or Guardian of: _____

This week we are learning about the social communication skill:

BODY LANGUAGE

This social skill is very important in interpersonal relationships.

The students have learned that a person's body language tells us a lot. It is important to "read" the body language of other people and to use appropriate body language ourselves.

Before the due date, please complete one of the following activities with your son or daughter: (put a check mark by your choice)

_____ A. We acted out the role play situation listed below.

_____ B. I observed my son/daughter using this social skill in a real-life situation. (I have described the situation below.)

Description of real-life observation:

Role play situation:

YOUR GREAT-AUNT FROM CALIFORNIA IS VISITING. SHE'S NICE, BUT SHE TALKS TOO MUCH. YOU WANT TO BE POLITE AND INTERESTED IN WHAT SHE IS SAYING. USE GOOD BODY LANGUAGE AND LOOK INTERESTED WHILE YOU ARE LISTENING TO HER.

- -

Please circle the word below which best describes how your son or daughter did while using this social skill in either the role play or real-life situation.

NEEDS MORE HELP   GOOD   EXCELLENT

It is important for you to reinforce your child's use of this social skill at home in a positive way. Encourage and praise your child when you see the skill appropriately used. Remind him/her to use the social skill when necessary.

Thank you for your assistance.

Sincerely,

* *

PARENT/GUARDIAN SIGNATURE: _____

Name:_____

Body Language

Body language means *emotions/feelings that we express with our bodies.* We can learn a lot about people by "reading" their body language. We can often tell if they are excited, angry, bored, and so forth, just by reading their body language.

Sometimes, it's easy to read body language as in Picture #1. We know this boy is angry. Some people are more subtle (not as open) with their body language, like the girl in Picture #2. If we look closely, we can tell that this person is angry also. However, her body language is not as easy to read as the boy's in Picture #1.

Picture #1

Picture #2

SSS: Social Skill Strategies (Book A)

Name:_____

Our Body

We express emotions with our bodies. We use all parts of our bodies to do this. Below is a list of some of the body parts we use to express our feelings:

- arms
- head
- eyes
- mouth
- hands
- legs
- feet
- shoulders
- eyebrows

* *

DIRECTIONS: For each of the pictures below:
1. Tell which emotion the person is expressing.
2. Tell which body part(s) helps to express that emotion.

1. (emotion) _____
   (body parts) _____
   _____

2. (emotion) _____
   (body parts) _____

3. (emotion) _____
   (body parts) _____
   _____

4. (emotion) _____
   (body parts) _____

SSS: Social Skill Strategies (Book A)

Name:_____

Your Body Language

DIRECTIONS: Read the questions and answer them.

1. What type of posture would you use to let the teacher know you are interested and paying attention during class?

2. What could you do with your arms to let your friends know you are angry with them?

3. What could you do with your face to let your friends know you are angry with them?

4. What do people do with their eyes when they are apologizing, to let people know they are really sorry?

5. What facial expressions do your mother or father use which let you know when they are angry?

6. What body language does your teacher use which lets you know when he/she is angry?

7. What body language does your friend use which lets you know when he/she is in a good mood?

B.L. CHARADES

WINNING TEAM: The team that scores the highest points in the given amount of time will win.

GAME DIRECTIONS:

1. Divide into two teams.

2. Choose a team captain.

3. One player from either side chooses a body language card (body language cards can be found on the following page). The player chooses the card without looking, reads the card, and then returns the card to the box. Then that player acts out the emotion/action that is written on the body language card.

4. Both groups try to guess what emotion/action is being acted out. When a team member thinks he knows the emotion/action, he whispers it to the team captain. (Your teacher will give the teams a copy of the body language card sheet to make it easier.)

5. The team captain raises his hand to give the answer.

6. If the answer is correct, that team scores two points.

7. If the answer is incorrect, that team loses one point. The other team is then given a chance to answer. If neither team can answer after one try each, the player tells them what emotion/action he was acting out.

8. Then the next player (a person from the other team) chooses a card, acts it out, etc. Players from each team should continue taking turns acting out the body language cards until the time period allowed for "B.L. Charades" is over.

9. A team will lose a point for any "poor sport" comment that is made during the game.

10. The team with the highest points at the end of the time period wins the game.

11. Both teams will receive an "A" grade for the day if everyone is a good sport.

Name:_____

WORRIED	**HAPPY**
SAD	**SHY**
ANGRY	**SCARED**
TIRED	**SLOPPY**
SILLY	**DEPRESSED**
ACTING TOUGH	**HURRIED**
BORED	**RELAXED**

Name:_____

BODY LANGUAGE - BODY LANGUAGE - BODY LANGUAGE

1. Define the social skill of body language.

   _____

   _____

2. Explain how body language helps us express our feelings to others.

   _____

   _____

   _____

3. Describe the type of body language you might use in the following situations:

   You are walking down a dark street by yourself. _____

   _____

   Your friend tells you her father is dying._____

   _____

   You just won a special award. _____

   _____

4. Describe the difference between the body language you would use to express the following emotions.

	Anger	Happiness
(your eyes)	_____	_____
(your mouth)	_____	_____
(your arms)	_____	_____

5. Draw a picture of a person whose body language is expressing one of the following emotions/feelings:

- anger
- boredom
- joy
- fear
- sadness
- loneliness

Circle the emotion you choose.
Label the body parts that help to express the emotion/feeling you circled.

6. Evaluate one of your parents. Can you tell how your father(mother) is feeling by his(her) body language or is he(she) a person who keeps his(her) emotions hidden? Include some specific examples in your answer.

_____

_____

_____

_____

_____

SKILL HOMEWORK ACTIVITY

_____
(Due Date)

Dear Parent or Guardian of: _____

This week we are learning about the social communication skill:

MAKING A GOOD IMPRESSION

This social skill is very important in interpersonal relationships.

The students have learned that they can make a good impression in three ways:
1. By what they say
   (e.g., using formal and informal language at the correct times)
2. By what they do
   (e.g., giving a hand to people when they need help)
3. By how they look
   (e.g., looking neat and clean)

Before the due date, please complete one of the following activities with your son or daughter: (put a check mark by your choice)

_____ A. We acted out the role play situation listed below.

_____ B. I observed my son/daughter using this social skill in a real-life situation. (I have described the situation below.)

Description of real-life observation:

Role play situation:

PRETEND THAT YOU ARE MEETING YOUR MOTHER'S/FATHER'S BOSS FOR THE FIRST TIME. DEMONSTRATE WHAT YOU COULD DO AND SAY TO MAKE A GOOD IMPRESSION.

- -

Please circle the word below which best describes how your son or daughter did while using this social skill in either the role play or real-life situation.

NEEDS MORE HELP   GOOD   EXCELLENT

It is important for you to reinforce your child's use of this social skill at home in a positive way. Encourage and praise your child when you see the skill appropriately used. Remind him/her to use the social skill when necessary.

Thank you for your assistance.

Sincerely,

. . . .

PARENT/GUARDIAN SIGNATURE: _____

Name:_____

Making A Good **What?**

Making a good impression means that *you make other people think favorably about you because of what you say, what you do, and how you look.* There are situations when making a good impression is VERY IMPORTANT (e.g., when you are meeting your girlfriend's/boyfriend's parents for the first time, or when you are interviewing for a job).

DIRECTIONS: Put a " + " by the statement which should give a good impression.
Put a " − " by the statement which should give a bad impression.

_____ 1. The phone rings. You answer it by saying, "Ya! What do you want?"

_____ 2. You are a newspaper deliverer, and you leave someone's newspaper in the rain.

_____ 3. You spend two hours with people you have never met, and you never introduce yourself during that time.

_____ 4. You help an elderly woman unload the groceries from her car.

_____ 5. You meet a new person, and you use good eye contact when you introduce yourself.

_____ 6. You don't wash your hair for three weeks.

_____ 7. You are always honest with your friends.

_____ 8. You politely introduce yourself to your mother's friend.

_____ 9. You go into a restaurant and say in a loud voice, "Give me a Coke!"

_____10. You go to an interview and shake hands when you meet your potential boss.

_____11. You go to a job interview in the same jeans you have worn all week.

_____12. When you meet new people, you slouch so that they will think you are shorter than you really are.

_____13. You talk very softly in class, so people will think you are shy.

_____14. You burp loudly after eating.

_____15. You laugh and giggle when you meet new people.

_____16. You usually remember a person's name after you meet only once.

_____17. You offer to help when you have dinner at someone else's house.

_____18. You look at the ceiling or floor when you speak to someone.

_____19. You try to be a good listener when you have a conversation with someone.

_____20. You try to be optimistic and look at the "bright side" of things.

Table Practice

DIRECTIONS: Complete the following table by filling in the blank spaces. (In the rows where nothing is given under either the GOOD IMPRESSION column or the BAD IMPRESSION column, you should fill in something new.)

	GOOD IMPRESSION	BAD IMPRESSION
EXAMPLE →	You try to look at the person you are talking to, most of the time.	*You seldom look at the person you are talking to.*
	You say things like "Please" and "Thank you" whenever you should.	
		You talk in a very loud voice that is uncomfortable to those who are listening to you.
		You enjoy speaking to people with a sarcastic tone of voice, because you think it's funny.
		You "beat around the bush" whenever you are uncomfortable asking for something.
		You always jump from one topic to another, without warning your listener.
	You try to close every conversation you have as smoothly as possible.	

100   SSS: Social Skill Strategies (Book A)

Name:_____

Making A List And Checking It Twice

Make a list of five special occasions when you would want to make a good impression.

1. _____

2. _____

3. _____

4. _____

5. _____

Make a list of five things you could do to make a good impression by the way you look.

1. _____

2. _____

3. _____

4. _____

5. _____

Make a list of five things you could do to make a good impression by your actions (the things you do).

1. _____

2. _____

3. _____

4. _____

5. _____

Make a list of five things you could do to make a good impression by the things you say.

1. _____

2. _____

3. _____

4. _____

5. _____

GOOD IMPRESSION CERTIFICATE

DIRECTIONS: Pair up with someone in your group. Think of something about your partner that you think helps to make a good impression. (Remember - Someone can make a good impression by what he says, what he does, or how he looks.) Cut out the certificate, fill it in, and present it to your partner.

GREAT IMPRESSION

_____ makes a great

(Name)

impression because he/she:

_____

_____

_____

SUPER

Name:_____

The Search . . .

DIRECTIONS: Search through magazines to find two pictures. One should be of a person who would make a good impression based on the way he/she looks. The other should be of a person who would make a bad impression based on his/her looks. Attach your pictures below. Write a description of your pictures (optional).

GOOD IMPRESSION   **BAD IMPRESSION**

EDUCATOR PAGE: DO NOT DUPLICATE FOR STUDENTS

DIRECTIONS: Give a piece of plain white 8½" x 11" paper to each of your students. Make certain they each have something to draw with. Ask your students to sit comfortably in their chairs, with their spines straight but relaxed, their feet flat on the floor, and their hands in a resting position. You may want to turn off some or all of the lights in the room in order to create a more peaceful environment. Read aloud the script below, in a relaxed and slow manner. The script is a guided visualization/imagery session for making a good impression.

Close your eyes, and on the count of three take a very slow, deep breath. One . . . two . . . three . . . inhale slowly . . . hold it . . . and now exhale slowly . . . let all the air out. As you do this, you should feel your body relaxing. Take another slow, deep breath . . . only this time imagine that you are breathing in very clean, cool, relaxed air and that you are breathing out all the tension and tiredness you have in your muscles. Ready? One . . . two . . . three . . . take a slow . . . deep breath . . . hold it . . . and now exhale slowly. Remember to imagine that you are breathing in relaxed, clean air . . . and that when you exhale . . . you are letting go of all the tiredness and tension in your body. Take a minute to concentrate as you continue your deep, slow breathing. (pause) Now, you are going to imagine yourself dressed in your best clothes and going to a job interview. The interview can be for babysitting, mowing lawns, working in a fast food restaurant, or for any other job you might have an interest in. Try to imagine this interview with all your feelings and senses. Before the interview starts, imagine that you say to yourself, "I am going to make a good impression. I am going to make a good impression." As you enter the room to begin the interview, your posture is very straight and poised. You look the interviewer directly in the eyes, and your body language shows that you are confident and that you can do a good job. Imagine that you begin the conversation in a good way and you speak with a volume that is easily understood. Now, imagine that the interviewer begins asking you questions about yourself and why you think you would be the best person for the job. You get straight to the point when answering the questions and you use a very pleasant tone of voice, which makes the interviewer feel very impressed with your verbal skills. Picture yourself taking a moment to tell yourself that things are going very well. When the interviewer tells you about the job, you are an excellent listener. When the interviewer is finished, you ask questions which are relevant and on topic. Now, imagine that the interview is ending. You remember to use good manners and thank the person for the interview. You tell the interviewer you know that you would do a good job if you are hired for the job. You close the conversation smoothly and leave the room. You leave the room feeling confident that you will be hired because you know you did everything you could have to make a good impression during the interview. Take a moment to experience the feelings you have about yourself. Do you feel proud? Excited? Happy? (pause) Now prepare yourself to return to the classroom. On the count of three you will open your eyes and you will be asked to draw a picture of the interview or a picture showing how you look or feel. One . . . two . . . three . . . open your eyes and begin to draw your picture. Remember to try and make your picture as detailed as possible. If you want to add words to your picture you may do so.

SUGGESTION: Encourage your students to use this visualization technique before entering any situation when they want to make a good impression.

EDUCATOR PAGE: DO NOT DUPLICATE FOR STUDENTS

DISCUSSION: Discuss the idea that to make a good impression with other people, it is important that we first feel good about ourselves on the inside. Let your students know that people who feel good about themselves use positive self-talk, and people who feel bad about themselves use negative self-talk. SELF-TALK is everything you tell yourself inside your head: the thoughts you have about yourself and other people. POSITIVE SELF-TALK is when you think good things about yourself or other people. NEGATIVE SELF-TALK is when you think bad things about yourself or other people. Make the point that people give themselves thousands of self-talk messages everyday. Some people use mostly negative self-talk, and it makes them feel bad about themselves (powerless). People who feel bad about themselves have a more difficult time making a good impression on other people. Some people use mostly positive self-talk, and it makes them feel good about themselves (powerful). People who feel good about themselves have an easier time making a good impression on others.

ACTIVITY: Ask for a volunteer to come to the front of the room to take part in an experiment. The experiment will show that positive self-talk actually makes a person more powerful, and that negative self-talk actually drains energy and makes a person more powerless. Ask your volunteer to hold his strongest arm straight out to the side. Ask the person to use all his strength to hold his arm in place while you try to push his arm down. While this is happening, the person should keep repeating aloud, "I am a bad person. I don't like myself." Repeat the procedure, only this time have the person repeat aloud, "I am a good person. I like myself." It will be obvious to your volunteer, as well as to those observing the experiment, that the person has significantly more strength and power when speaking positively. Typically, students will not believe their eyes when they see the difference in strength, and more of them will want to be volunteers. After the activity is completed, let your students know that it was designed to show that the type of self-talk they use is a very important thing, and that it will make a significant difference in their lives.

MAKING A GOOD IMPRESSION - MAKING A GOOD IMPRESSION

1. Explain what *making a good impression* means.

   _____

   _____

2. Why is it important to make a good impression with your teachers during the first day of school?

   _____

   _____

3. Describe a situation at home, at school, and in the community when it would be important for you to make a good impression.

   (home) _____

   _____

   (school) _____

   _____

   (community) _____

   _____

4. Think of two people you know. Compare them with each other. Decide which of the two usually makes a better impression on people because of the things he/she says and does, and because of the way he/she looks.

   Write the person's first name: _____

   List three things about this person which you feel help him/her to make a better impression than the other person.

   (1) _____

   (2) _____

   (3) _____

5. Write or tell a short story about a character who makes a good impression when he/she goes out on a first date. (Use the back of this page if you need more space.)

   _____

   _____

   _____

   _____

6. Evaluate your success in making a good impression with the person who gave you this sheet to fill out. Do you feel you have made a good or bad impression today? Explain your answer.

   _____

   _____

SKILL HOMEWORK ACTIVITY

_____
(Due Date)

Dear Parent or Guardian of: _____

This week we are learning about the social communication skill:

FORMAL/INFORMAL LANGUAGE

This social skill is very important in interpersonal relationships.

The students have learned that they should use informal language (more relaxed speech that includes slang and shorter forms of words) when they talk to friends and adults they feel close to (e.g., "Hi, what's up?"). They have also learned that they should use formal language (more traditional language which uses the longer forms of words) when they want to make a good impression with individuals in respected positions (e.g., "Hello, how are you today?").

Before the due date, please complete one of the following activities with your son or daughter: (put a check mark by your choice)

_____ A. We acted out the role play situation listed below.

_____ B. I observed my son/daughter using this social skill in a real-life situation. (I have described the situation below.)

Description of real-life observation:

Role play situation:

YOU HAVE JUST FINISHED INTERVIEWING FOR A JOB AND IT IS TIME TO CLOSE THE CONVERSATION. DEMONSTRATE HOW YOU WOULD USE FORMAL LANGUAGE. (REMEMBER — "GOOD-BYE" IS MORE FORMAL THAN "BYE" AND THE PHRASE "IT HAS BEEN NICE MEETING YOU" IS MORE FORMAL THAN "NICE TO MEET YA.")

- -

Please circle the word below which best describes how your son or daughter did while using this social skill in either the role play or real-life situation.

NEEDS MORE HELP   GOOD   EXCELLENT

It is important for you to reinforce your child's use of this social skill at home in a positive way. Encourage and praise your child when you see the skill appropriately used. Remind him/her to use the social skill when necessary.

Thank you for your assistance.

Sincerely,

* *

PARENT/GUARDIAN SIGNATURE: _____

Name:_____

Formal - *Informal*
What Is the Difference?

There is a difference between formal clothes and informal clothes. People usually dress formally when they go to a wedding or a special dance. People usually dress informally when they go to a casual party, or to a football game.

There is a difference between a formal dinner and an informal dinner. A formal dinner usually includes fancy dishes and calls for using special manners. At an informal dinner, you might use paper plates and serve yourself.

There is also a difference between using
FORMAL AND INFORMAL LANGUAGE.

Formal language is used when you want to make a good impression with people in respected positions (e.g., principal, teacher). You should speak in a more *traditional* way and use the longer forms of words when you want to be formal.

Informal language is used when you talk to peers, or adults that you feel close to. You should speak in a more *relaxed* way, by using shorter forms of words and slang, when you want to be informal.

Formal or Informal?

DIRECTIONS: For each of the following word or phrase pairs, identify which is formal and which is informal. Write **F** for formal and **I** for informal.

1. _____ Bye

   _____ Good-bye

2. _____ Are you able to join us?

   _____ Are ya comin'?

3. _____ Hey, get that for me.

   _____ Would you please pick that up for me?

4. _____ Can

   _____ Could

5. _____ Hello, how have you been doing?

   _____ Hi, how's it goin'?

6. _____ You want something else?

   _____ Will there be anything else for you?

7. _____ I can't stand spinach.

   _____ I do not care for spinach.

8. _____ Sorry about that!

   _____ I want to apologize.

9. _____ Why not?

   _____ Could you please tell me the reason?

10. _____ I am unable to attend.

    _____ I can't go.

Change It

DIRECTIONS: Change the following informal words and phrases to be formal.

1. Hi.

2. Sure!

3. Will ya?

4. Ya gotta do it!

5. What do you want?

DIRECTIONS: Change the following formal words and phrases to be informal.

1. I would be delighted!

2. I certainly appreciate this!

3. It has been a pleasure meeting you.

4. Could you possibly give me a hand with this project?

5. You are a wonderful human being!

DIRECTIONS: List three situations where you would want to use informal language.

1._____

2._____

3._____

DIRECTIONS: List three situations where you would want to use formal language.

1._____

2._____

3._____

Name:_____

Finding Examples

DIRECTIONS: Cut out pictures and words from magazines or newspapers that show examples of things which are formal and informal. Use what you find to create a collage on a piece of construction paper. Below is an example of what your collage might look like.

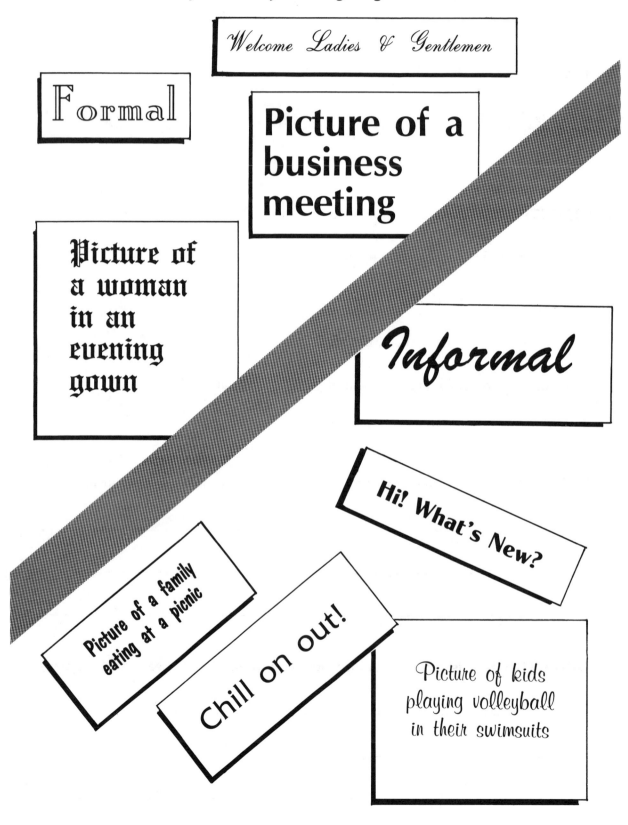

Welcome Ladies & Gentlemen

Formal

Picture of a business meeting

Picture of a woman in an evening gown

Informal

Hi! What's New?

Picture of a family eating at a picnic

Chill on out!

Picture of kids playing volleyball in their swimsuits

What to Be?

DIRECTIONS: For each of the situations described below, decide if you should use formal language or informal language. Write **F** for formal and **I** for informal.

_____ 1. You called your dad at work and his boss answered the phone.

_____ 2. You are asking a girl/guy out on a date.

_____ 3. You are talking to your parents at the dinner table.

_____ 4. You are running for class president and you need to give a speech to the student body.

_____ 5. You are applying for a babysitting job.

_____ 6. You are ordering a meal at a fancy restaurant.

_____ 7. You are calling your favorite aunt on the phone.

_____ 8. You are talking to your friends at lunch.

_____ 9. You are trying to convince the assistant principal to drop the detention you were given.

_____ 10. You are being introduced to your brother's new girlfriend.

What do you think would happen if you made the mistake of sounding formal when you spoke to your friends or to adults you knew well?

What do you think would happen if you were talking to an authority figure in a respected position and you spoke informally?

FORMAL/INFORMAL LANGUAGE

1. Define *formal* and *informal language.*

   (formal) _____

   _____

   (informal) _____

   _____

2. Write a strategy you could use when you want to speak formally and informally.

   (formal) _____

   _____

   (informal) _____

   _____

3. Describe a situation when you should speak in a formal way and an informal way, out in the community.

   (formal) _____

   _____

   (informal) _____

   _____

4. Read the situation below and then answer the questions which follow.

   When Beth entered the principal's office, the principal said, "Good morning Beth." Beth said, "Hi! What's up?" The principal said, "I would like to speak with you about your attendance record." Beth answered, "I ain't gonna talk to you about that."

   Did Beth choose to speak in a formal or informal way to the principal?

   _____

   Did Beth make a good or bad choice? _____ Explain your answer.

   _____

   _____

5. Write down the words you would say if you were being introduced to the President of the United States of America.

   _____

   _____

6. Choose one of the following people to evaluate, and circle your choice.

   Your grandmother   Your favorite teacher   Your father

   When you talk with this person, do you speak more formally than you do when you are with your friends? Why or why not?

   _____

   _____

GENERAL INTERACTION SKILLS

SKILL HOMEWORK ACTIVITY

_____
(Due Date)

Dear Parent or Guardian of: _____

This week we are learning about the social communication skill:

GIVING REASONS

This social skill is very important in interpersonal relationships.

The students have learned that when they give reasons for their wishes, beliefs, and actions, they need to make their reasons relevant and specific.

Before the due date, please complete one of the following activities with your son or daughter: (put a check mark by your choice)

_____ A. We acted out the role play situation listed below.

_____ B. I observed my son/daughter using this social skill in a real-life situation. (I have described the situation below.)

Description of real-life observation:

Role play situation:

PRETEND THAT YOU FAILED SCIENCE. DEMONSTRATE HOW YOU WOULD EXPLAIN THE REASONS FOR GETTING THE "F" TO ONE OF YOUR PARENTS.

- -

Please circle the word below which best describes how your son or daughter did while using this social skill in either the role play or real-life situation.

NEEDS MORE HELP   GOOD   EXCELLENT

It is important for you to reinforce your child's use of this social skill at home in a positive way. Encourage and praise your child when you see the skill appropriately used. Remind him/her to use the social skill when necessary.

Thank you for your assistance.

Sincerely,

* *

PARENT/GUARDIAN SIGNATURE: _____

The Reason for Reasons

Explaining reasons is a very important skill. It helps your listener to better understand your wishes, beliefs, or actions.

DIRECTIONS: Below is a list of situations when you would need to explain reasons. The list is long and it should convince you that giving reasons is an important skill. As you read through the list, put a star next to the situations when you think you are good at providing reasons.

1. If you are able to give specific reasons, it helps to make a good impression.

2. When you need to interrupt anyone, you should tell your reason for interrupting.

3. When you say "Thank you" to someone, you should tell the reason for thanking him.

4. When you ask someone for help, you need to explain your reason for asking.

5. When you make an apology, you also give your reason for apologizing.

6. When you tell your opinion about a certain topic, you should give your reasons for believing the way you do.

7. When you tell someone that you disagree, it is necessary to explain your reason for disagreeing.

8. When you want to convince others to believe the way you do, you need to give them good reasons.

9. When you say "No" to peer pressure, you may want to give the reason you do not want to do the things they are pressuring you to do.

10. When you ask to join into an activity, you may want to give your reason for asking.

11. Teachers often ask you to give specific reasons for certain things on a test.

12. When you make a complaint, you should give the reason you are complaining.

13. When you accuse someone, you should give your reason for making the accusation.

14. When you give advice to a person, you also give your reason for giving that advice.

15. When you tell someone you are angry, you should explain your reason for being upset.

16. When someone has embarrassed you, you may want to tell your reason for feeling embarrassed.

17. When you are afraid of something, you may want to decide what your reasons are for being afraid.

Name:_____

Reason or No Reason?

DIRECTIONS: Read each of the following statements. If the statement gives a reason, write its number in the left hand column of the table below. If the statement does not give a reason, write its number in the right hand column. Hint: Not all reason statements begin with the word *because*. Notice that some numbers of statements have been written in the table already.

1. I want a pizza because I'm hungry.

2. This coat is very warm.

3. I am allergic to strawberries.

4. I'd like to get my hair cut so it looks good at the school dance.

5. I'm sorry, I don't have it. I left it at home.

6. I don't think I'll go out for softball because I'd rather be in track.

7. I'll loan you a dollar if you do the dishes for me.

8. I don't raise my hand in class. I'm pretty shy.

9. Last night I got home 35 minutes late.

10. I think he has to be the best looking guy in our class.

11. If it rains this weekend, I'll really be mad.

12. The grass needs mowing. It's really long.

13. I don't think you should be friends with him. He's always pressuring you.

14. I wish I didn't have to share a room with you. You're very messy.

15. That movie is said to be a complete waste of money.

16. I'd rather get sausage and mushrooms on the pizza.

EXAMPLE →

REASON	**NO REASON**
#1	#2

Name:_____

Make It Good

For a reason to be good, it must be RELEVANT and SPECIFIC.

When a reason is **RELEVANT,** it means that *it relates to the topic*. Pretend your parents ask why you came home late. You say, "Because Cindy had a fight with her boyfriend." Your parents probably would not like your reason, because they would think it was not relevant. They might say, "Cindy and her boyfriend have nothing to do with you. You could have been home on time whether Cindy and her boyfriend had a fight or not." An example of a relevant reason for being late would be, "Because Cindy had a fight with her boyfriend. She was so upset! I was afraid to leave her alone so I stayed and talked to her."

When a reason is **SPECIFIC,** it means that *it explains something exactly*. Pretend your dad says you may not go to a movie you would like to see. When you ask him why, he says, "Because I said so." You probably would not like his reason because it is not specific. His answer would leave you still wondering why you couldn't go. An example of a specific reason for not being allowed to go see a movie would be, "Because the movie is rated 'R' and you know that I will not allow you to go to 'R' rated movies."

DIRECTIONS: Read each of the following questions and answers. If you think the answer provides a reason that is relevant and specific, then mark it with a " + ." If the reason is not good, then mark it with a " − ."

1. Why didn't you turn in your assignment on time?

    _____ My brother had a date last night.

    _____ Because I just didn't.

    _____ Because I left it sitting on the kitchen table this morning.

2. Why can't you go to the football game with me this Friday?

    _____ I just can't, that's all.

    _____ I have a babysitting job this Friday night.

    _____ Because my parents told me I have to go up north with them.

3. Why did you strike out in the last inning?

    _____ I kept swinging too soon.

    _____ I didn't have hotdogs for lunch.

    _____ Because I felt like it, why do you think?

4. Can you please help me on my math?

    _____ No, I can't.

    _____ Ask Mary instead of me.

    _____ No, I have an appointment and I'm late for it.

Name:_____

What Are Your Reasons?

DIRECTIONS: Answer the following questions, and explain your reasons. Make certain that your reasons are *relevant* and *specific.*

1. Do you think it is good for students to have a part-time job during high school? Explain why.

2. Explain why it is important to be organized if you want to do well in school.

3. Do you think parents should set a curfew for their teen-agers? Explain your answer.

4. Explain why schools need to have rules for discipline.

5. Do you think everyone in your family should share in the household chores? Explain why.

6. Tell why it is important for everyone to have a good friend.

7. Describe your best quality, and then explain why you believe it is your best.

8. Tell what your favorite class is this year. Explain why.

9. Do you think you are trying your best in school this year? Explain why.

10. Explain why good social communication skills are important if you want to get along with other people.

GIVING REASONS - GIVING REASONS - GIVING REASONS

1. Explain what two things make a reason good.

   (1) _____

   (2) _____

2. Why is it important to be able to give a good reason?

   _____

   _____

3. Describe a situation at home, at school, and in the community when you may need to explain your reasons to someone.

   (home) _____

   _____

   (school) _____

   _____

   (community) _____

   _____

4. Compare the following two comments. Tell one way they are the same and one way they are different.

   | "Because I said so." | "Because if you stay up too late, you'll be tired." |

   (same) _____

   (different) _____

5. Pretend you are a boss. Create a list of five reasons you would consider to be good for one of your employees being late and five reasons you would consider to be bad.

   Good Reasons

   (1)_____

   (2)_____

   (3)_____

   (4)_____

   (5)_____

   Bad Reasons

   (1)_____

   (2)_____

   (3)_____

   (4)_____

   (5)_____

6. On a scale of one to ten, how good are you at giving relevant and specific reasons (one being bad, and ten being good)? Circle the number that represents your choice.

   1   2   3   4   5   6   7   8   9   10

   Explain why you rated yourself the way you did.

   _____

   _____

SKILL HOMEWORK ACTIVITY

_____
(Due Date)

Dear Parent or Guardian of: _____

This week we are learning about the social communication skill:

PLANNING WHAT TO SAY

This social skill is very important in interpersonal relationships.

The students have learned to plan ahead about what they are going to say when they have something important to say to someone. They can plan in two ways:

1. Thinking things out in their head (using self-talk)
2. Writing down important points to say

Before the due date, please complete one of the following activities with your son or daughter: (put a check mark by your choice)

_____ A. We acted out the role play situation listed below.

_____ B. I observed my son/daughter using this social skill in a real-life situation. (I have described the situation below.)

Description of real-life observation:

Role play situation:

YOU WANT TO TALK WITH YOUR PARENTS ABOUT GETTING A RAISE IN YOUR ALLOWANCE. PLAN OUT WHAT YOU ARE GOING TO SAY TO THEM BY WRITING THE IMPORTANT POINTS ON A PIECE OF PAPER. USE YOUR NOTES WHEN YOU TALK WITH THEM.

- -

Please circle the word below which best describes how your son or daughter did while using this social skill in either the role play or real-life situation.

NEEDS MORE HELP   GOOD   EXCELLENT

It is important for you to reinforce your child's use of this social skill at home in a positive way. Encourage and praise your child when you see the skill appropriately used. Remind him/her to use the social skill when necessary.

Thank you for your assistance.

Sincerely,

• •

PARENT/GUARDIAN SIGNATURE: _____

PLANNING what to Say

Has this ever happened to you? You go to talk to someone and you really mess up what you say. If you answered "Yes," don't feel bad because it happens to many people. Sometimes, there's nothing you can do about things coming out of your mouth in the wrong way. But other times, you could have prevented your garbled message by planning ahead what you wanted to say.

Here's an example: Linda wanted to tell her new neighbors that she was available if they ever needed a babysitter. She didn't really plan ahead what she was going to say. Here's the conversation.

> Linda: Hi, you have little kids, don't you?
> Mrs. Sine: Yes, we do.
> Linda: Do you ever go anywhere by yourself?
> Mrs. Sine: (puzzled) Yes, I do sometimes.
> Linda: Well, you know, I'm right next door.
> Mrs. Sine: Oh, you're the girl from next door.
> Linda: Well, give me a call then.

Linda didn't get her message across to her new neighbor. Mrs. Sine probably thought that Linda was a little strange. Linda forgot some things that she should have said.

Make a list of things that Linda should have said:

-
-
-
-
-

It's good to plan ahead sometimes before you speak. You can plan ahead in two ways:

1. Thinking things out in your head (using self-talk)
2. Writing down important points to say

It's also a good idea to think about what the other person might say or ask. That helps you think of how you will respond.

Name:_____

Plan Before you Speak

DIRECTIONS: Read the story below. Answer the questions at the end of the story.

Bryon needed to talk with his teacher about his book report. He wanted to get some help because he couldn't find a good book to read. Bryon did not really plan out what he was going to say beforehand. When he got to his teacher's office, Bryon said, "I can't find one!" Bryon's teacher looked at him strangely because she didn't know what he was talking about. She said, "What do you want, Bryon?" "There aren't any good ones," he said. Again, Bryon's teacher didn't know what he was talking about. She was getting angry. "Bryon, what do you want?" Bryon looked at her like she was crazy. He had just finished telling her what he wanted. When he didn't say anything, his teacher said, "Bryon Johnson, please get out of my office, I'm very busy!" Bryon got upset and said, "Oh, you never help me!" He stomped out of the room.

1. Did Bryon tell his teacher what he wanted?

2. Why did Bryon's teacher get upset?

3. What should Bryon have done before he went to talk to his teacher?

4. Write or tell what Bryon should have said to his teacher.

Your Friends

DIRECTIONS: In each of the situations below, you would want to plan ahead what you were going to say to your friend. Choose one of the situations and write what you would say to that friend.

1. Your good friend has been saying things about you behind your back. You feel really bad and want to talk with him/her about it. What will you say?

2. Your girlfriend/boyfriend has started to go out with someone else. You want to talk with her/him about it. What will you say?

3. Your good friend won an award at school. You want to let your friend know how proud you are of him/her. What will you say?

4. You are going out with a group of your friends tonight. You think that they will be drinking and smoking and you don't want to do those things. What will you say?

5. One of your friends has been really nice to you lately. You really appreciate his/her friendship. You would like to let him/her know it. What will you say?

I have chosen situation #_____

I would say:

126   SSS: Social Skill Strategies (Book A)

Name:_____

THINK ABOUT . . .

DIRECTIONS: Write down a situation

(circle one)   *at school*   *at home*   *in the community*

when you need to plan what you are going to say to someone. Then write down what you would think about in your head.

Situation:

EDUCATOR PAGE: DO NOT DUPLICATE FOR STUDENTS

PURPOSE OF ACTIVITY: To demonstrate that people speak more smoothly when they plan ahead about what they are going to say.

* *

ACTIVITY: 1. Ask for three volunteers. Have two of the volunteers leave the room to go someplace where they will not hear what is being said.

2. Tell volunteer #1 to pretend he is on a job interview. Tell him you would like him to tell all about himself for two minutes. Tell him to start talking immediately. (The educator should not say anything for two minutes even if volunteer #1 does not use the entire two minutes to talk.)

3. Next, ask volunteer #2 to return to the room. Give volunteer #2 the same instructions as volunteer #1. However, allow volunteer #2 about one to two minutes to prepare what he will say.

4. After volunteer #2 finishes speaking, ask volunteer #3 to return to the room. Give volunteer #3 the same instructions as the other volunteers received. However, allow volunteer #3 five minutes to prepare what he will say. Tell volunteer #3 he may use notes if he wishes.

5. Afterwards, discuss the differences among the three speakers. Emphasize to the students that people usually sound smoother and make better sense when they have time to plan what they are going to say. Point out that in a real job interview, people would not be allowed preparation time before answering questions. Thus, it is a good idea to try to anticipate which questions will be asked. Also, discuss the benefits of verbally rehearsing beforehand.

PLANNING WHAT TO SAY - PLANNING WHAT TO SAY

1. Tell two ways you can plan ahead about what you are going to say to someone.

   _____

   _____

2. Explain why it is helpful to plan ahead about what you are going to say.

   _____

   _____

3. Describe a situation from home, school, and the community when you would want to plan ahead for what you want to say.

   (home) _____

   _____

   (school) _____

   _____

   (community) _____

   _____

4. Describe a time when you didn't plan ahead about what you said.

   _____

   _____

   Describe a time when you planned ahead about what you said.

   _____

   _____

   Compare how you felt in each of the above situations.

   _____

   _____

5. Ashley wants to ask her parents to let her stay out later on week nights. Develop a list of things Ashley could say. Also develop a list of the things you think Ashley's parents might say.

   (what Ashley could say) _____

   _____

   _____

   (what Ashley's parents might say) _____

   _____

   _____

6. Rate yourself from 1-10 on how good you are at planning ahead what to say (1 = poor, 10 = excellent). Then, explain why you rated yourself as you did and give possible suggestions for improvement.

   1   2   3   4   5   6   7   8   9   10   (Circle one)

   (explanation) _____

   _____

   _____

   (suggestions for improvement) _____

   _____

   _____

SKILL HOMEWORK ACTIVITY

_____
(Due Date)

Dear Parent or Guardian of: _____

This week we are learning about the social communication skill:

INTERRUPTING

This social skill is very important in interpersonal relationships.

This skill can be broken down into the following skill steps. Please watch for all of the steps in your role play practice.

1. **G**et the person's attention appropriately:
   a. Knock on the door
      and/or
   b. Say, "Excuse me"
      or
   c. Stand close enough so the person sees you waiting.

2. **A**pologize for interrupting.

3. **G**ive the reason for interrupting.

We taught the students to think of the word **GAG** to help them remember the steps in order.

Before the due date, please complete one of the following activities with your son or daughter: (put a check mark by your choice)

_____ A. We acted out the role play situation listed below.

_____ B. I observed my son/daughter using this social skill in a real-life situation. (I have described the situation below.)

Description of real-life observation:

Role play situation:

PRETEND YOUR MOM IS CHATTING ON THE PHONE. DEMONSTRATE HOW YOU WOULD INTERRUPT TO TELL HER SOMEONE IS AT THE FRONT DOOR, WANTING TO TALK TO HER.

Please circle the word below which best describes how your son or daughter did while using this social skill in either the role play or real-life situation.

NEEDS MORE HELP   GOOD   EXCELLENT

It is important for you to reinforce your child's use of this social skill at home in a positive way. Encourage and praise your child when you see the skill appropriately used. Remind him/her to use the social skill when necessary.

Thank you for your assistance.

Sincerely,

* *

PARENT/GUARDIAN SIGNATURE: _____

Name:_____

When To Interrupt and When Not To

One very important thing to know about interrupting is that sometimes it is appropriate to interrupt, and sometimes it is not.

It is OK to interrupt when what you have to say needs to be taken care of right away.

It is not OK to interrupt when what you have to say can wait.

This activity page will give you practice deciding between good and bad times to interrupt.

DIRECTIONS: Read each of the situations below. If the person should interrupt, write INTERRUPT on the blank line provided. If the person should not interrupt, write WAIT.

1. It is Monday night. Shelly just remembered that she has to have one of her parents sign a permission slip that she needs to return to school by Friday. Her parents are in the kitchen playing cards with the neighbors.

   _____

2. The school secretary asks Mark to go to Mr. Morgan's room and ask him if he can take a long distance phone call in the office. When Mark gets to his room, he sees that Mr. Morgan is lecturing to his students.

   _____

3. Toby is three years old and his mother has told him never to touch the stove. She is talking on the phone. Toby sees that something is cooking on the stove, and it is starting to bubble over.

   _____

4. Grandpa Jackson is watching his favorite show on TV. It is just about over. His grandson Pete wants to ask him if he will fix the chain on his bike.

   _____

5. Two sales clerks behind the checkout counter are chatting about the weather. Sue is in a hurry, and she can't find what she is looking for in the store. Sue wants to ask for help.

   _____

6. Whitney's teacher is helping another student with a math problem at her desk. Whitney decides she needs to ask for help also.

   _____

Name:_____

WHAT TO DO
(When you don't want to interrupt)

When what you want to say or ask can wait, it is important not to interrupt, but that can be very difficult.

Here is an idea for something you can try, to stop yourself from making an unnecessary interruption:

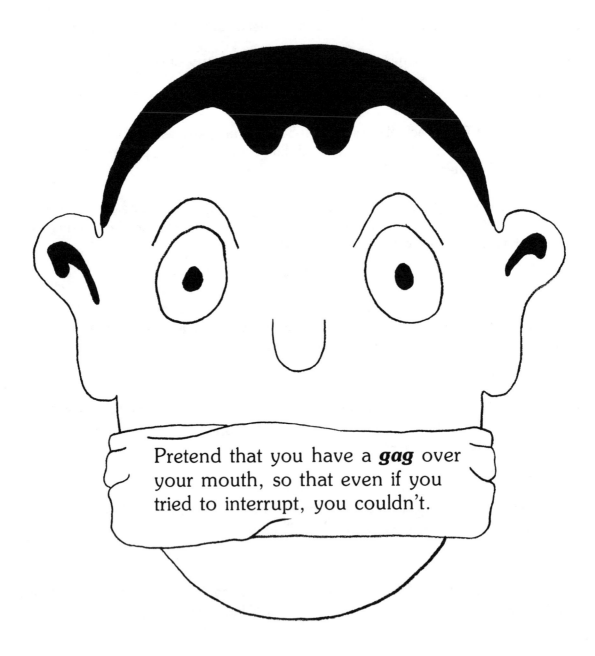

Pretend that you have a **gag** over your mouth, so that even if you tried to interrupt, you couldn't.

A **gag** *is something tied over the mouth to prevent speech or outcry.*

SSS: Social Skill Strategies (Book A)

Name:_____

WHAT TO DO
(When you do need to interrupt)

Interrupting can be broken down into these three skill steps:

1. **G**et the person's attention.
2. **A**pologize for interrupting.
3. **G**ive the reason for interrupting.

The cartoons below show the three skill steps for interrupting. Each one shows a different way to get someone's attention.

(1) Get the person's attention by knocking on the door.

(2) Apologize for interrupting.

(3) Give the reason for interrupting.

(1) Get the person's attention by saying, "Excuse me."

(2) Apologize for interrupting.

(3) Give the reason for interrupting.

(1) Get the people's attention by standing close enough for them to see you.

(2) Apologize for interrupting.

(3) Give the reason for interrupting.

Name:_____

Interrupting the Right Way!

REMEMBER these three skill steps for interrupting:

1. **G**et the person's attention

2. **A**pologize for interrupting

3. **G**ive the reason for interrupting

> **HINT!** Think of the word **GAG**, to help yourself remember the skill steps for making an interruption. The word **GAG** should also remind you to interrupt only when it is necessary.

DIRECTIONS: After reading each situation below, choose the best way for the person to make the interruption. Circle the correct letter.

1. Aldo's grandmother said she would drive him to his softball game. It was time for them to leave, but his grandmother was involved in watching a good movie. Aldo decided he had better interrupt her, or he would miss his game.

   A. "Man, is that all you ever do is watch that TV?"

   B. "Come on! Let's go. I'm gonna be late."

   C. "Excuse me, Grandma. I'm sorry for interrupting, but my game starts in ten minutes. I think we had better leave soon, or I'll be late."

2. Melissa's school bus was approaching her house when she suddenly remembered that she needed money to order her yearbook. It was the last day to order one. She ran into the kitchen to ask her mom for the money and saw that her mom had just gotten a call on the telephone. Melissa knew she had better interrupt in a polite way, or her mom might not give her the money.

   A. "Mom, sorry to interrupt, but the bus is coming. I wonder if you could give me $5.00 for a yearbook. Today is the last day I can order."

   B. "Mom! You never gave me that money you promised me, and now I'm gonna miss the bus. You can't get mad at me because it was your fault."

   C. "Mom, give me that $5.00 now, or I'll miss my bus!"

3. One of Josh's teachers asked him to run and get the principal because there was an emergency in the gym. When Josh got to the principal's office, he could see that she was having a meeting with a student's parents. He quickly knocked on the door and said:

   A. "Ms. Welch, get down to the gym now!"

   B. "Hello, Ms. Welch. Could you please come to the gym?"

   C. "I'm sorry to interrupt. You're needed in the gym. There is an emergency!"

Name:_____

Transferring The Social Skill

To interrupt in an appropriate way, follow these three steps:

1. Get the person's attention
2. Apologize for interrupting
3. Give the reason for interrupting

DIRECTIONS: Every time you remember to interrupt someone correctly, ask the person to sign below, verifying that you used the skill appropriately.

- -

1. _____ interrupted me for the following reason:

    He/she remembered to follow the three steps listed above for interrupting correctly.

    Signed: _____

- -

2._____ interrupted me for the following reason:

He/she remembered to follow the three steps listed above for interrupting correctly.

Signed: _____

- -

3._____ interrupted me for the following reason:

He/she remembered to follow the three steps listed above for interrupting correctly.

Signed: _____

- -

4._____ interrupted me for the following reason:

He/she remembered to follow the three steps listed above for interrupting correctly.

Signed: _____

- -

INTERRUPTING - INTERRUPTING - INTERRUPTING

---

1. List the three skill steps for interrupting correctly.

   (1) _____

   (2) _____

   (3) _____

2. Explain why it is sometimes not appropriate to interrupt, even if you follow the three skill steps listed above.

   _____

   _____

3. Describe a situation when it would be appropriate to interrupt, and a situation when it would not be.

   (appropriate)_____

   _____

   (not appropriate) _____

   _____

4. Compare interrupting one of your parents with interrupting one of your teachers. Should the way you interrupt each of them be the same or different? Explain your answer.

   _____

   _____

5. Tell three consequences of interrupting people for things that are not important and can wait.

   (1) _____

   (2) _____

   (3) _____

6. Evaluate the way you usually interrupt one of your parents.

   Do you interrupt only when it is absolutely necessary? YES   NO

   (explain) _____

   When you do interrupt, do you usually follow the three skill steps for interrupting in a good way? YES   NO

   (explain) _____

SKILL HOMEWORK ACTIVITY

_____
(Due Date)

Dear Parent or Guardian of: _____

This week we are learning about the social communication skill:

GIVING A COMPLIMENT

This social skill is very important in interpersonal relationships.

The students have learned that there is a difference between giving an _outside_ compliment (about the way a person looks, or what a person owns) and an _inside_ compliment (about a person's personality, or what the person does and says). Both compliments are nice, but _inside_ compliments usually mean more. _Inside_ compliments, however, are harder to give.

They have also learned that it is important to use a sincere tone of voice when giving a compliment, so it is not mistaken as sarcasm.

Before the due date, please complete one of the following activities with your son or daughter: (put a check mark by your choice)

_____ A. We acted out the role play situation listed below.

_____ B. I observed my son/daughter using this social skill in a real-life situation. (I have described the situation below.)

Description of real-life observation:

Role play situation:

DEMONSTRATE HOW YOU WOULD GIVE AN _OUTSIDE_ COMPLIMENT TO ONE OF YOUR PARENTS, AND THEN AN _INSIDE_ COMPLIMENT.

- -

Please circle the word below which best describes how your son or daughter did while using this social skill in either the role play or real-life situation.

NEEDS MORE HELP   GOOD   EXCELLENT

It is important for you to reinforce your child's use of this social skill at home in a positive way. Encourage and praise your child when you see the skill appropriately used. Remind him/her to use the social skill when necessary.

Thank you for your assistance.

Sincerely,

* *

PARENT/GUARDIAN SIGNATURE: _____

Compliments Can Mean a Great Deal

When you give someone a compliment, it means that you say something nice about that person. When compliments are given correctly, they can mean a lot to the people who receive them. A good compliment should include:

1. A reference to something specific about the person (e.g., the person's shoes, hair, personality, sports ability).

2. A positive word or remark (e.g., great, nice, I like, good).

An example of a good compliment would be, "You are really a good listener!" This compliment includes both parts. The word *listener* refers specifically to the person's listening skills, and the word *good* is a positive word about that skill. If you gave this compliment to a person, he would know that you like the way he listens.

An example of a bad compliment would be, "You got a new pair of shoes." This compliment only includes one of the two parts. The person who receives this compliment would know that you were talking specifically about his shoes, but he wouldn't know if you liked them or not. This compliment does not include a positive word or remark about the shoes.

DIRECTIONS: (1) Read each of the statements below.

(2) If the statement is a good compliment which includes both parts, write **GOOD**.

(3) If the statement is a bad compliment which includes only one of the two parts, write **BAD** and then rewrite the statement so that it would be considered a good compliment.

1. You have a new watch.

2. You are a great friend.

3. Good.

4. I like how you write.

5. You have a beautiful wardrobe.

6. You have a different shirt on today, don't you?

7. I see you got your project finished.

8. You gave a terrific party last night.

9. Nice.

in/SIDE/out

There are two kinds of compliments:

#1. **OUTSIDE COMPLIMENT**

This kind of compliment says something positive about the way a person looks, or what a person owns or has.

For example: "You have beautiful hair."

"Those pants are great."

"Nice track shoes."

"I like your haircut."

#2. **INSIDE COMPLIMENT**

This kind of compliment says something positive about a person's personality, or what the person does and says. An inside compliment is sometimes harder to give because it is more personal than an outside compliment. Both kinds of compliments are nice to give, but inside compliments usually mean more to the people who receive them.

For example: "I wish I could be more like you. You're always so patient."

"I really admire your willpower. You really stick to your goals."

"I'm glad you're my friend. I don't know what I would do without you!"

Write two outside compliments you could give to your best friend.

1.

2.

Write two inside compliments you could give to your best friend.

1.

2.

Write two outside compliments you could give to one of your parents.

1.

2.

Write two inside compliments you could give to one of your parents.

1.

2.

Name:_____

to Give Is Better than to Receive

DIRECTIONS: Draw a circle around the statement below which is most like you.

I SELDOM GIVE SOMEONE A COMPLIMENT.

Because:

1. I just don't ever think about giving compliments.

2. I feel embarrassed giving a compliment.

3. There is not much I like about other people.

4. (other)

I LIKE TO COMPLIMENT PEOPLE AND I AM ALWAYS TRUTHFUL WHEN I GIVE A COMPLIMENT.

I AM ALWAYS GIVING PEOPLE COMPLIMENTS, BUT SOMETIMES I DON'T REALLY MEAN WHAT I SAY.

Because:

1. I am afraid that people won't like me if I don't give them compliments all the time.

2. I can get more of what I want if I "butter people up" with compliments first.

3. (other)

Try to start giving people compliments. There is usually something good you can find in everybody. You may want to start with "outside" compliments, since they are easier to give. The more compliments you give, the more comfortable you will feel. You may find that people enjoy being around you more.

Try to give compliments only when you mean them. People can usually tell when you give an insincere compliment, or when you give a compliment just to get something in return.

Keep up the good job! Don't change a thing.

SSS: Social Skill Strategies (Book A)

Name:_____

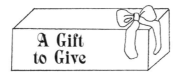

A Gift
to Give

DIRECTIONS: Read the story below, and then complete the compliment activity.

STORY: It was Christmas eve. Soon Sue's family would gather around the tree to open their gifts. Sue was nervous. She wanted to get something for her mother, but when she went shopping, nothing she saw seemed special enough. Sue knew she needed to think of something fast. Time was running out. At last, she had an idea. Sue decided to write a letter to her mom telling her why she is so special and what she does that is so helpful.

Finally, it was time to open gifts. Sue's gift to her mother was under the tree along with all the other colorfully wrapped packages. After a few of the gifts were opened, Sue's mother reached down and picked up the gift from her. Sue felt worried. She knew her gift was the best she could give, but compared with all the clothes and jewelry her mom had received, Sue wondered if it would be good enough.

Sue watched as her mom read the complimentary letter. Tears came to her mom's eyes. Everyone was watching. She got up and whispered in Sue's ear, "Thank you! This was the best gift I could ever get." Sue felt very happy.

ACTIVITY: 1. Write your name on a small piece of paper. Put your name into a container along with the names of all the other people in your group.

2. Choose a name from the container.
(If you choose your own name, put it back and pick another.)

3. Do not let anyone know whose name you picked.

4. Think of a compliment to give the person you chose. (Remember, there are inside and outside compliments. Inside compliments are the best to give.)

5. Write down your compliment using your best writing. You may even want to decorate your compliment.

6. Put your compliment in an envelope or a box, and gift wrap it. Put a name tag on the present that tells who the compliment is for and who it is from.

7. Exchange the gifts after everyone has finished.

REMEMBER: Compliments are made to help people feel good about themselves.

Your Tone Makes a Difference

When you compliment someone, it is important to use a sincere tone of voice.

Decide who will read the lines for each character in the script below. For a demonstration of just how important tone of voice can be, the following script should be read aloud two times.

The first time, the person who reads Jill's lines should talk in a way that lets the character, Mark, know that she really means what she says and wants to have Mark feel good about himself.

The second time, Jill's lines should be read with a sarcastic tone of voice, letting Mark know that she really means to put him down and hurt his feelings. (To accomplish this, Jill could laugh during her lines, and her facial expression should be one of teasing.)

Character Description:

Jill - A teen-age student

Mark - A teen-age student

Scene Description:

Mark comes back to school after a holiday break with a brand new outfit on. Jill notices the new outfit and talks to Mark about it.

Jill: Mark, are those new clothes?

Mark: Yeah, they are.

Jill: Where did you get them?

Mark: My mom gave them to me for Hanukah.

Jill: Boy, they're really something! I bet you'll get a lot of comments from people today.

Mark: Do you really think so?

Jill: I really do. Those are nice clothes, Mark, really nice.

Notice that both times the script was read, the words were exactly the same. What changed was the **WAY** the words were said. If you are trying to decide if someone is being serious or sarcastic, pay attention to tone of voice and body language.

GIVING A COMPLIMENT - GIVING A COMPLIMENT

1. Write the two things that a good compliment should include.

   (1) _____

   (2) _____

   Give the definitions for the following two terms:

   Inside compliment: _____

   _____

   Outside compliment: _____

   _____

2. Explain why an inside compliment can sometimes be more difficult to give.

   _____

   Explain why inside compliments usually mean more to the people receiving them than outside compliments.

   _____

3. Pretend you are going to interview one of your teachers to find out how he/she feels about compliments. Write down three questions you could ask.

   (1) _____

   (2) _____

   (3) _____

4. Compare an inside compliment with an outside compliment. Tell one way they are the same, and one way they are different.

   (same) _____

   (different) _____

5. Pretend you are a teacher and that many of your students rarely give compliments. Create an activity you could do with your students to help them learn how to give more compliments.

   _____

   _____

   _____

6. Write down the last three compliments you gave, and indicate whether they were inside or outside compliments.

   (1) _____

   Inside or outside? _____

   (2) _____

   Inside or outside? _____

   (3) _____

   Inside or outside? _____

SKILL HOMEWORK ACTIVITY

_____
(Due Date)

Dear Parent or Guardian of: _____

This week we are learning about the social communication skill:

ACCEPTING A COMPLIMENT

This social skill is very important in interpersonal relationships.

The students have learned to say "Thank you" when someone compliments them. Many of us ruin a compliment when someone gives us one by saying things like, "Oh, I'm not cute," or "This old shirt?"

Before the due date, please complete one of the following activities with your son or daughter: (put a check mark by your choice)

_____ A. We acted out the role play situation listed below.

_____ B. I observed my son/daughter using this social skill in a real-life situation. (I have described the situation below.)

Description of real-life observation:

Role play situation:

YOUR MOM TELLS YOU THAT YOU DID A GOOD JOB CLEANING UP THE YARD. ACCEPT THE COMPLIMENT APPROPRIATELY AND SAY, "THANK YOU."

- -

Please circle the word below which best describes how your son or daughter did while using this social skill in either the role play or real-life situation.

NEEDS MORE HELP   GOOD   EXCELLENT

It is important for you to reinforce your child's use of this social skill at home in a positive way. Encourage and praise your child when you see the skill appropriately used. Remind him/her to use the social skill when necessary.

Thank you for your assistance.

Sincerely,

* *

PARENT/GUARDIAN SIGNATURE: _____

Thank You

Sometimes it's hard to accept a compliment when someone gives you one. Pretend your friend says, "Hey, I like your shirt!" You might be tempted to say, "Oh, this old thing?" because it might be difficult to say, "Thank you."

It's important for us to learn to accept compliments by saying "Thank you." If we don't, people will stop giving us compliments. If you give someone a compliment such as, "You did a really nice job on that picture," and the person you compliment says, "I think it's really ugly," you won't feel like giving a compliment again.

There is a short, simple phrase that you can use to accept compliments. Just say, "**Thank you**." It's nice and easy to remember. Just say, "**Thank you**." It's hard to say "Thank you" at first if you're not used to it. The more you say it, the easier it will get for you. Remember, just say, "**Thank you**."

* *

DIRECTIONS: Answer the following questions.

1. What is a compliment?

2. What should you say when someone gives you a compliment?

3. Why do you think people have a hard time accepting compliments (saying "Thank you")?

4. How do you feel when someone you compliment doesn't say, "Thank you"?

Just Say Thanks!

REMEMBER: THE BEST WAY TO ACCEPT A COMPLIMENT IS JUST TO SAY, "THANK YOU!"

DIRECTIONS: Read each compliment and response below. Decide if the person accepted the compliment in the appropriate manner. Write GOOD after those people who accepted the compliment in the right way. Write BAD after those people who accepted the compliment in the wrong way.

1. (Compliment): "Boy, John I really like that T-shirt!"
   (Response): "Oh, this old thing?"   _____

2. (Compliment): "You got your hair cut. I like it."
   (Response): "Thanks."   _____

3. (Compliment): "Melissa, you really do a good job here."
   (Response): "Thank you, Mr. Simon."   _____

4. (Compliment): "Nice picture, that's really good!"
   (Response): "Oh, I'm terrible at drawing."   _____

5. (Compliment): "Good job on your homework assignment!"
   (Response): "Who cares?"   _____

6. (Compliment): "You did a terrific job cleaning your room!"
   (Response): "Thanks, Mom."   _____

7. (Compliment): "Your behavior has greatly improved."
   (Response): "Oh, thanks. It's about time you noticed!"   _____

8. (Compliment): "You got a 'B+' on your test? That's good."
   (Response): "I should have gotten an 'A'."   _____

9. (Compliment): "Neat pants! Where'd you get them?"
   (Response): "Oh, thanks. At the mall."   _____

10. (Compliment): "That's a cute dress, Maria."
    (Response): "Oh, thanks. This rag?"   _____

Name:_____

HOW DO YOU RESPOND TO COMPLIMENTS?

REMEMBER: THE BEST WAY TO ACCEPT A COMPLIMENT IS JUST TO SAY, "THANK YOU!"

DIRECTIONS: In each of the boxes below, write a compliment that you think that person would give you. Then write how you would respond.

Write a compliment that a teacher might give you.

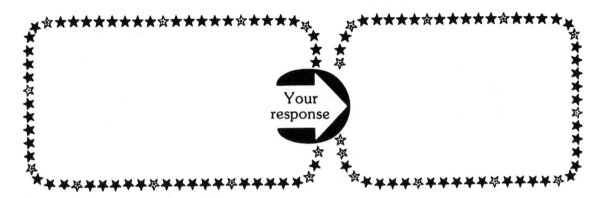

Write a compliment that a parent might give you.

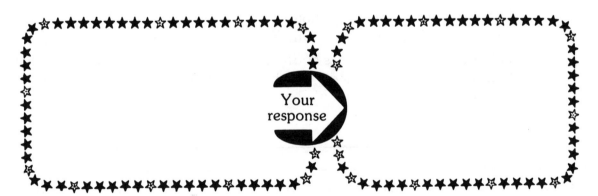

Write a compliment that a friend might give you.

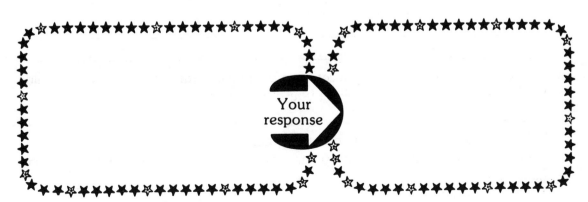

ACCEPTING A COMPLIMENT - ACCEPTING A COMPLIMENT

1. Write the rule to remember about accepting a compliment.

   _____

2. Explain why it's important to accept a compliment correctly.

   _____

   _____

3. Write a compliment that each of the following people might give you. Then write the exact words you would use to accept the compliment.

   (your teacher) _____

   (your response) _____

   (your parent) _____

   (your response) _____

   (your friend) _____

   (your response) _____

4. Read the following situations. Compare the way each person accepted a compliment. Tell which person you think accepted the compliment in a better manner and explain why.

   > Anna went over to her friend's house. Her friend said, "Anna, I really like that shirt. Is it new?" Anna replied, "Oh, thanks. No, I borrowed it from my sister."

   > Carla went over to her friend's house. Her friend said, "Carla, I really like that shirt. Is it new?" Carla replied, "Oh, this old shirt? I can't stand it but I couldn't find anything else to wear."

   (which person) _____

   (explanation) _____

   _____

5. Write a short story about a boy who doesn't accept compliments in the correct manner. Tell what happens to him. (Use the back of this page if you need more space.)

   _____

   _____

   _____

6. Rate yourself on how well you accept compliments. Mark an "X" below on the line. Explain why you rated yourself as you did.

   ●————————————————●————————————————●

   I always accept   I sometimes accept   I never accept
   compliments correctly.   compliments correctly.   compliments correctly.

   (explanation) _____

   _____

   _____

SKILL HOMEWORK ACTIVITY

_____
(Due Date)

Dear Parent or Guardian of: _____

This week we are learning about the social communication skill:

SAYING THANK YOU

This social skill is very important in interpersonal relationships.

This skill can be broken down into the following skill steps. Please watch for all of the steps in your role play practice or real-life observation.

1. Decide if the person has done something for you or said something to you that you appreciate (e.g., given you a compliment, a favor, a gift).
2. Thank the person, using words that express your appreciation (e.g., thanks, thank you, I appreciate . . . , I am grateful . . .)
3. Tell what you are thanking the person for.

Before the due date, please complete one of the following activities with your son or daughter: (put a check mark by your choice)

_____ A. We acted out the role play situation listed below.

_____ B. I observed my son/daughter using this social skill in a real-life situation. (I have described the situation below.)

Description of real-life observation:

Role play situation:

YOUR MOM/DAD MADE YOUR FAVORITE MEAL ON YOUR BIRTHDAY. DEMONSTRATE HOW YOU WOULD EXPRESS YOUR APPRECIATION.

- -

Please circle the word below which best describes how your son or daughter did while using this social skill in either the role play or real-life situation.

NEEDS MORE HELP   GOOD   EXCELLENT

It is important for you to reinforce your child's use of this social skill at home in a positive way. Encourage and praise your child when you see the skill appropriately used. Remind him/her to use the social skill when necessary.

Thank you for your assistance.

Sincerely,

* *

PARENT/GUARDIAN SIGNATURE: _____

Name:_____

Giving Thanks

Saying thank you means *to express your appreciation to someone who has done something for you or said something nice to you.*

Knowing when to say *thank you* is very important! If you do not thank people, you may find that they stop doing you favors, complimenting you, and giving you gifts.

DIRECTIONS: List eight things that you appreciate and would want to say *thank you* for. Each one must begin with the letter given. You can list things that people might say to you or do for you.

 **T**elling me you like my new haircut.

Name:_____

THANK YOU CONTEST

DIRECTIONS: Divide into three groups. Group one will be assigned the category of "parents," group two "friends," and group three "brothers/sisters." Each group will be given five minutes to brainstorm and list things that the people in their category might do or say that they would want to say *thank you* for (e.g., in the parent category, making my favorite meal on my birthday, might be listed). Every idea thought of should be written down. At the end of the five minutes, each group will read their list aloud. Each group should try to list at least 15 ideas. (Groups may not list different gifts that they might receive.) The groups should write on the front and back of this sheet. If more space is needed, ideas can be written on another piece of paper.

Name:_____

The How To's

Saying *thank you* can be broken down into three steps:

Step 1 - Decide if the person has done something for you or said something to you that you are happy about and appreciate (e.g., given you a compliment, done you a favor, or given you a gift).

Step 2 - Thank the person, using words that express your appreciation (e.g., thanks, thank you, I appreciate . . . , I am grateful . . .).

Step 3 - Tell what you are thanking the person for.

Example #1: If your best friend carries your books for you when you break your arm, you could say, "Thanks a million for carrying my books."

Example #2: If your mom compliments you on how you rearranged your room, you could say, "Thank you for the compliment."

DIRECTIONS: Read each of the situations below. If it is a situation where you would want to say *thank you*, write down the words you would say. Make certain to follow steps two and three above. If a thank you is not necessary in the situation, write *none*.

1. You are in the middle of repairing your bike and your hands are greasy. Your friend is watching you, and answers the phone for you when it rings.

2. When you get home from school, you notice that your mom has rearranged the furniture in her bedroom.

3. At Christmas, you receive a gift from your aunt, who lives in a different state.

4. You've been working hard to stop biting your fingernails. One of your friends notices, and comments about how much better they look.

5. Your teacher gives you extra help on your math after school, and then gives you a ride home because it is raining.

6. At the beginning of class each day, your teacher takes attendance.

Formal / Informal

In **formal** situations, when you are with adults in respected positions, there are several ways to say *thank you*. A few are listed below:

"I am grateful . . . . . ."

"I appreciate . . . . . ."

"I want to thank you . . . . . ."

In **informal** situations, when you are with friends or a relative you know well, there are many ways to say *thank you*. A few are listed below:

"Thanks for . . . . . ."

"Thanks a lot . . . . . ."

"Thank you . . . . . ."

DIRECTIONS: In each of the situations below, it would be appropriate to say *thank you*. Decide if the situation is formal or informal, and then circle the correct word. Next, write down the words you would say to express your appreciation. You may use the phrases listed above. Remember to also tell what you are thanking the person for.

1. You just finished interviewing for a new job. You want to thank the boss for giving you the opportunity to interview.

   Formal   Informal

2. Your best friend compliments you on your new shirt.

   Formal   Informal

3. Your mom bakes you a batch of cookies for a party you are going to.

   Formal   Informal

4. Your school principal takes the time to talk to you about a problem you are having with a teacher.

   Formal   Informal

5. Your brother does the dishes for you because he knows you have a huge test tomorrow, and you need the extra time to study.

   Formal   Informal

SAYING THANK YOU - SAYING THANK YOU

1. Tell what saying *thank you* means and write the three skill steps.

   (definition) _____

   _____

   (step 1) _____

   _____

   (step 2) _____

   _____

   (step 3) _____

   _____

2. Explain what might happen if you do not thank people when they do something for you or say something nice to you.

   _____

   _____

   Pretend a friend at school complimented you on your new haircut. When would be the best time to say *thank you* and why?

   _____

   _____

3. Describe a situation in the community when you would want to say *thank you* to someone.

   _____

   _____

4. Compare the following two comments. Tell one way they are the same and one way they are different.

   "Thanks for the help." "I appreciate the help you gave me."

   (same) _____

   (different) _____

5. Pretend you have a bad habit of forgetting to say *thank you* and you want to start remembering. Write down two things you could do to help yourself reach your goal.

   (strategy 1) _____

   (strategy 2) _____

6. Read the short script below. Decide if David said *thank you* in an appropriate way or not. Explain your answer.

   Patty: David, here are the notes you missed when you were absent from school last week. I made a copy for you because I thought you might like to have them when you study for the test tonight.

   David: Thanks, but it's a little late, don't you think? Everyone knows you should study more than one night before a test!

   Did David say *thank you* in a good way? YES   NO

   (explain) _____

   _____

SKILL HOMEWORK ACTIVITY

_____
(Due Date)

Dear Parent or Guardian of: _____

This week we are learning about the social communication skill:

INTRODUCING YOURSELF

This social skill is very important in interpersonal relationships and can be broken down into the following skill steps. Please watch for all of the steps in your role play practice or real-life observation.

The students have learned to use formal language (e.g., Hello, my name is . . .) and to shake hands when introducing themselves to an adult.

The skill steps are:

1) Walk up to the person.
2) Say: "Hi, I'm . . ."
3) Make small talk.

Before the due date, please complete one of the following activities with your son or daughter: (put a check mark by your choice)

_____ A. We acted out the role play situation listed below.

_____ B. I observed my son/daughter using this social skill in a real-life situation. (I have described the situation below.)

Description of real-life observation:

Role play situation:

NEW NEIGHBORS HAVE JUST MOVED IN NEXT DOOR. YOUR MOTHER TOLD YOU THAT THE FAMILY'S NAME IS MATSON. WHEN YOU ARE OUTSIDE, YOU SEE ONE OF THE MATSON BOYS. WALK OVER TO HIM AND INTRODUCE YOURSELF.

Please circle the word below which best describes how your son or daughter did while using this social skill in either the role play or real-life situation.

NEEDS MORE HELP   GOOD   EXCELLENT

It is important for you to reinforce your child's use of this social skill at home in a positive way. Encourage and praise your child when you see the skill appropriately used. Remind him/her to use the social skill when necessary.

Thank you for your assistance.

Sincerely,

• •

PARENT/GUARDIAN SIGNATURE: _____

Name:_____

Introducing Yourself

There are many, many times when you need to introduce yourself to someone. The manner in which you introduce yourself is very important. You want to make a good first impression. When you introduce yourself to an adult, you will do it differently than when you introduce yourself to someone your own age. When you introduce yourself to an adult, you will use **formal** language. For example, "Hello, Mrs. Blink. I'm David Thomas." You can use **informal** language when you are introducing yourself to someone your age. For example, "Hi, I'm Dave."

DIRECTIONS: Make a list of times when you would need to introduce yourself to an adult and to your peers.

Adults	Peers

Name:_____

Do It *Right!*

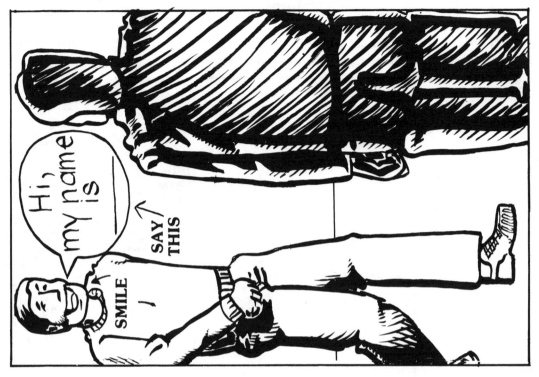

INFORMAL

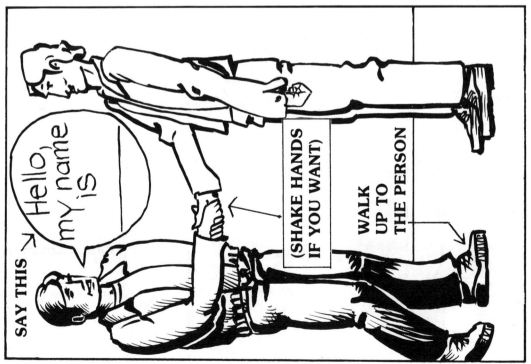

FORMAL

SSS: Social Skill Strategies (Book A)

Name:_____

Hi, I'm . . .

Informal

DIRECTIONS: Write the exact words you would say if you were introducing yourself to a new kid in your neighborhood.

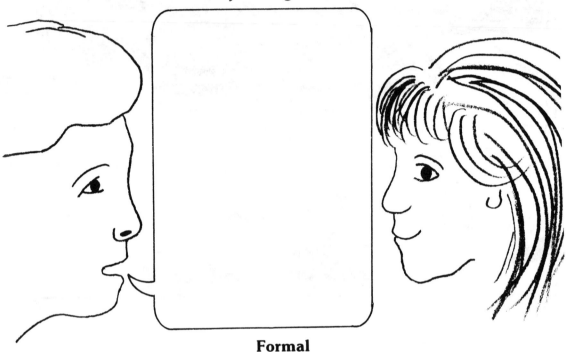

Formal

DIRECTIONS: Write the exact words you would say if you were introducing yourself to your friend's dad, Mr. Whitley.

Name:_____

INTRODUCING YOURSELF - INTRODUCING YOURSELF

1. Tell the three skill steps for the social skill of introducing yourself.

   (step 1) _____

   (step 2) _____

   (step 3) _____

2. Explain why it is important to introduce yourself to people.

   _____

   _____

3. Write the exact words you would use to introduce yourself to Ms. Jenks, who is the manager of a grocery store. You hope to get a job at the store someday.

   _____

   _____

   _____

4. Compare an informal introduction with a formal introduction. Tell one way they are the same and one way they are different.

   (same) _____

   _____

   (different) _____

   _____

5. Pretend you are teaching a younger brother or sister the social skill of introducing yourself. Explain how you would teach the skill. Tell the exact things you would say and do. (Use the back of this page if you need more space.)

   _____

   _____

   _____

6. Read the following story. Decide if you feel Malory introduced herself in an appropriate manner or an inappropriate manner. Explain your answer.

   Malory had just started in a new school where she didn't know anyone. A girl came and opened the locker next to Malory's locker. Malory smiled at her and said, "Hi, my name's Malory Draft. I'm new at this school. I was wondering if you could help me find room 434? I'd really appreciate it."

   (circle one)   appropriate   inappropriate

   (explanation) _____

   _____

SKILL HOMEWORK ACTIVITY

_____
(Due Date)

Dear Parent or Guardian of: _____

This week we are learning about the social communication skill:

INTRODUCING TWO PEOPLE TO EACH OTHER

This social skill is very important in interpersonal relationships.

The students have learned that they need to decide whether to make a formal or informal introduction (for a formal introduction, you would use more formal words such as, "Hello, I would like you to meet Mr. . . ."). The introduction should be two-way (e.g., "John, meet Pam. Pam, meet John."). After you have introduced the two people, say something that will help the people get a conversation started.

Before the due date, please complete one of the following activities with your son or daughter: (put a check mark by your choice)

_____ A. We acted out the role play situation listed below.

_____ B. I observed my son/daughter using this social skill in a real-life situation. (I have described the situation below.)

Description of real-life observation:

Role play situation:

YOU HAVE BROUGHT HOME A NEW FRIEND WHO JUST MOVED INTO THE NEIGHBORHOOD. INTRODUCE YOUR FRIEND TO YOUR MOTHER/FATHER.

- -

Please circle the word below which best describes how your son or daughter did while using this social skill in either the role play or real-life situation.

NEEDS MORE HELP   GOOD   EXCELLENT

It is important for you to reinforce your child's use of this social skill at home in a positive way. Encourage and praise your child when you see the skill appropriately used. Remind him/her to use the social skill when necessary.

Thank you for your assistance.

Sincerely,

* *

PARENT/GUARDIAN SIGNATURE: _____

Introductions

You will often need to introduce two people to each other. Introductions are of two types: formal and informal. A **formal introduction** should be used any time there is an adult who needs to be introduced. When you make a formal introduction, you use more formal words, such as: "Mrs. Potter, I would like to introduce you to my mother and father, Mr. and Mrs. Rothenberger. Mom and Dad, this is my music teacher, Mrs. Potter."

You can use an **informal introduction** if you are introducing people your own age to one another. You can use more informal words, such as: "Hi, Bob! This is Cindy and Karen. Karen, Cindy, meet Bob."

The Steps:

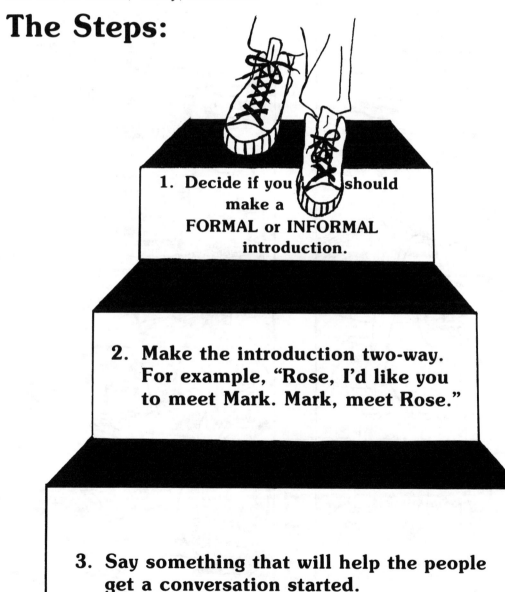

1. Decide if you should make a FORMAL or INFORMAL introduction.

2. Make the introduction two-way. For example, "Rose, I'd like you to meet Mark. Mark, meet Rose."

3. Say something that will help the people get a conversation started.

                   SSS: Social Skill Strategies (Book A)

INTRODUCTIONS

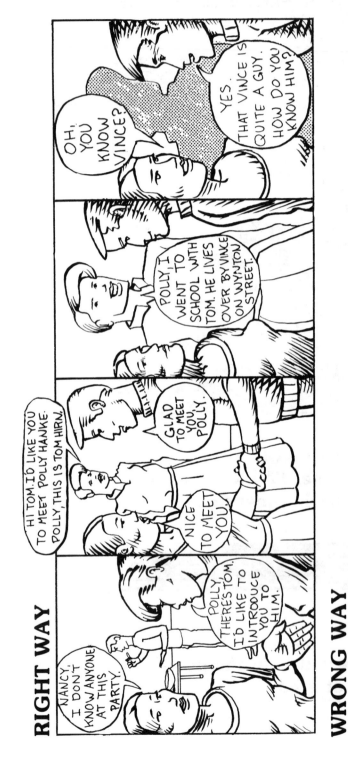

Name:_____

Making Introductions

DIRECTIONS: In the talk bubbles, write the exact words you would use to make the following introductions. On the line, write whether the introduction would be formal or informal.

1. Introducing: your mother or father
   your principal   _____

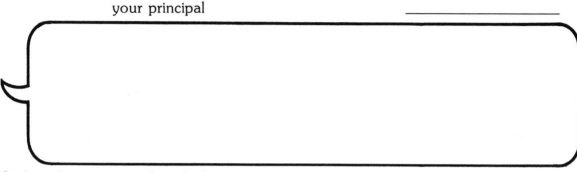

2. Introducing: your friend, Jean
   your cousin, Kristin   _____

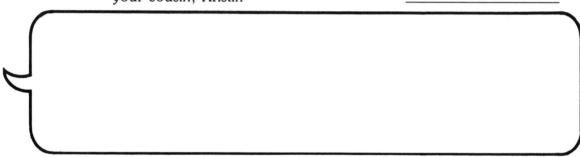

3. Introducing: your brother
   your boss, Mr. Wolfe   _____

4. Introducing: your friend, Tom
   your friend, Angela   _____

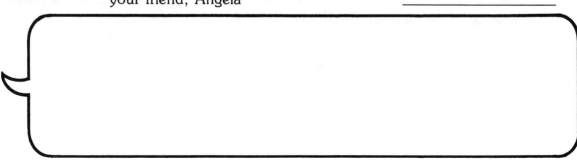

QUESTIONS

DIRECTIONS: Answer the questions about making introductions.

1. Why is it important to introduce people to one another?

2. Why is it a good idea to use formal language when introducing adults?

3. Why is it important to say something that will help the people start a conversation?

4. What should you do if you are not sure whether two people know each other?

5. Write down the exact words you would use if you had to introduce your cousin, Jamie, to a group of three of your friends. (When you are introducing a person to a group of people, the introductions do not have to be two-way.)

INTRODUCING TWO PEOPLE TO EACH OTHER

1. Write three things you should do when introducing two people to each other.

   (1) _____

   (2) _____

   (3) _____

2. Why is it important to introduce two people to each other?

   _____

   _____

   _____

   _____

3. Describe a situation from home, school, and the community when you may need to introduce two people to each other.

   (home) _____

   _____

   (school) _____

   _____

   (community) _____

   _____

4. Compare introducing yourself to someone to introducing two people to each other. Tell one way they are the same and one way they are different.

   (same) _____

   _____

   (different) _____

   _____

5. Write a short play about a girl who has to introduce her parents to her teacher at parents' night at school. (Use the back of this page if you need more space.)

   _____

   _____

   _____

6. Write about a time when you had to introduce two people to each other. Then, evaluate how well you think you did at your introduction.

   (situation) _____

   _____

   (evaluation) _____

   _____

SKILL HOMEWORK ACTIVITY

_____
(Due Date)

Dear Parent or Guardian of: _____

This week we are learning about the social communication skill:

MAKING A REQUEST

This social skill is very important in interpersonal relationships.

The students have learned that when they make a request of someone, they should ask/request instead of tell/demand. (e.g., "Give me some money" is a demand and "Could you please loan some money to me?" is a request.)

Before the due date, please complete one of the following activities with your son or daughter: (put a check mark by your choice)

_____ A. We acted out the role play situation listed below.

_____ B. I observed my son/daughter using this social skill in a real-life situation. (I have described the situation below.)

Description of real-life observation:

Role play situation:

PRETEND YOU WANT TO ASK YOUR PARENTS FOR A NEW PAIR OF SHOES. DEMONSTRATE HOW YOU WOULD MAKE YOUR REQUEST.

- -

Please circle the word below which best describes how your son or daughter did while using this social skill in either the role play or real-life situation.

NEEDS MORE HELP   GOOD   EXCELLENT

It is important for you to reinforce your child's use of this social skill at home in a positive way. Encourage and praise your child when you see the skill appropriately used. Remind him/her to use the social skill when necessary.

Thank you for your assistance.

Sincerely,

* *

PARENT/GUARDIAN SIGNATURE: _____

No More Demands!

DIRECTIONS: Read the following story about Mrs. Fletcher and her family. Then answer the questions at the bottom of the page.

Scene 1

Mrs. Fletcher was dressed for work and sitting in the kitchen. Her two children, Wayde and Brenda, came in to get something to eat for breakfast. Brenda said, "I've still got to iron this shirt. Mom, put in a bagel for me while I'm ironing." Mrs. Fletcher thought to herself, "She sure is bossy!" Wayde said, "Mom, you gotta give me $10.00. Our field trip is today and I'm broke." Again Mrs. Fletcher thought to herself, "It would be nice if he asked!" Next, Mr. Fletcher walked in and said, "Good morning! Honey, I've got a tennis game right after work today. You'll have to pick up my suit at the dry cleaners. I won't be able to make it before they close." Mrs. Fletcher shook her head. She got up and said, "If you would like me to do something for you, you will have to ask me if I will do it. I'm tired of everyone demanding things from me!" Mrs. Fletcher picked up her purse and keys, and left. Mr. Fletcher and Wayde both looked confused. Wayde said, "What was that about?"

Scene 2

Wayde and Brenda both got home from school at the same time. The front door was open so they knew that their mom was home. They walked inside but didn't see her anywhere. Wayde said, "Hey, Brenda! Look at this note on the mirror. It says, *'A REQUEST IS ALWAYS MORE POLITE THAN A DEMAND!'"* Brenda said, "Let me see that. Hey, it looks like Mom's handwriting. Look! There is another note on the clock. Let's see what it says." Wayde walked over and read it aloud. It said, *"THERE IS A BIG DIFFERENCE BETWEEN 'ASKING' AND 'TELLING.' YOU'LL HAVE BETTER RESULTS IF YOU ASK!"* Wayde and Brenda both went upstairs to see if they could find their mom. They both had notes taped to their bedroom doors. The notes said the same thing: *DON'T FORGET THE "PLEASE" WORD.* Brenda said, "I think Mom is trying to make a point. Now I know why she left this morning." "Me too," said Wayde.

* *

QUESTIONS:

1. Write the demand that Brenda made of her mom in Scene 1.

2. Write the demand that Wayde made of his mom in Scene 1.

3. Write the demand that Mr. Fletcher made of his wife in Scene 1.

4. How do you think Mrs. Fletcher felt in Scene 1? Why?

5. Explain the point that Mrs. Fletcher was trying to make to her family when she wrote the notes in Scene 2.

Name:_____

Ask, Don't Tell
Request, Don't Demand

When you make a **request**, it means that *you ask someone to do something in a polite way*. (e.g., "Please pass the rice.")

When you make a **demand**, it means that *you tell someone to do something*. (e.g., "Give me some more rice.")

If you want to get along with people, it is important that you make requests instead of demands (or ask instead of tell).

DIRECTIONS: Read each of the statements below. If it is a demand, change it into a polite request. Remember to use the word *please*. If it is already a polite request, then write *OK*.

1. "Hey! I need a pencil."

2. "Mom, you gotta give me five dollars for a yearbook."

3. "Would you please pass the potatoes?"

4. "Tell me what the homework assignment is."

5. "Give me a ride home."

6. "Pick up my pencil. It fell on the floor."

7. "Mom, I told you I needed clean clothes."

8. "Will you please sit down?"

9. "Give me some gum."

10. "Get out of my desk."

11. "Give me some help on this."

12. "Could you please help me with this problem?"

13. "Dad, pick me up at 4:00."

14. "You've got to let me stay out until 11:00 tonight."

Know When To Ask

You have learned that when you want someone to do something for you, it is important to ask or request it in a polite way.

Something else to think about is the time and place to make your request. If you want to ask your teacher if you can go to the bathroom, it would be better to ask during work time than it would be while she is lecturing. If you ask people at a good time and place, they will be more likely to say *yes*.

DIRECTIONS: Circle the best time and place to make the following requests.

1. You want to ask your parents for a new bike.

   - Ask them after you bring home your poor report card.

   - Ask them after you bring your grades up.

2. You want to ask your mom for $10.00.

   - Ask her two days before pay day.

   - Ask her the day after pay day.

3. You want to ask your brother if he'll show you how to play his guitar.

   - Ask him when he is in a good mood.

   - Ask him after he has a fight with his girlfriend.

4. You want to ask your teacher for an extra day on your assignment.

   - Ask her before school when she isn't so busy.

   - Ask her after class begins, when she is trying to take attendance.

5. You want to ask your friend if he could help you with your typing skills.

   - Ask him on a day when he has a lot of homework himself.

   - Ask him on a day when he doesn't have much homework.

6. You want to ask your principal if he would consider putting another candy machine in the school.

   - Ask him when he is in his office and doesn't look very busy.

   - Ask him right after a prank fire alarm.

Name:_____

The Magic Word

The most important word to remember when you make a request is **PLEASE.**

DIRECTIONS: 1. Choose one of the phrases listed below:

   PLEASE - the magic word!
   Don't forget to say *please!*
   Please say *Please!*

2. Create a poster which includes your phrase.

3. Consider displaying your completed poster in a location where several people will see it and be reminded of the importance of the word *please.*

DIRECTIONS: 1. From a magazine, cut out pictures of two people.

2. Glue the pictures below, or on the back of this page, so that the people are facing each other.

3. Draw a "talk bubble" coming out of one person's mouth to make the picture look like a cartoon.

4. Write down what the person would say to make a request of the other person.

MAKING A REQUEST - MAKING A REQUEST

1. Tell what *making a request* means.

   _____

   _____

   Tell what *making a demand* means.

   _____

   _____

2. Explain two benefits of making a request rather than making a demand.

   (1) _____

   (2) _____

3. Describe a situation at home, in school, and in the community when you may need to make a request.

   (home) _____

   _____

   (school) _____

   _____

   (community) _____

   _____

4. Tell one similarity and one difference between making a request and making a demand.

   (similarity) _____

   (difference) _____

5. Write or tell a short story about "Dean, The Demander" while he is at school, and tell what happens to him because he doesn't know how to make a request. (Use the back of this page if you need more space.)

   _____

   _____

   _____

6. Read the short story below. Decide if Mylo made his request in a good way or a bad way. Explain your answer.

   Mylo was babysitting for his younger brother. He was making dinner, when he decided he could use some help. He said to his brother, "Would you please set the table while I finish making supper?"

   _____

   _____

   _____

SKILL HOMEWORK ACTIVITY

_____
(Due Date)

Dear Parent or Guardian of: _____

This week we are learning about the social communication skill:

OFFERING HELP

This social skill is very important in interpersonal relationships.

The students have learned that when they want to help someone, they should not just "take over." They need to remember that people may not want their help. When they want to help they should ask first by saying something like this:

"Can I help you with that?"
"Would you like a hand?"
"Do you want some help with that?"

Before the due date, please complete one of the following activities with your son or daughter: (put a check mark by your choice)

_____ A. We acted out the role play situation listed below.

_____ B. I observed my son/daughter using this social skill in a real-life situation. (I have described the situation below.)

Description of real-life observation:

Role play situation:

YOU NOTICE THAT YOUR MOM IS HAVING DIFFICULTY GETTING A LADDER DOWN. DEMONSTRATE HOW YOU WOULD OFFER TO HELP.

Please circle the word below which best describes how your son or daughter did while using this social skill in either the role play or real-life situation.

NEEDS MORE HELP   GOOD   EXCELLENT

It is important for you to reinforce your child's use of this social skill at home in a positive way. Encourage and praise your child when you see the skill appropriately used. Remind him/her to use the social skill when necessary.

Thank you for your assistance.

Sincerely,

. . . .

PARENT/GUARDIAN SIGNATURE: _____

When To Help

DIRECTIONS: The list below describes times when you may want to offer to help someone. Add seven new situations to the list.

1. Your mom comes home from the grocery store and has several bags to bring into the house.

2. Your brother is complaining about how difficult his math homework is. He is doing division, and that is something you like.

3. Your sister is very excited because she is sewing her first skirt at home. She is having trouble pinning up the hem by herself and getting it straight.

4. _____

   _____

5. _____

   _____

6. _____

   _____

7. _____

   _____

8. _____

   _____

9. _____

   _____

10. _____

   _____

Name:_____

A Helping Hand

Offering help means *to offer to assist someone who is in need.* When you think you can help someone, don't just take over, ask first! Remember, the person may not want your help at all. The best bet is to ask first.

Below is a list of some ways to ask:

"Could you use a hand with that?"

"Do you want any help?"

"Can I help you with that?"

"I think I know how to do that. Would you like me to help?"

If you offer to help and the person says *no,* it means that the person wants to try it on his or her own.

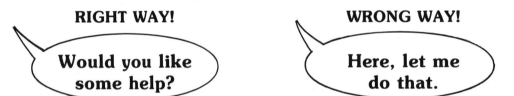

RIGHT WAY!

Would you like some help?

WRONG WAY!

Here, let me do that.

DIRECTIONS: For each of the situations below, write down what you would say to offer your help. You may use the examples from above or think of new ways to ask.

1. Your friend is trying to type a letter, but she hasn't had typing class yet. You learned how to type last semester.

2. You see a person in a wheelchair trying to get through a door. You don't know if he wants help or not.

3. You heard that the decoration committee was looking for people to draw murals. You are good at drawing.

4. One of the kids in your class isn't sure how to work the computer. You know quite a bit about it.

5. You notice that one of the seventh graders who is new to your school can't find a room he needs to find. You have been going to school in the building for three years and know your way around very well.

Name:_____

Don't Be a Score Keeper

Me	You
5	2

DIRECTIONS: Read the script below. It is a conversation between two students, Nicky and Pat, who are doing a computer project together. They are talking about Annette, who unfortunately is a "score keeper."

Nicky: It would be great if we could add some graphics to this computer system. I bet we'd really get a good grade then!

Pat: That would be neat! I've never done any graphics before though, have you?

Nicky: No, I haven't. Maybe Annette could help us. She is really good with computers. I bet she could show us how.

Pat: Are you sure you want Annette's help? She'd never let us hear the end of it.

Nicky: What do you mean by that?

Pat: Well, she offered to help me once before. She had this way of making me feel like I owed my life to her because she helped me.

Nicky: Really? It's too bad some people have to be like that.

Pat: No kidding! It's like she's keeping score or something, and only offers to help if she thinks she can get something in return.

Nicky: Did you thank her for the help?

Pat: Of course I did! Do you know what she said? She said, "Don't forget you owe me one, Pat!" Don't get me wrong. I really appreciated her help, but she made it sound like she had given me the world.

Nicky: That reminds me of my brother, Mike. Whenever he helps me, he acts like he's so smart and I'm so dumb. I never ask him for help anymore, because he makes me feel like such a pea brain.

Pat: Well, let's see. Who else could we ask besides Annette?

(Nicky and Pat continue their conversation)

When you offer help to someone, remember these tips:

1. Don't be a "score keeper" and have the person you help feel that he owes you something in return.

2. Don't let the person you help feel that you're smart and he's dumb.

3. When someone thanks you for helping, say something like, "Sure, anytime."

Name:_____

Transferring the Social Skill

To offer help in an appropriate way,
follow these suggestions:

1. Ask if you can help.
2. Don't "take over."
3. Don't make the person feel that he/she
   owes you something because of your
   help.

DIRECTIONS: Every time you offer help in an appropriate manner, ask the person
you helped to sign below, verifying that you used the social skill
correctly.

---

1. _____offered help to me for the following reason:

   He/she remembered to follow the three suggestions listed above for offering help
   correctly.

   Signed:_____

---

2. _____offered help to me for the following reason:

   He/she remembered to follow the three suggestions listed above for offering help
   correctly.

   Signed:_____

---

3. _____offered help to me for the following reason:

   He/she remembered to follow the three suggestions listed above for offering help
   correctly.

   Signed:_____

---

4. _____offered help to me for the following reason:

   He/she remembered to follow the three suggestions listed above for offering help
   correctly.

   Signed:_____

OFFERING HELP - OFFERING HELP - OFFERING HELP

1. Define the social skill of offering help, and write an important tip to remember.

   _____

   _____

2. Explain why you should not make a person feel he owes you something when you help him.

   _____

   _____

3. Describe a situation at home, in school, and in the community when you could offer help to someone.

   (home) _____

   _____

   (school) _____

   _____

   (community) _____

   _____

4. Compare the following two comments. Tell one way they are the same and one way they are different.

   "Would you like me to help you with that?"   "Let me do that for you."

   (same) _____

   (different) _____

5. Pretend your friend is trying to sew a button on his/her shirt, but is having a difficult time. You know how to sew, so you want to offer some help. Write down the words you would say.

   _____

   _____

6. Think of one of your friends, and tell how well you think he/she does at offering help to other people. Explain your answer.

   _____

   _____

   _____

SKILL HOMEWORK ACTIVITY

_____
(Due Date)

Dear Parent or Guardian of: _____

This week we are learning about the social communication skill:

ASKING FOR HELP

This social skill is very important in interpersonal relationships and can be broken down into the following skill steps. Please watch for all of the steps in your role play practice or real-life observation.

1. Try to do it on your own first.

    If you can't,
2. Ask for help (explain yourself clearly).
3. Pay attention when the person helps you.
4. Thank the person for helping you.

Before the due date, please complete one of the following activities with your son or daughter: (put a check mark by your choice)

_____ A. We acted out the role play situation listed below.

_____ B. I observed my son/daughter using this social skill in a real-life situation. (I have described the situation below.)

Description of real-life observation:

Role play situation:

YOU ARE WORKING ON YOUR SOCIAL STUDIES HOMEWORK. YOU CAN'T FIND THE ANSWER TO QUESTION #11 IN THE BOOK. ASK ONE OF YOUR PARENTS TO HELP YOU.

- -

Please circle the word below which best describes how your son or daughter did while using this social skill in either the role play or real-life situation.

NEEDS MORE HELP   GOOD   EXCELLENT

It is important for you to reinforce your child's use of this social skill at home in a positive way. Encourage and praise your child when you see the skill appropriately used. Remind him/her to use the social skill when necessary.

Thank you for your assistance.

Sincerely,

* *

PARENT/GUARDIAN SIGNATURE: _____

Name:_____

Asking for Help

Everyone needs to ask for help at different times. If you ask for help, it does not mean you are stupid. **REMEMBER, EVERYONE ASKS FOR HELP!**

Rate yourself on how often you ask for help. Put an "X" below where you think you are.

I never ask.	I sometimes ask.	I ask all the time.

☐☐☐☐☐☐☐☐☐☐☐☐☐☐☐☐☐☐☐☐☐☐☐☐

People like this sometimes get in trouble. They mess up because they do not ask for help when they should. They are worried people will think they are stupid if they ask for help.

People like this are always asking for help. They don't try to do it on their own first. They usually get on people's nerves because they are pesty or a bother.

Why:

Tell why you marked your "X" where you did.

?

The skill steps for asking for help are:	
1) Try to do it on your own first. If you can't do it, then . . .	See if you can figure it out on your own, unless it's an emergency and you need help right away.
2) Ask for help (explain yourself clearly).	Remember, others don't know what you need help with.
3) Pay attention when someone helps you.	The person who helps you will get angry if it seems as though you're not listening.
4) Thank the person for helping.	We should never forget this.

Name:_____

HELP!

DIRECTIONS: In the left-hand column, write ten situations when you would need to ask for help. In the right-hand column, write the name of the best person to get help from.

EXAMPLE ➡

	Situation	Person to Ask
1.	*I don't understand the new math formula.*	*Math teacher*
2.		
3.		
4.		
5.		
6.		
7.		
8.		
9.		
10.		

SSS: Social Skill Strategies (Book A)

Name:_____

How You Ask

It's important to ask for help in the right way. Remember to explain what you want carefully. Thank the person for helping you.

DIRECTIONS: In each of the talk bubbles, write the exact words you would use to ask for help.

You have been working on a homework assignment and you really don't understand question #3.

You are fixing one of the electrical outlets in the kitchen. You want to ask someone for help to make sure you're doing it the right way.

You work at a fast-food restaurant. You need to ask someone to help you get some heavy cases of ketchup down off the shelf.

Your dad has been hitting you around a lot lately. You want to ask a counselor at school for help.

SSS: Social Skill Strategies (Book A)

"Asking for Help" Questions

DIRECTIONS: Answer the questions in complete sentences.

1. Tell about a time when you didn't ask for help and you should have. What happened?

2. Why do you think some people are afraid to ask for help?

3. How do you feel about a person in your class who asks for help too much?

4. Why is it important to try to do it on your own first?

5. Why is it important to explain yourself clearly when asking for help?

6. Why is it important to pay attention when a person is helping you?

7. Why is it important to choose the right time and place to ask for help?

Name:_____

ASKING FOR HELP
Contract

I agree to observe_____for the next

(name of student)

week. I will evaluate the manner in which the above named student asks for help from

either myself or other people. At the end of the week, I will complete the evaluation form

below.

_____

(teacher signature)

ASKING FOR HELP
Evaluation

DIRECTIONS: The evaluator should put his/her initials next to those behaviors that were observed.

The student

_____ asked for help instead of becoming frustrated.

_____ asked for help using the right tone of voice.

_____ asked for help at the right time and place.

_____ asked for help after first trying to do it on his/her own (didn't ask for help too often).

_____ paid attention to the person giving help.

_____ thanked the person for giving help.

_____

(teacher signature)

ASKING FOR HELP - ASKING FOR HELP - ASKING FOR HELP

1. List the four skill steps for the social skill of asking for help.

   (1) _____

   (2) _____

   (3) _____

   (4) _____

2. Explain why it's important to ask for help in an appropriate manner.

   _____

   _____

   _____

   _____

   _____

3. Tell a situation for each class when you may need to ask for help.

   (math class) _____

   _____

   _____

   (science class) _____

   _____

   _____

   (gym class) _____

   _____

4. Compare how the following people asked for help. Tell one way they were the same and one way they were different.

   Story #1: Allison was working on her math assignment. She was having some trouble solving problem #6. Allison saw that her teacher was talking to someone at the door, so Allison waited before she went to ask for help. When Allison went up to the teacher's desk she said, "Mr. Jaywalk, I've been having some trouble with this problem. I wonder if you could help me?"

   Story #2: Liz was working on her math assignment. She really didn't like math because it was difficult for her. Liz had looked over the assignment and told herself that it was too hard. Her teacher was busy, so Liz couldn't ask for help. She decided to talk to the boy behind her. When the teacher told Liz to start her assignment, Liz said, "It's too hard. I need some help."

   (same) _____

   _____

   _____

   (different) _____

   _____

   _____

5. Create a rhyme or a slogan about the social skill of asking for help. (Use the back side of this paper.)

6. Evaluate whether the following situations are the right time and place to ask for help. Circle *yes* or *no* for each and explain your answer.

   Your mother is on the phone with someone.   yes   no

   (explanation) _____

   _____

   Your teacher is sitting at her desk.   yes   no

   (explanation) _____

   _____

   Your teacher is helping another student.   yes   no

   (explanation) _____

   _____

SKILL HOMEWORK ACTIVITY

_____
(Due Date)

Dear Parent or Guardian of: _____

This week we are learning about the social communication skill:

ASKING PERMISSION

This social skill is very important in interpersonal relationships.

Because teen-agers are growing up and becoming more independent, they sometimes have difficulty asking for permission. The students have discussed the reasons why, despite these feelings, it is still important for them to ask permission.

They have learned the following skill steps for asking permission:

1. Decide if it is necessary to ask permission to do what you want to do.
2. Decide whom you should ask for permission.
3. Choose a good time and place to ask.

Before the due date, please complete one of the following activities with your son or daughter: (put a check mark by your choice)

_____ A. We acted out the role play situation listed below.

_____ B. I observed my son/daughter using this social skill in a real-life situation. (I have described the situation below.)

Description of real-life observation:

Role play situation:

DEMONSTRATE HOW YOU WOULD ASK PERMISSION FROM ONE OF YOUR PARENTS TO HAVE A PARTY AT YOUR HOUSE.

Please circle the word below which best describes how your son or daughter did while using this social skill in either the role play or real-life situation.

NEEDS MORE HELP   GOOD   EXCELLENT

It is important for you to reinforce your child's use of this social skill at home in a positive way. Encourage and praise your child when you see the skill appropriately used. Remind him/her to use the social skill when necessary.

Thank you for your assistance.

Sincerely,

PARENT/GUARDIAN SIGNATURE: _____

Name:_____

Two Decisions

Asking permission means *asking if you may be allowed to do something.*

These are the first two steps:

1. Decide if it is necessary to ask permission to do what you want to do.

2. Decide whom you should ask for permission.

For example, if you want to use your brother's catcher's mit, it would be necessary to ask permission, and your brother would be the person to ask.

DIRECTIONS: Complete the following table by filling in the blank spaces. (In the rows where nothing is filled in under either column, fill in something new.)

EXAMPLE

TIMES WHEN IT IS NECESSARY TO ASK PERMISSION	THE PERSON FROM WHOM YOU SHOULD ASK PERMISSION
When you want to go to the bathroom during class at school	*The teacher*
When you want to paint your bedroom a different color	
	The salesclerk
	Your brother/sister
	Your boss
When you want to use someone's phone because you ran out of gas	

STEP 3

You have already learned that the social skill of **asking permission** includes two decisions: 1) Deciding if it is necessary to ask permission to do what you want to do. 2) Deciding whom you should ask for permission.

The third and final step for asking permission is to choose a good **time and place** to ask permission.

For example, if you want to ask permission from your boss to have the weekend off, the best time and place to ask would be when your boss is not busy and is alone.

DIRECTIONS: Read each of the situations below. If you think it would be a good time and place to ask permission, write **good**. If it would be a bad time and place to ask permission, write **bad**.

_____ 1. You want to ask for your sister's permission to use her camera. She comes home from work and is really in a good mood. She notices that you did all of the dishes without her and thanks you for doing them.

_____ 2. You want to ask for your dad's permission to get a musical instrument and take lessons. Your mom and dad are trying to pay the monthly bills and are having trouble coming up with the money to do so.

_____ 3. You want to ask for your teacher's permission to hand in your assignment late because you have had so much other homework lately. Your teacher just finished telling the class how disappointed she is that so few students are handing in their work on time.

_____ 4. You want to ask for your best friend's permission to borrow his tennis racket during the weekend. Your friend just told you that he has to help his parents with a garage sale all weekend, and won't be able to play any tennis.

DIRECTIONS: For each of the following situations, write down what you think would be the best time and place to ask for permission.

1. You want to ask permission from the secretary in the office to use her masking tape to hang homecoming posters.

2. You want to ask permission from your teacher to go get a drink of water.

3. You want to ask permission from your mom to buy a mini-bike.

4. You want to ask permission from the office to stay in the halls after school to hang valentines on classmates' lockers.

Name:_____

Another *Perspective*

As you become older, and feel you are able to make decisions on your own, it becomes more difficult to ask for someone else's permission.

By taking another person's perspective, it becomes easier to understand why it is still necessary to ask for permission.

DIRECTIONS: For each of the situations below, explain why you would want the person to ask for your permission.

1. Pretend that you are an eighth grade science teacher. You have at least 30 students in each one of your classes. Explain why you would want your students to ask for your permission before going to the bathroom during class time.

2. Pretend that you are a parent of two teen-agers. Explain why you would want them to ask for your permission to stay out past their curfew.

3. Pretend that you have one brother and one sister. Explain why you would want them to ask for your permission before using any of your personal belongings.

4. Pretend you are a home owner. Explain why you would want the neighborhood kids to ask for your permission to cut through your back yard to walk to school.

5. Pretend you are a salesclerk at a clothing store. Explain why you would want a customer to ask your permission to exchange an article of clothing for a different size.

6. Pretend you are a babysitter. Explain why you would want the kids you are sitting for to ask your permission to go over to a friend's house before leaving.

7. Pretend you are a boss. Explain why you would want your employees to ask for your permission before leaving early.

Avoid It Like the Black Plague

When it comes to asking for permission, there are three things to avoid (i.e., three things you should NOT do).

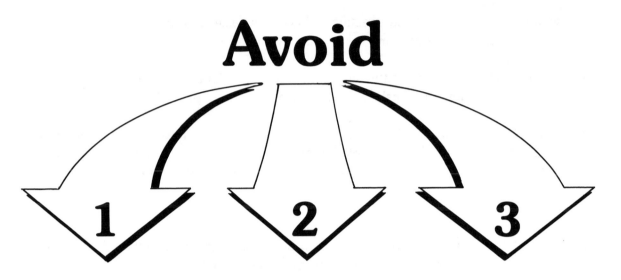

Being the type of person who refuses to ask for permission when it is necessary to do so. This type of person often ends up having privileges taken away. Remember, we all have authorities. Even adults do!

Describe a time when adults have to ask for permission:

_____
_____
_____
_____
_____
_____

Being the type of person who asks for permission when it is not necessary to do so. If you ask for permission too often, people will be annoyed and may get angry!

Describe something you can do without asking for permission:

_____
_____
_____
_____
_____
_____

Being the type of person who gets impulsive when told *no* after asking for permission. If you get upset and impulsive, the person will be more likely to say *no* the next time you ask too.

Describe a time when you were not permitted to do something and how you reacted:

_____
_____
_____
_____
_____
_____

Name:_____

Transferring the Social Skill

To ask for permission appropriately, follow these three steps:

1. Decide if it is necessary to ask permission to do what you want to do.
2. Decide whom you should ask for permission.
3. Choose a good time and place to ask permission.

DIRECTIONS: Each time you remember to ask for permission correctly, ask the person to sign below to verify that you used the skill appropriately.

1. _____ asked for permission from me for the following reason:

He/she remembered to follow the three steps listed above for asking permission correctly.

Signed: _____ Date: _____

2. _____ asked for permission from me for the following reason:

He/she remembered to follow the three steps listed above for asking permission correctly.

Signed: _____ Date: _____

3. _____ asked for permission from me for the following reason:

He/she remembered to follow the three steps listed above for asking permission correctly.

Signed: _____ Date: _____

4. _____ asked for permission from me for the following reason:

He/she remembered to follow the three steps listed above for asking permission correctly.

Signed: _____ Date: _____

ASKING PERMISSION - ASKING PERMISSION

1. Define the social skill of asking permission and tell what the three skill steps are.

   (definition) _____

   (step 1) _____

   (step 2) _____

   (step 3) _____

2. Explain why it is not a good idea to ask for permission using a "snotty" tone of voice.

   _____

   _____

   Explain why it is a bad idea to get impulsive when told *no* after asking for permission.

   _____

   _____

3. Describe a situation at school and in the community when you should ask permission and tell whom you should ask for each situation.

   (school) _____

   (who should be asked) _____

   (community) _____

   (who should be asked) _____

4. Compare a person who asks permission too often with a person who never asks permission in situations when he should. Tell one way they are the same and one way they are different.

   (same) _____

   (different) _____

5. List two things for which you should ask permission, and two things for which you do not need to ask permission.

   Should ask permission: (1) _____

                                   (2) _____

   Should not ask permission: (1) _____

                                   (2) _____

6. Evaluate your skill at asking permission. Circle the statement that best describes you and then explain your choice.

I don't like to ask permission from anyone.	I ask for permission when I should and I ask at a good time and place.	I ask for permission even when it is not necessary to do so.

   (explanation) _____

   _____

SKILL HOMEWORK ACTIVITY

_____
(Due Date)

Dear Parent or Guardian of: _____

This week we are learning about the social communication skill:

ACCEPTING NO

This social skill is very important in interpersonal relationships and can be broken down into the following skill steps. Please watch for all of the steps in your role play practice or real-life observation.

1. Decide whether the NO is coming from an authority figure.
2. Stay calm. Don't get impulsive.
3. Think about the consequences of not following the authority's decision.
4. Respond by saying "O.K." or don't say anything at all.
5. Follow the authority's decision.

Before the due date, please complete one of the following activities with your son or daughter: (put a check mark by your choice)

_____ A. We acted out the role play situation listed below.

_____ B. I observed my son/daughter using this social skill in a real-life situation. (I have described the situation below.)

Description of real-life observation:

Role play situation:

YOU ASK YOUR MOTHER/FATHER IF YOU CAN HAVE A FRIEND STAY OVER FOR THE WEEKEND. YOUR PARENT SAYS _NO_. DEMONSTRATE HOW YOU CAN ACCEPT _NO_ IN A MATURE WAY.

- -

Please circle the word below which best describes how your son or daughter did while using this social skill in either the role play or real-life situation.

NEEDS MORE HELP   GOOD   EXCELLENT

It is important for you to reinforce your child's use of this social skill at home in a positive way. Encourage and praise your child when you see the skill appropriately used. Remind him/her to use the social skill when necessary.

Thank you for your assistance.

Sincerely,

* *

PARENT/GUARDIAN SIGNATURE: _____

Name:_____

Authority Figures

Everyone in this world has to follow rules. Believe it or not, even your parents and your teachers have rules to follow. Everyone has people he/she must listen to. Authority figures are people who make sure we follow the rules.

DIRECTIONS: Add to this list of authority figues.

- Teacher
- Principal
- President
-
-
-
-
-
-
-
-
-

DIRECTIONS: Add to this list of situations when an authority figure tells you NO and you aren't able to do what you wanted to do.

- My mom says I can't go out Friday night.
- The teacher said I can't get a drink of water.
-
-
-
-
-
-
-

Name:_____

ules

DIRECTIONS: Answer these questions.

1. Write down four rules that you have to follow at home.
   -
   -
   -
   -

2. Write down four rules that you have to follow at school.
   -
   -
   -
   -

3. Write down two rules that you might have to follow at a job.
   -
   -

4. Write down two rules that your teacher has to follow.
   -
   -

5. Write down two rules that your mother/father must follow.
   -
   -

6. Write down two rules that you have to follow at a grocery store.
   -
   -

7. Tell what would happen if there were no rules.

DIRECTIONS: Read the information below and follow the directions on this page.

> *When someone says NO to you and you don't get your way, how do you handle it?*

Do you . .

1) Accept the NO in a mature way (e.g., you do what the person asks without making faces, comments, or arguing)?

   IF YOU DO, YOU ARE VERY ADULT-LIKE!

2) Accept the NO in a bad way (e.g., you make rude faces, inappropriate comments, or argue)?

   IF YOU DO, YOU MAY BE VIEWED AS CHILDISH!

DIRECTIONS: In each of the rectangles below, draw what each type of person looks like when he accepts NO in a bad way.

Are you a face maker?

Do you have temper tantrums?

Do you talk back?

Are you a beggar?

QUESTION: How do you act when someone says NO and you aren't able to do something you wanted to do?

Name:_____

How to Accept NO in a Mature Way

Here are the skill steps for accepting NO in a mature way.

1) Decide if the NO is coming from an **AUTHORITY** figure.

(Authority figures are parents, teachers, etc.)

2) Stay **CALM.** Don't get impulsive.

(Don't get excited. See the *Staying Calm* page [Accepting NO - F] if you have problems with this.)

3) Think about the **CONSEQUENCES** of not following the authority's decision.

(Think about what will happen to you if you do it anyway.)

4) **RESPOND** by saying "O.K." or don't say anything at all.

(Refrain from making negative comments/gestures.)

5) **FOLLOW** the authority's decision.

(Do what the authority wants you to do.)

Here's a funny sentence to help you remember the skill steps:

All **C**ops **C**an **R**un **F**ast!

A = **A**uthority

C = **C**alm

C = **C**onsequences

R = **R**espond

F = **F**ollow

If an authority figure says NO to you, just remember, ALL COPS CAN RUN FAST!

DIRECTIONS: Tell about a time when you will need to accept NO from an authority figure.

Staying Calm

DIRECTIONS: Read the information below.

Staying calm is a very difficult thing to do and takes a lot of self-control. Some people need practice at staying calm because they get upset easily. It's important to stay calm when an authority figure tells you NO. But it's often difficult to stay calm in these situations. Here are some techniques that will help you:

1) Take a deep breath and let the air out slowly.

2) Tell yourself to calm down.

3) Walk away for a few seconds.

4) Count to five before saying or doing anything.

5) Picture yourself calming down.

Don't expect a miracle right away. Pick one technique and practice that one. It takes effort just to remember to try a technique when you are upset. Everyone has to find out what techniques work best.

DIRECTIONS: Do each role play with a partner. Try to get really upset when the authority figure says NO. Make your body feel upset. Then use one of the techniques from above to help yourself calm down.

1. Your father/mother just told you that you cannot go to the carnival because you are grounded. All of your friends are going. Your father/mother will not change his/her mind.

2. You ask your teacher if you can go outside for lunch recess. She says NO and reminds you that you have to finish your homework.

3. You ask the principal if you can get out of being suspended and he says NO.

Name:_____

Accepting NO Proof

DIRECTIONS: Get this sheet signed by authority figures (at home, in school, or in the community). When you accept NO in a mature way, ask the authority figure to sign his/her name to show that you accepted NO in a mature way. Do this three different times.

I feel that the student accepted NO in a mature way (refrained from making faces, talking back) and then followed my directions.

Situation (describe what the student was asking for when you said NO):

_____

_____   _____
(signature of authority figure)   (date)

I feel that the student accepted NO in a mature way (refrained from making faces, talking back) and then followed my directions.

Situation (describe what the student was asking for when you said NO):

_____

_____   _____
(signature of authority figure)   (date)

I feel that the student accepted NO in a mature way (refrained from making faces, talking back) and then followed my directions.

Situation (describe what the student was asking for when you said NO):

_____

_____   _____
(signature of authority figure)   (date)

Name:_____

Accepting NO Questions

DIRECTIONS: Answer the questions.

1. Make a list of two authority figures who tell you NO the most often.

   •

   •

2. Write down the skill steps to accepting NO in a mature way. (Use the "cop" sentence to help you remember the steps.)

   •

   •

   •

   •

   •

3. Explain why you think it's important to accept NO in a mature way.

4. What do you think about a student who does not accept NO in a mature way (e.g., talks back, makes faces, tries to argue, etc.)?

5. Pretend you are a parent. You have a child who is fourteen years old. Write four rules you would make for your child.

   A rule about curfew:

   A rule about chores:

   A rule about respect for parents:

   A rule about school work:

6. Tell about a situation when an authority figure may not be fair in saying NO.

7. Explain each of the following ways of handling a situation when an authority figure says NO unfairly.

   A. Do what the authority figure says anyway

   B. Become angry and upset

   C. Be assertive and talk to the authority figure

   Which do you think is the best option? _____ Why?

201

ACCEPTING NO - ACCEPTING NO - ACCEPTING NO

1. Write the skill steps for the social skill of accepting NO.

    (step 1) _____

    (step 2) _____

    (step 3) _____

    (step 4) _____

    (step 5) _____

2. Explain some problems that can arise when a person does not accept NO in a mature manner.

    _____

    _____

    _____

    _____

3. Write a situation for each of the following people when you might need to accept NO from them in an appropriate manner.

    (your English teacher)_____

    _____

    (your parent) _____

    _____

    (your boss) _____

    _____

4. Compare the way you accept NO to the way your best friend accepts NO. Tell one similarity and one difference between the two of you.

    (similarity) _____

    _____

    (difference) _____

    _____

5. Create a memory device to help you remember the skill steps for the social skill of accepting NO.

6. Rate yourself from 1-10 on how well you accept NO (1 = poor, 10 = good). Give reasons for why you rated yourself as you did.

    Rating = _____

    Reasons: _____

    _____

    _____

SKILL HOMEWORK ACTIVITY

_____
(Due Date)

Dear Parent or Guardian of: _____

This week we are learning about the social communication skill:

MAKING AN APOLOGY

This social skill is very important in interpersonal relationships.

This skill can be broken down into the following skill steps. Please watch for all of the steps in your role play practice or real-life observation.

1. Choose a good time and place to apologize.
2. Say you are sorry in a sincere way (to show you really mean it).
3. Tell what you are sorry about.
4. Offer a solution (if necessary).

Before the due date, please complete one of the following activities with your son or daughter: (put a check mark by your choice)

_____ A. We acted out the role play situation listed below.

_____ B. I observed my son/daughter using this social skill in a real-life situation. (I have described the situation below.)

Description of real-life observation:

Role play situation:

YOU WERE HORSING AROUND IN THE HOUSE AND BROKE A WINDOW. DEMONSTRATE HOW YOU WOULD APOLOGIZE TO ONE OF YOUR PARENTS AND OFFER A SOLUTION.

Please circle the word below which best describes how your son or daughter did while using this social skill in either the role play or real-life situation.

NEEDS MORE HELP   GOOD   EXCELLENT

It is important for you to reinforce your child's use of this social skill at home in a positive way. Encourage and praise your child when you see the skill appropriately used. Remind him/her to use the social skill when necessary.

Thank you for your assistance.

Sincerely,

* *

PARENT/GUARDIAN SIGNATURE: _____

When To Apologize

Making an apology means *to say you are sorry when you have made a mistake or done something wrong.*

DIRECTIONS: Read each of the situations below. If you think the main character made a mistake or did something wrong and should apologize, write *YES*. If you think the main character has nothing to apologize about, write *NO*. Explain your answers.

1. Mike got mad at his best friend one day and said, "I wish you and I had never met." After he cooled down, Mike felt bad about what he said.

   Should Mike apologize to his best friend? _____ Why?

2. Renee made plans to meet her friend downtown at 2:00. She had to do extra house chores and didn't get there until 3:00. Renee could tell that her friend was upset about having to wait for an hour.

   Should Renee apologize to her friend? _____ Why?

3. Wess did the long jump in the first track meet of the season. He had practiced a lot. He did his best and ended up taking third place in his event. Wess's team took second overall in the meet.

   Is it Wess's fault that the team didn't take first place? _____ Why?

4. Tracy and her family finally left on the trip they had been planning all year. Tracy became sick with the flu on the trip.

   Is it Tracy's fault that she got sick? _____ Why?

5. Oliver's mom asked him to drive to the store to get some groceries. While Oliver was in the store, someone backed into his parked car and dented the fender. Whoever did the damage was nowhere to be found.

   Should Oliver apologize to his mom? _____ Why?

6. While Jackie was babysitting, she accidently broke a vase. She wasn't watching where she was going and bumped into it.

   Should Jackie apologize to the people she was babysitting for? _____ Why?

About Apologizing . . .

There are four steps to remember when you apologize to someone:

Step 1: Choose a good time and place to apologize.

(For example, you would not apologize to your boss for being late to work when the boss is in a meeting with someone else.)

Step 2: Say you are sorry in a sincere way. Don't apologize unless you really mean it. People can tell if it is a "fake" apology.

(It is best to apologize in person. If you feel uncomfortable, you could write your apology, which would be better than not apologizing at all.)

Step 3: Tell what you are sorry about.

(For example, if you scratch someone's record, you should say, "I'm sorry, I accidently scratched your record." If you just walk up, say "I'm sorry," and walk away, the person wouldn't know what you were apologizing for.)

Step 4: Offer a solution, if appropriate, or an explanation.

(For example, if you break something, you might want to explain how it happened and offer to replace it.)

DIRECTIONS: Read each of the situations below. First, write down the time and place to apologize, and then write down what you would say. Remember to follow the four steps listed above.

1. During class, your teacher intercepts a note that you are passing to your friend. Your note says some pretty bad things.

   What time and place would you choose to apologize to the teacher?

   What would you say?

2. While your dad is on the phone, you are in the garage playing with his golf clubs. He has asked you never to use his clubs. You break his putter.

   What time and place would you choose to apologize to your dad?

   What would you say?

Avoid *NEVER* And *ALWAYS*

Nobody is perfect! Because we are human and make mistakes, we all need to say we are sorry sometimes.

There are some people who **NEVER** say they are sorry. When they make a mistake or do something wrong, they refuse to apologize.

Do you know anyone like this?

Do you think it is all right for someone to be like this? Why or why not?

How do you feel when you're around someone who never apologizes?

Why do you think it is so hard for some people to say they are sorry?

There are other people who are just the opposite. They **ALWAYS** say they are sorry, even when they haven't done anything wrong.

Do you know anyone like this?

Do you think it is good to apologize all the time? Why or why not?

How do you feel when you're around someone who is always apologizing?

Why do you think a person might apologize too much?

Put a circle around the comment below that is most like you:

I HAVE A REALLY HARD TIME APOLOGIZING. I DON'T SAY *I'M SORRY* ENOUGH.	I DO APOLOGIZE, BUT ONLY WHEN I HAVE MADE A MISTAKE OR DONE SOMETHING WRONG.	I TEND TO SAY *I'M SORRY* WAY TOO MUCH, EVEN WHEN I DON'T NEED TO APOLOGIZE.

                   SSS: Social Skill Strategies (Book A)

Who's Who?

DIRECTIONS: Read each of the situations below, and decide who should apologize to whom. Sometimes, the person should apologize to more than one person.

1. Marcia and Angie were talking in the locker room. Angie was telling Marcia about the funny-looking shoes that Ruth wore to school that day. Angie said she wouldn't be caught dead wearing anything like that. As the girls left, Angie noticed that Ruth was in the locker room and had overheard every word.

   _____ should apologize to _____

   Why?

2. Mrs. Pieper said she would pick up her daughter, Kathy, from school at 3:30 to take her to a dental appointment. Mrs. Pieper didn't watch the time. She got to Kathy's school at 3:45. Kathy ended up being 15 minutes late for her appointment. Mrs. Pieper went into the dentist's office with Kathy and saw that the receptionist looked a little annoyed.

   _____ should apologize to _____

   Why?

3. Bart, Chris, and Jesse decided to go on a camp-out. They divided the responsibilities for bringing supplies. Jesse was in charge of the food, Chris was in charge of the cooking equipment, and Bart was in charge of the sleeping equipment. At the camp sight, they discovered that they had no tent or sleeping bags.

   _____ should apologize to _____

   Why?

4. Mrs. Clark called Greg at home to see if he could come to work an hour earlier tomorrow. Greg wasn't home, but his sister Joyce took a message. Joyce saw Greg that night at supper, but forgot to tell Greg that his boss had called.

   _____ should apologize to _____

   Why?

5. It was parents' night at the basketball game. Kenton was excited that his parents would get a chance to see him. The coach promised to let everyone play. During the game, the coach put in his first, second, and third string players. He forgot about Kenton, who ended up sitting on the bench the whole game. At the end of the game, the coach realized he had not played Kenton.

   _____ should apologize to _____

   Why?

Sincere or Fake?

There are two types of apologies: The kind that is given sincerely, and the kind that is fake.

THE FAKE APOLOGY
A person who gives a fake apology, says he is sorry just to get out of trouble, or because someone else makes him say it.

THE SINCERE APOLOGY
A person who gives a sincere apology, says he is sorry and truly means it.

> I'm sorry I called you that mean name. Now, can I still get my allowance this week?

> I'm really sorry that I called you that mean name! Sometimes when I get mad, I say things that I don't mean.

DIRECTIONS: Read the following situations and decide whether the person made a SINCERE apology or a FAKE apology. Write **S** if the apology was sincere, and **F** if it was fake.

_____ 1. Wanda got upset in math class because she didn't understand something. She said some mean things to the teacher and received a detention. Wanda didn't want a detention, so after class she went and told the teacher she was sorry. The teacher accepted Wanda's apology but didn't take back the detention. Wanda called her an "old bag" when she left the room.

_____ 2. Jacob hit his little sister. Later he felt really bad about it. He went into her room and apologized to her and asked her if she wanted to go to the ice-cream shop.

_____ 3. Tracy stole something from a gym locker. She felt bad afterwards. She turned herself in to the principal. She apologized to him and to the gym teacher.

_____ 4. Matt called his mother a "fat cow." She told him he couldn't go outside until he apologized to her. Matt said in a snotty tone, "Okay, I'm sorry!"

_____ 5. John was really disruptive in class. He got a detention from the teacher. The next day John brought a note to his teacher. The note said:
    Dear Mrs. Gajewski: I am sorry about how I acted. I will try to be better from now on.
John's behavior was much better for the rest of the week.

_____ 6. Carrie was late for work one day. She apologized to her boss and said it would not happen again. She was late for work the next day.

MAKING AN APOLOGY - MAKING AN APOLOGY

1. Tell what *making an apology* means and list the four skill steps for the social skill.

   (definition) _____

   _____

   (step 1) _____

   (step 2) _____

   (step 3) _____

   (step 4) _____

2. Explain why it is important to apologize when you have done something wrong.

   _____

   _____

   _____

3. Describe a situation when you would expect someone to apologize to you.

   _____

   _____

   _____

4. Explain how you can tell the difference between a fake apology and a sincere apology.

   _____

   _____

5. Describe what you think a school might be like if nobody in it ever apologized.

   _____

   _____

   _____

6. Read the situation below. Decide if Craig apologized in an appropriate or inappropriate way. Explain your answer.

   Craig was two hours late for dinner. He didn't call his family to tell them he would be late. When he finally got home, he could see they were very worried and angry. Craig said, "Sorry, what's for supper? I'm really hungry."

   _____

   _____

SKILL HOMEWORK ACTIVITY

_____
(Due Date)

Dear Parent or Guardian of: _____

This week we are learning about the social communication skill:

STATING AN OPINION

This social skill is very important in interpersonal relationships.

The students learned the difference between a fact and an opinion. They learned to use phrases such as "I feel . . .," "I believe . . .," and "In my opinion . . ." when they are stating an opinion.

Before the due date, please complete one of the following activities with your son or daughter: (put a check mark by your choice)

_____ A. We acted out the role play situation listed below.

_____ B. I observed my son/daughter using this social skill in a real-life situation. (I have described the situation below.)

Description of real-life observation:

Role play situation:

YOU AND YOUR BROTHER ARE TALKING ABOUT YOUR FAVORITE ROCK GROUPS. STATE YOUR OPINION ABOUT YOUR FAVORITE ROCK GROUP. MAKE SURE YOU STATE YOUR OPINION BY USING ONE OF THE OPINION PHRASES.

Please circle the word below which best describes how your son or daughter did while using this social skill in either the role play or real-life situation.

NEEDS MORE HELP   GOOD   EXCELLENT

It is important for you to reinforce your child's use of this social skill at home in a positive way. Encourage and praise your child when you see the skill appropriately used. Remind him/her to use the social skill when necessary.

Thank you for your assistance.

Sincerely,

* *

PARENT/GUARDIAN SIGNATURE: _____

COOPERATION ACTIVITY

I feel . . .
I think . . .
I believe . . .
In my opinion . . .
Personally, I feel . . .

When you state an opinion, it is a good idea to start off your sentence with one of these phrases. If you do, people will know you are stating an opinion.

Definitions	**Examples**
FACT: *Something that can be proven*	That is a 100% cotton shirt.
OPINION: *A person's belief*	That is the cutest shirt I ever saw.

DIRECTIONS:
1. You will be working in small groups. (Your teacher will assign the groups.)
2. Work cooperatively with your team members to complete the three activities on the following pages.
3. Choose one member of the group to be the secretary, to write the answers on each activity page.
4. Complete the activities by the end of the class period.
5. Every member should help complete the activities. Your teacher will be giving extra points to those groups that cooperate.
6. Each team member will take a quiz on all of the activities. Your group's quiz scores will be averaged, and everyone will receive the average grade.

Group Members:_____
_____
_____

Activity #1
FACT OR OPINION

DIRECTIONS: Read each statement below. Decide if it is a fact or an opinion. Write *F* for fact and *O* for opinion.

1. _____ Root beer is the best kind of soda pop.

2. _____ That is the ugliest dress I have ever seen.

3. _____ There are twelve hundred students in this school.

4. _____ The music store sold 169 albums this week.

5. _____ The United States is a great country.

6. _____ She is the nicest person in this school.

7. _____ Mr. Smith is an excellent teacher.

8. _____ The population of our town is 32,100.

9. _____ Our town is a big town.

10. _____ This shirt is really a good bargain.

11. _____ Jocks are so dumb.

12. _____ McDonald's® hamburgers are on special for 69 cents.

13. _____ Lincoln was our greatest president.

14. _____ McDonald's® has the best hamburgers.

15. _____ Lincoln was our 16th president.

16. _____ Chocolate chip cookies are the best kind.

17. _____ My wife is the worst cook.

18. _____ Our football team can beat any other team.

19. _____ Our football team needs a better quarterback.

20. _____ Our team's record is 10 wins, 8 losses.

Activity #2
REWRITE THE OPINION

DIRECTIONS: Read each opinion. Rewrite it to make it sound more like an opinion. Use one of the following phrases to rewrite the opinion:

I feel . . .   I think . . .   I believe . . .   In my opinion . . .
Personally, I feel . . .   This is just my opinion, but . . .

1. This is the worst school in the world.

2. Pepsi® is the best soda pop.

3. Laurie is the best cheerleader.

4. My parents are the strictest people in the world.

5. That is the cutest skirt around.

6. Rob Cruise is the cutest boy in this school.

7. She has a big mouth.

8. They are the number one rock group.

9. Mr. Rogers is the best science teacher.

10. Pizza is the tastiest food.

Group Members:_____

_____

_____

Activity #3
YOUR OPINIONS

DIRECTIONS: Write ten opinions on any topic. Use phrases like:

I feel . . .   In my opinion . . .
I believe . . .   Personally, I feel . . .
I think . . .

1. _____

2. _____

3. _____

4. _____

5. _____

6. _____

7. _____

8. _____

9. _____

10. _____

Name:_____

Stating an Opinion Quiz

DIRECTIONS: Write **F** if the sentence is a fact and **O** if it is an opinion.

_____ 1. He is the most popular boy at school.

_____ 2. He is the student council president.

_____ 3. I think that is the worst song I've heard.

_____ 4. That song was ranked number twelve on the pop charts.

_____ 5. In my opinion, he's the funniest comedian.

DIRECTIONS: Rewrite these opinions using the opinion phrases.

1. Rocky is the most intelligent animal.

   _____

2. Mrs. Finklebinkle is the crabbiest teacher.

   _____

3. Rob Gobber has the neatest hair.

   _____

DIRECTIONS: Write three opinions on any topic. Use the correct phrases.

1._____

2._____

3._____

Name:_____

STATING AN OPINION - STATING AN OPINION

1. Define the terms *fact* and *opinion*.

(fact) _____

(opinion) _____

2. Explain why it is important to know the difference between a fact and an opinion.

_____

_____

_____

3. Read the following story. Answer the questions below.

> Buddy and Jonathon were listening to the radio. Buddy said, "The *Purple Cement* is my favorite music group. They are the best music group there is." Jonathon said, "No, *Doco Moco* is the best group. They have the best sound." Buddy and Jonathon continued to argue about which music group was the best until Buddy got angry and went home.

Was Buddy's statement (i.e., "*Purple Cement* is the best music group.") a fact or an opinion?　　FACT　　OPINION

Did Buddy state his idea correctly?　YES　　NO

Explain why it was useless for Buddy and Jonathon to argue about which music group was the best.

_____

_____

_____

4. Tell whether each statement is a fact or an opinion by circling **F** or **O**. If the statement is an opinion, write the word in the sentence that helps to make it an opinion.

Lilacs are the prettiest flowers.	F	O	_____
Some lilacs are purple.	F	O	_____
Pappy's has the tastiest pizza.	F	O	_____
Pappy's sold 100,000 pizzas last year.	F	O	_____
Janet is the best singer.	F	O	_____
Janet is in the chorus.	F	O	_____

5. Write three facts.

   (1) _____

   (2) _____

   (3) _____

   Write three opinions.

   (1) _____

   (2) _____

   (3) _____

6. Evaluate how well you understand the social skill of stating an opinion. Do you know the difference between a fact and an opinion? Do you use phrases such as "I feel . . ." and "I believe . . ."? Describe your use of the skill and tell whether you use the skill appropriately.

   _____

   _____

   _____

SKILL HOMEWORK ACTIVITY

_____
(Due Date)

Dear Parent or Guardian of: _____

This week we are learning about the social communication skill:

AGREEING AND DISAGREEING

This social skill is very important in interpersonal relationships.

This skill can be broken down into the following skill steps. Please watch for all of the steps in your role play practice or real-life observation.

1. Listen carefully to the other person's idea or opinion.
2. Decide if you agree or disagree.
3. Use a nice tone of voice.
4. Tell the person you agree or disagree.
5. Explain your reason.

Before the due date, please complete one of the following activities with your son or daughter: (put a check mark by your choice)

_____ A. We acted out the role play situation listed below.

_____ B. I observed my son/daughter using this social skill in a real-life situation. (I have described the situation below.)

Description of real-life observation:

Role play situation:

PRETEND THAT YOUR MOM BELIEVES YOUR FAMILY SHOULD BE UP AT 6:00 A.M. ON SATURDAY MORNINGS SO EVERYONE CAN GET HIS/HER CHORES DONE SOONER. DEMONSTRATE HOW YOU WOULD EXPRESS YOUR DISAGREEMENT IN AN APPROPRIATE WAY.

- -

Please circle the word below which best describes how your son or daughter did while using this social skill in either the role play or real-life situation.

NEEDS MORE HELP   GOOD   EXCELLENT

It is important for you to reinforce your child's use of this social skill at home in a positive way. Encourage and praise your child when you see the skill appropriately used. Remind him/her to use the social skill when necessary.

Thank you for your assistance.

Sincerely,

* *

PARENT/GUARDIAN SIGNATURE: _____

 SSS: Social Skill Strategies (Book A)

Do You Agree or Disagree?

When you **agree**, it means that *you have the same opinion as another person.*

When you **disagree**, it means that *you have a different opinion than another person.*

DIRECTIONS: Read the following statements. If you agree, circle the word *AGREE*. If you do not agree, circle the word *DISAGREE*. Next, write down why you agree or disagree.

1. I really like watching professional football on TV.

   AGREE   DISAGREE

   Why?_____

2. I hate reading.

   AGREE   DISAGREE

   Why?_____

3. If students want to continue their education after high school, I think they should work a few years first just to make sure.

   AGREE   DISAGREE

   Why?_____

4. I believe that soap operas are stupid and anyone who watches them is wasting time.

   AGREE   DISAGREE

   Why?_____

5. Parents should force their kids to do daily housechores.

   AGREE   DISAGREE

   Why?_____

6. I like corn on the cob.

   AGREE   DISAGREE

   Why?_____

Name:_____

Disagreements

DIRECTIONS: Write down or tell five things that teen-agers and parents disagree about, that teen-agers and teachers disagree about, and that brothers and sisters disagree about. Tell why you think the disagreements occur.

TEEN-AGERS AND PARENTS

EXAMPLE ➡

Disagreements	*Reasons*
1. curfew	1. Because teenagers usually want to stay out late and parents worry.
2.	2.
3.	3.
4.	4.
5.	5.

TEEN-AGERS AND TEACHERS

Disagreements	*Reasons*
1.	1.
2.	2.
3.	3.
4.	4.
5.	5.

BROTHERS AND SISTERS

Disagreements	*Reasons*
1.	1.
2.	2.
3.	3.
4.	4.
5.	5.

Name:_____

Remember the Skill Steps

The social skill of agreeing and disagreeing can be broken down into these five steps:

1. Listen carefully to the other person's idea or opinion.

2. Decide if you agree or disagree.

3. Use a nice tone of voice.

4. Tell the person you agree or disagree.

5. Explain your reason.

Because this social skill has five skill steps, it is important that you develop a strategy that will help you remember them. In this case, an **acrostic** would work well.

An acrostic is one type of strategy to help you remember something. It is a sentence in which the first letters of each word in the sentence are the same as the first letters of the words or phrases you wish to remember.

For example, the order of the planets in our solar system can be remembered with this acrostic:

Many	**V**ery	**E**arly	**M**en	**J**ust	**S**at	**U**nderneath	**P**luto.
e	e	a	a	u	a	r	e	l
r	n	r	r	p	t	a	p	u
c	u	t	s	i	u	n	t	t
u	s	h		t	r	u	u	o
r				e	n	s	n	
y				r			e	

Your acrostic should be as wild and wacky as possible, to help you remember it.

An example of an acrostic to help you remember the five skill steps above would be: **L**arry **D**isagreed **U**nder **T**he **E**gg. Because the sentence is silly, it is easy to remember. The letter **L** in Larry should help you remember the word *listen* in step one, the letter **D** in Disagreed should help you remember the word *decide* in step two, and so on.

DIRECTIONS: Create your own acrostic for the five skill steps to agreeing and disagreeing. Remember to make your acrostic wild and wacky.

There is a Right Way and a *Wrong* Way

Agreeing with someone is a simple thing to do. When you tell a person that you feel the same way he does, it is a comfortable situation.

Disagreeing, however, is not always as simple. No two people will agree on everything! It is fine to express your disagreement as long as you do it in a good way. If you follow the skill steps properly, you should be able to disagree without either one of you getting angry.

When you disagree, avoid putting the other person's ideas down and telling him that his ideas are stupid. Avoid using an angry tone of voice. Pretend someone says to you, "How about if we go to a movie tonight?" and you say, "That's a stupid idea. You know I don't like going to movies." The person will probably get angry or feel bad because of the way you expressed your disagreement. You should say something like, "No, I don't think so. I know you enjoy going to movies, but personally I don't like to." Stated like this, the other person knows that you do not agree with his idea, but you don't make him feel bad.

DIRECTIONS: 1. Read each of the situations below and the follow-up comments.

2. If the follow-up comment is a statement of agreement, write ***agree***.

3. If the comment is a good statement of disagreement, write ***disagree/good***.

4. If the comment is a bad statement of disagreement, write ***disagree/bad***.

Situation#1:

The class finished brainstorming. They had come up with a list of ideas for a class party. Next, they went back and discussed each idea to try to narrow the list. When they got to Joe's idea of going roller-skating, these were the comments made:

_____ 1. "That's a stupid idea, Joe. Don't you remember we went roller-skating last time?"

_____ 2. "It was fun last time we went roller-skating, but I think we should do something different this time."

_____ 3. "Skating was a blast last time. Let's go again."

_____ 4. "Forget it! If you're going skating instead of renting a movie, then I'm just not gonna go!"

_____ 5. "I disagree with the skating idea. I would rather do something where we wouldn't have to waste time traveling."

Situation#2:

Five hundred dollars were donated to your school. Five students were chosen to be on a committee with the principal to decide how to use the money. The principal suggested building a marquee in front of the school to highlight upcoming events. Here are the comments that the five students made:

_____ 1. "I'm not sure if we really need a marquee. The video and screen in front of the library already let us know about upcoming events."

_____ 2. "You've got to be kidding! I don't even know what a marquee is."

_____ 3. "I think that is an excellent suggestion. A marquee is something that everyone would benefit from. Even the adults in the community could use it."

_____ 4. "I like that idea."

_____ 5. "I think there might be things the teachers and students would prefer more than a marquee."

_____ 6. "Come on, get with it! Nobody cares about marquees anymore."

Name:_____

How Would You Say It?

When you want to tell someone that you agree with an idea or opinion, you can begin by saying something like:

"I agree . . ."   "I do too . . ."

"I think so too . . ."   "So do I . . ."

"Me too . . ."   "I feel the same way . . ."

When you want to tell someone that you disagree with an idea or opinion, you can begin by saying something like:

"I don't agree . . ."   "Not me . . ."

"My opinion is different . . ."   "I don't think so . . ."

"I feel differently . . ."   "It seems to me . . ."

DIRECTIONS: For each of the following situations, write down what you would say to express your agreement or disagreement. You may use any of the phrases above or create your own. Remember also to explain why you agree or disagree.

1. One of your friends says, "I think I'm going to start smoking. It will make me look cool, and older too."

2. Your sister says, "I want to do my best in school. I think an education is important if I want to get a good job."

3. Your teacher says, "I like starting school earlier in August, so we can get out earlier in the spring."

4. Your dad says, "I like to exercise at least four times a week. It gives me more energy and stops me from gaining weight."

5. Your friend says, "I think cheerleaders are wasting their time. I think they should go out for a sport themselves."

6. The people you babysit for say, "If my son misbehaves, you should send him to his room. I do not believe in spanking."

AGREEING AND DISAGREEING

1. Tell what it means to agree and to disagree.

   (agree) _____

   (disagree) _____._____

2. Write the five skill steps for the social skill of agreeing and disagreeing. Explain why each step is important.

   (**step 1**) _____

   (Why?) _____

   (**step 2**) _____

   (Why?) _____

   (**step 3**) _____

   (Why?) _____

   (**step 4**) _____

   (Why?) _____

   (**step 5**) _____

   (Why?) _____

3. Describe a situation in the community when you might agree with someone and a time when you might disagree with someone.

   (agree) _____

   (disagree) _____

4. Compare agreeing with disagreeing. Decide which is harder to do correctly and explain why.

   _____

   _____

   _____

5. Pretend you have an assignment to design a poster to hang in your school to help students understand how to disagree correctly. What would your poster say?

   _____

   _____

   _____

6. Think about someone you know. Evaluate that person's skill at disagreeing appropriately. Decide if you think the person usually does a good job at disagreeing, or if you think he/she needs improvement. Explain your answer.

   _____

   _____

   _____

   _____

SKILL HOMEWORK ACTIVITY

_____
(Due Date)

Dear Parent or Guardian of: _____

This week we are learning about the social communication skill:

CONVINCING OTHERS

This social skill is very important in interpersonal relationships and can be broken down into the following skill steps. Please watch for all of the steps in your role play practice or real-life observation.

1. Plan what you are going to say.
2. Choose a good time and place.
3. Give good reasons.
4. Stay calm when talking to the person.

Before the due date, please complete one of the following activities with your son or daughter: (put a check mark by your choice)

_____ A. We acted out the role play situation listed below.

_____ B. I observed my son/daughter using this social skill in a real-life situation. (I have described the situation below.)

Description of real-life observation:

Role play situation:

YOU WANT TO CONVINCE YOUR PARENTS THAT YOU ARE MATURE ENOUGH TO STAY BY YOURSELF FOR THE WEEKEND WHEN THEY GO OUT OF TOWN. REMEMBER TO FOLLOW THE ABOVE STEPS SO THAT YOU WILL BE A BETTER CONVINCER.

- -

Please circle the word below which best describes how your son or daughter did while using this social skill in either the role play or real-life situation.

NEEDS MORE HELP   GOOD   EXCELLENT

It is important for you to reinforce your child's use of this social skill at home in a positive way. Encourage and praise your child when you see the skill appropriately used. Remind him/her to use the social skill when necessary.

Thank you for your assistance.

Sincerely,

* *

PARENT/GUARDIAN SIGNATURE: _____

CONNIE CONVINCER

Connie Convincer often gets what she wants. She has a skill in which she can get people to think like she does. No, she doesn't have a magic potion or a magic wand. No, she doesn't get her way by bullying people. Connie knows how to CONVINCE people. When you **convince** someone, *you get them to believe as you do.* Knowing how to convince people really can come in handy. Here are some times when you may need to convince someone of something:

- You want to convince your parents to give you more allowance.
- You want to convince your teacher to give you an extra day on an assignment.
- You want to convince your boss to give you a raise.
- You want to convince your friend to join the baseball team.

Connie Convincer doesn't always get her way. But, her convincing skills improve her chances of getting what she wants. Last week she wanted to get a new pair of tennis shoes. She knew that her mom probably wouldn't let her get them. She looked in the newspaper ads and found a pair that were on sale. Then she got out her old pair of tennis shoes (which were pretty shabby). Connie asked her mom if she could talk to her after supper. When Connie sat down to talk to her mom, she knew exactly what she was going to say to her. Connie explained that she needed a new pair of tennis shoes for gym class. She showed her mom the old pair of shoes and reminded her that they were two years old. Connie remained calm the whole time (even though her mom didn't look like she would get her the shoes). Connie then showed her mom the ad with the shoe sale. Connie told her mom that the shoes were a good deal and she really needed a new pair. Connie's mom was convinced. She told Connie she could get a new pair of shoes next payday.

Connie did some things that helped her get what she wanted. First of all, she planned out what she was going to say. Then, she chose a good time and place to talk to her mother. Connie gave reasons why she needed a new pair of shoes. When Connie was talking to her mother, she remained calm and didn't start screaming and yelling. All of these things helped Connie get what she wanted.

Remember these steps! *Plan what you are going to say.*
Choose a good time and place to convince the person.
Give good reasons.
Stay calm when you are talking to the person.

> **Caution:** There will be times when even if you follow these skills, you will still not be able to convince someone. Remember, stay calm if this happens. If you get upset and act like a baby, it will decrease your chances for getting what you want the next time.

Planning How to Convince

DIRECTIONS: You and your partner should choose one of the following situations to role play. Plan out what you will say to convince the other person, and then actually do the role play. Answer the questions below when you finish.

Situations

1. You are trying to convince your mother/father to let you have your own bedroom (or a phone in your room).

2. You are trying to convince your friend to stay out of trouble. He/she has started to hang around with some kids who get in a lot of trouble.

Questions

1. Why is it important to plan what to say before you try to convince someone of something?

2. Explain why you should choose a good time and place to convince someone.

3. Do you think you did a good job of convincing your partner during the role play? Tell why or why not.

Name:_____

Student Council

DIRECTIONS: You want to be nominated for the student council. To get nominated, you have to fill out the form below. A committee will then read all the forms and choose ten people to run in the student council election. You should do the following:

1) Fill out the nomination form below.
2) Pretend that you have been nominated to run in the elections. Make a poster which convinces other students that you are the best person for the job.

Student Council Nomination Form

Name: _____

Date: _____

Why do you want to be a student council member?

Describe your positive qualities.

Describe your communication skills.

SSS: Social Skill Strategies (Book A)

You've Got Me Convinced

DIRECTIONS: Read each pair of situations below. Choose the person who did the best job of convincing. (Remember - convincing does not mean bullying someone.) Tell why that person was a better convincer.

Set A

Michael and Sean are both applying for a job at a grocery store. Read what each of the boys said at the interview and decide which person did a better job of convincing the employer to hire him.

SEAN'S INTERVIEW

Sean had practiced for the interview at home. His mom had given him interview questions and he had answered them. Sean felt confident when he went to the interview. Mrs. Wildman, the store owner, asked Sean why he wanted the job. Sean said, "I think I would enjoy working in a grocery store and I really do need a job!" Mrs. Wildman told Sean to convince her that he was the best person for the job. (Sean was ready for this question because he had practiced it with his mom). Sean said, "I'm a hard worker, I get along well with other people, and I haven't missed a day of school in the past three years. I've had lawn jobs and I was a paper boy. I've got a list of people you can call for references. I would be glad to work on the weekends when other kids want off. I think I would do a good job." Mrs. Wildman told Sean that she was really impressed with his interview and would let him know at the end of the week. He thanked her.

MICHAEL'S INTERVIEW

Michael was nervous about his interview. He had tried to put the interview out of his mind. At the interview, Mrs. Wildman asked Michael why he wanted the job. Michael said, "Well, I really need a job, and I think I'd like it here." Mrs. Wildman told Michael to convince her that he was the best person for the job. Michael said, "Well, I'm a hard worker, I really do a good job when I do things." Mrs. Wildman thanked Michael for coming to the interview and told him she would let him know at the end of the week. Michael thanked her.

Which boy was a better convincer? _____

Why? _____

_____

_____

Set B

Jenny and Mary are both trying to convince a friend to do something. Read what each girl says, and decide which person does a better job of convincing her friend.

JENNY AND HER FRIEND

Jenny is trying to convince her friend Ann to go to the movies with her. Jenny said, "Ann, let's go to the movies tonight." Ann told Jenny that she couldn't go because she had to study for a test. Jenny said, "Aw, come on! You're smart enough! You'd better go with me or I'll be mad." Ann still looked like she didn't want to go. Jenny said, "Ann, if you don't go, I'll tell everyone about the time your pants ripped."

MARY AND HER FRIEND

Mary is trying to convince her friend Katie to go to the movies with her. Mary said, "Katie, let's go to the movies tonight." Katie told Mary that she couldn't go because she had to study for a test. Mary said, "Well, I have to study for that test, too. Hmmm, what could we do? How about if we study after school and then we could go to the movies tonight? I'll quiz you on the way to the movies and on the way home, too."

Which girl was a better convincer? _____

Why? _____

_____

_____

_____

Set C

Chad and Sam are each trying to convince their parents to let them sleep over at a friend's house. Read what each boy says and decide who is the better convincer.

CHAD AND HIS PARENTS

Chad asked his parents if he could sleep over at a friend's house. Chad said, "I'd like to sleep over at John's house tomorrow night. His parents will be home. I haven't slept over at anyone's house for awhile." Chad's parents didn't say anything. Chad said (smiling), "Just think, you could have a night all to yourselves without me pestering you. I really want to sleep over at his house!"

SAM AND HIS PARENTS

Sam asked his parents if he could sleep over at his friend's house. Sam said, "I want to sleep over at Jim's house tomorrow night. Can I?" Sam's parents didn't say anything. Sam said, "Come on, I want to sleep over! You never let me do anything. You treat me like a baby all the time. Can I sleep over or not?"

Which boy was a better convincer? _____

Why? _____

_____

_____

_____

Name:_____

NEW PRODUCT

Advertisers try to convince you to buy something. Commercials make a product look good so that people will purchase that item.

MATERIALS NEEDED: an empty pop can or an empty cereal box
construction paper
magic markers or paint
scissors
tape or glue

DIRECTIONS: 1. Design a new type of soda pop or a new cereal. Make up a new name and design a new container.

2. Cover the old can or box with construction paper.

3. Draw on the new design.

4. Make sure that it looks neat and attractive.

5. Write a one-minute commercial to advertise your new product.

6. Give your commercial to the rest of the class.

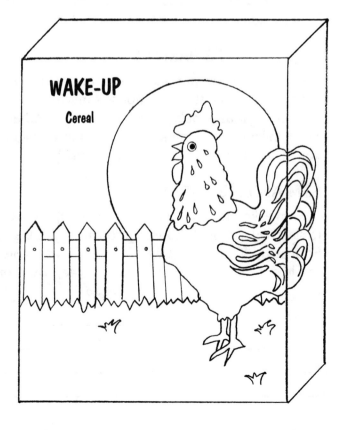

CONVINCING OTHERS - CONVINCING OTHERS

1. Tell what it means to convince someone of something.

   _____

   _____

2. Explain why it is important to be able to convince someone to believe as you do.

   _____

   _____

3. Tell what you could do and say to convince one of your parents to quit smoking.

   _____

   _____

   _____

   _____

4. Compare the following situations in which you want to convince someone. What would you do the same in both situations? What would you do differently?

   (1) convincing your parents to   (2) convincing your parents to
       give you a raise in your   let you have your own bedroom
       allowance

   (same) _____

   _____

   _____

   (different) _____

   _____

   _____

5. Pretend you have to make a poster to convince someone of something. What would your poster say?

   _____

   _____

6. Describe a situation when you tried to convince someone.

   (situation) _____

   _____

   _____

   Were you able to convince the person?   YES   NO

   If you were able to convince the person, evaluate what things you did that helped you convince him/her.

   If you were not able to convince the person, evaluate what things you could have done to help you convince that person.

   (evaluation) _____

   _____

   _____

   _____

SKILL HOMEWORK ACTIVITY

_____
(Due Date)

Dear Parent or Guardian of: _____

This week we are learning about the social communication skill:

GIVING INFORMATION

This social skill is very important in interpersonal relationships.

There are many times when people need to give information (e.g., when they answer questions on a test, when they give directions, when they explain a problem).

The students have learned the following tips to use when giving information:
1. Give the information in order.
2. Use specific names and words. (Avoid words such as "stuff" and "thing.")
3. Give enough information to be understood. (Don't give too little.)
4. Only include information which is relevant. (Don't give too much.)
5. Check with your listener to see if you're being understood.
   (If you are not understood, restate it in a different way.)

Before the due date, please complete one of the following activities with your son or daughter: (put a check mark by your choice)

_____ A. We acted out the role play situation listed below.

_____ B. I observed my son/daughter using this social skill in a real-life situation. (I have described the situation below.)

Description of real-life observation:

Role play situation:

PRETEND YOU ARE GOING ON A SCHOOL FIELD TRIP. DEMONSTRATE HOW YOU WOULD TELL YOUR PARENTS INFORMATION ABOUT IT. (BE CERTAIN TO INCLUDE INFORMATION ABOUT THE COST, DATE, TIME, LOCATION, AND PURPOSE.)

Please circle the word below which best describes how your son or daughter did while using this social skill in either the role play or real-life situation.

NEEDS MORE HELP   GOOD   EXCELLENT

It is important for you to reinforce your child's use of this social skill at home in a positive way. Encourage and praise your child when you see the skill appropriately used. Remind him/her to use the social skill when necessary.

Thank you for your assistance.

Sincerely,

* *

PARENT/GUARDIAN SIGNATURE: _____

COOPERATION

Giving information means *to provide specific knowledge or facts.* There are many times when we need to provide information to another person. Some examples are listed below:

- When you answer questions on a test.
- When you explain a problem you are having.
- When you give directions to someone.
- When you tell a story to someone.

Here is a list of five tips to remember when you give information to someone:

1. Give the information in order.
2. Use specific names and words. (Avoid words such as *stuff* and *thing*.)
3. Give enough information to be understood. (Don't give too little.)
4. Only include information that is relevant. (Don't give too much.)
5. Check with your listener to see if you're being understood.
   (If you are not understood, restate your message in a different way.)

DIRECTIONS: 1. You will be given an activity page for one of the five tips listed above. (If your class has less than five students, you will be assigned more than one tip. If your class has more than five students, you will be working with a partner on your assigned tip.)

2. The activity page you receive will include specific information about your assigned tip, along with questions for you to answer.

3. Work by yourself (or with your partner) to make certain that you understand the tip and that you are able to answer correctly the questions at the bottom of your page. Do not write the answers on the activity page. If you need assistance, ask for help from the teacher (or from your partner, if you have one.) You need to understand the tip thoroughly, because you will be in charge of "teaching" your assigned tip to the entire class.

4. When everyone is fully prepared, meet back together as a class to begin teaching.

5. When you (or you and your partner) take your turn to teach, explain your assigned tip to the class, and help the class members to answer the questions on the activity page. Offer help as needed. When the class agrees on an answer and you judge it as being correct, write it on the page.

6. When each student is teaching his/her tip, all students in class should be very cooperative. When everyone is finished teaching, the class should turn in the five completed activity pages to be graded and averaged. Each student in class will receive the same averaged grade.

7. Everyone will take a quiz on the five tips at the end of this activity. If everyone in your class receives a grade of "C" or better, everyone will be given 5 extra credit points.

Giving Information - Tip #1

GIVE THE INFORMATION IN ORDER. BE ORGANIZED. (TELL IT IN ORDER.)

When you give directions to someone, give the directions in the same order you want the listener to follow them:

Correct order	Incorrect order
Drive down Pine Street until you come to the first set of stop lights. Next, turn right and go four blocks to Elm Street. Then, turn left onto Elm Street. The house is the second one on the left.	The house is on Elm Street, but first you have to go to the first set of stop lights. It will be the second house on the left. Oh yeah, turn left when you get to Elm.

When you tell a story to someone, tell the story from beginning to end, so it is in the correct order:

Correct order	Incorrect order
When I was in English class, I got called to the principal's office. He asked me if I had taken any of Bill's lunch tickets out of his locker without asking. I told the principal that I didn't do it. I told him I didn't even know Bill's locker combination.	I can't believe the principal said I took Bill's lunch tickets. I'm never going to English class again. I'd be too embarrassed after getting called out of class. I can't believe someone took Bill's lunch tickets. I told him, the principal that is, that I couldn't have done it. I was in English class when it all started. I don't even know Bill's combination.

DIRECTIONS: Read each of the statements below. If the statement is organized and in the correct order, then write **organized**. If it is disorganized and not in the correct order, then write **disorganized** and rewrite the statement so that it is organized.

1. Bake it for 20 minutes at 350°. Put the batter into a greased 9" x 13" pan. Mix all the ingredients together.

2. The first thing I cleaned was my bedroom. Then I took out the trash. The last thing I did was wash the kitchen floor.

3. Wash these clothes using the gentle cycle setting. You have to add soap to the washing machine first. Don't forget to spray the stains before you wash the clothes.

 SSS: Social Skill Strategies (Book A)

Giving Information - Tip #2

USE SPECIFIC NAMES AND WORDS. (AVOID WORDS SUCH AS *STUFF* AND *THING*.)

When you give information to someone, you want to be specific, so that the person understands exactly what you are talking about:

Specific words	Nonspecific words
Could I borrow some of your **clothes** for the **party** I'm going to?	Can I use some of your **stuff** for the **thing** I'm going to?
Would you please tell me what our **history assignment** is again? I forgot what it is.	What is **it** again?
Please get me the **socket wrench** out of my **tool box**.	Get me the **thing-a-ma-jig** out of my **what-cha-ma-call-it.**

DIRECTIONS: Read each of the statements below. If all the words in the statement are specific, write **specific**. If any of the words in the statement are nonspecific, write **nonspecific** and circle the word or words that should be more specific.

1. What am I supposed to bring for the things tomorrow?

2. Your report is very well-written. It has an excellent summary at the end.

3. If you bring any more of that stuff in here, you'll really get it.

4. I think that thing at the bottom needs to be replaced.

5. The computer is in room 213, at the back of the room.

6. Tell the person all about it.

Giving Information - Tip #3

GIVE ENOUGH INFORMATION TO BE UNDERSTOOD. (DON'T GIVE TOO LITTLE.)

When you give information to someone, you want to make certain to tell the person enough so that there is no misunderstanding:

Enough information	Not enough information
You will be taking an essay test this Friday. It will be on chapters four and five from your book.	You will be taking a test soon.
The library is on 34th Avenue, across the street from City Hall.	The library is three blocks away.

When you answer questions on a test, it is important to give enough information by writing down everything you know. If you don't, you may be cheating yourself by not getting the points you deserve.

DIRECTIONS: Write down what you would say to answer each of the following questions. Make certain to include enough information.

1. How do you get to the main office in this building from the room you are in now?

2. How do you make a peanut butter and jelly sandwich?

3. How do you find and check out a book from your library?

Giving Information - Tip #4

ONLY INCLUDE INFORMATION THAT IS RELEVANT. (DON'T GIVE TOO MUCH.)

When you give information to someone, make certain that you only include information that is important and deals with the main topic. If you add information that is irrelevant and unnecessary, it will only confuse your listener:

Relevant information	Irrelevant information
Walk down this hall until you come to a staircase. Walk down the steps and turn left. The room will be the second one on the right side of the hall.	Walk down this hall until you come to a staircase. *Those are the stairs where I tripped my first year here. I was so embarrassed.* Anyway, walk down the steps and take a left. The room will be the second one on the right. *The first room on the right is Mrs. Walker's room. She is a strict teacher. Just wait until you have her.*

DIRECTIONS: Each of the directions/stories below contains information that is unnecessary and irrelevant. Circle the parts that are irrelevant and should be left out.

1. To make soup, first you have to open the can. I think the label on this can is really stupid looking. The electric can-opener is on the counter. Next, you empty the contents of the can into this pan. The bottom of the pan is really getting dark. I think I should scrub it better when I wash it. Anyway, then you add one can of water to the pan. Heat it on the stove over medium heat for about five minutes. Stir it every once in a while.

2. Go down this street until you come to the second stop sign. There are some beautiful houses on this street. They must be really expensive. Turn left onto George Street and go three blocks. You'll go past the movie theater. I hear there is a bad movie playing there this week. I wouldn't go to it if I were you. The bank you are looking for is on the right side of the street, just past the theater.

3. You'll need to bring $10.00 for our field trip tomorrow. We're going to the state capital building. We will be leaving right after attendance is taken first hour. The $10.00 will cover the bus ride, the entrance fee, and meals. We will be getting back to school around 1:30 in the afternoon. I hope you all eat a good meal tonight at home.

Giving Information - Tip #5

CHECK WITH YOUR LISTENER TO SEE IF YOU'RE BEING UNDERSTOOD. (IF YOU ARE NOT UNDERSTOOD, RESTATE YOUR MESSAGE IN A DIFFERENT WAY.)

When you give information to someone, you should ask your listener if he understands you (e.g., "Does that make sense?" or "Do you understand?"):

Checked with the listener	Didn't check
. . . And that is how you get to the swimming pool. Do you understand my directions?	. . . And that is how you get to the swimming pool. Bye, see you later.

If your listener doesn't understand you, then give the information again, but state it differently than you did the first time:

Stated differently	Not stated differently
Teacher: Combine the two chemicals after the test tube has been heated. See what I mean? Student: No, I don't understand. Teacher: First, heat this test tube, and then put the two chemicals into it. OK? Student: OK, now I understand.	Teacher: Combine the two chemicals after the test tube has been heated. See what I mean? Student: No, I don't understand. Teacher: I said to combine the two chemicals after the test tube has been heated. Student: I still don't get it.

DIRECTIONS: Restate each of the following directions.

1. Your report will have to be rewritten after your rough draft is corrected.

2. Turn the water off when it fills up to this line.

3. I want you to use this edger to cut the grass you can't get with the lawn mower.

Name:_____

QUIZ

Five tips for giving information:

1. Give the information in order.

2. Use specific names and words. (Avoid words such as *stuff* and *thing*.)

3. Give enough information to be understood. (Don't give too little.)

4. Only include information that is relevant. (Don't give too much.)

5. Check with your listener to see if you're being understood. (If you are not understood, restate your message in a different way.)

DIRECTIONS: Each of the directions below has one or more problems. Describe what is wrong with each one.

1. Take the turkey out when it is browned and remember to baste it about every half hour. Bye, I have to get going.

2. The bank is downtown.

3. I need you to get the thing for me.

4. Bring the mixture to a boil. Oh yeah, but before that you need to chop up the nuts. The first thing you have to do is measure out all the dry ingredients.

5. The store you are looking for is right down the street. You should make sure to have some of their cherry ice cream while you are there. It is on the left side, about four stores down.

DIRECTIONS: Write or tell about how to get to your house from where you are now. Make certain you follow all five tips listed above.

GIVING INFORMATION - GIVING INFORMATION

1. Tell what *giving information* means and write the five tips to remember for that social skill.

   (definition) _____

   _____

   (tip #1) _____

   (tip #2) _____

   (tip #3) _____

   (tip #4) _____

   (tip #5) _____

2. Explain why it is important to be able to give information clearly.

   _____

   _____

3. Describe a situation at home, in school, and in the community when you would need to give information to someone.

   (home) _____

   (school) _____

   (community) _____

4. Describe the difference between information that is relevant and information that is not relevant.

   _____

   _____

   _____

5. Imagine that you are unable to speak or write. List three ways you would be able to give information to another person.

   (1) _____

   (2) _____

   (3) _____

6. Review the five tips for giving information correctly. Which tip is the one you need to improve on the most? Explain your answer.

   _____

   _____

   _____

SKILL HOMEWORK ACTIVITY

_____
(Due Date)

Dear Parent or Guardian of: _____

This week we are learning about the social communication skill:

DEALING WITH CONTRADICTIONS

This social skill is very important in interpersonal relationships and can be broken down into the following skill steps. Please watch for all of the steps in your role play practice or real-life observation.

Sometimes two people give contradictory (opposite) messages. The students learned that if two people give them opposite messages, they should:

1. Tell one or both of the people about the contradiction (using a good tone of voice).
2. Ask the people involved what to do.

Sometimes one person gives contradictory messages. When this happens, the student should:

1. Point out the contradiction.
2. Ask the person what was really meant.

Before the due date, please complete one of the following activities with your son or daughter: (put a check mark by your choice)

_____ A. We acted out the role play situation listed below.

_____ B. I observed my son/daughter using this social skill in a real-life situation. (I have described the situation below.)

Description of real-life observation:

Role play situation:

YOUR MOTHER TELLS YOU THAT YOUR FAMILY HAS DECIDED TO GO TO FLORIDA THIS SPRING. WHEN YOU ASK YOUR DAD ABOUT IT, HE SAYS THAT HE DOESN'T KNOW ANYTHING ABOUT IT AND HE'S NOT GOING TO FLORIDA. DEMONSTRATE WHAT YOU WOULD SAY TO YOUR PARENTS ABOUT THIS CONTRADICTION.

- -

Please circle the word below which best describes how your son or daughter did while using this social skill in either the role play or real-life situation.

NEEDS MORE HELP   GOOD   EXCELLENT

It is important for you to reinforce your child's use of this social skill at home in a positive way. Encourage and praise your child when you see the skill appropriately used. Remind him/her to use the social skill when necessary.

Thank you for your assistance.

Sincerely,

* *

PARENT/GUARDIAN SIGNATURE: _____

?? CONFUSION ??

	YES (✓)	NO
1. Has something like this ever happened to you?	____	____
If you said *yes*, answer questions 2, 3, and 4.		
2. Did you feel confused?	____	____
3. Did you feel frustrated?	____	____
4. Did you get angry?	____	____

IF YOU ANSWERED *YES* TO QUESTION #1, WE HAVE JUST THE LESSON FOR YOU:

DEALING WITH CONTRADICTIONS

Name:_____

Contradictions

Dealing with contradictions means *handling messages that are unclear and opposite of each other.*

> *Please turn off the VCR.*

Two-People Contradictions

Sometimes different people will tell you two different things. These messages can become really confusing. Your mom might tell you to be home at 9:00 and your dad might tell you to be home at 7:00. You get mixed up about when you are supposed to be home.

> *Could you please turn on the VCR?*

When you get contradictory messages from two people, you should:

1) Tell either or both about the contradiction. (Use a good tone of voice and a normal volume.)

2) Ask the people involved what to do.

One-Person Contradiction

Sometimes a person will say one thing and then say something totally different later. This can be really confusing. Sometimes a person says one things with words, but his body language says another thing. Your friend might tell you he isn't angry, but his body language says he's angry. This is also a contradiction.

When you get contradictory messages from the same person, you should:

1) Point out the contradiction (in a nice way).

2) Ask the person what was really meant.

DIRECTIONS: Tell about a situation in your life when you had to deal with a contradiction. Describe how you felt and tell how you handled the contradiction.

OR

Make up a situation involving a contradiction and tell how you could deal with the contradiction.

Name:_____

What Would You Do?

DIRECTIONS: Read each situation. Tell how you would handle the contradiction. (Tell what you would do.)

1. John works in a grocery store. When he got to work one day, the head bagboy told John to go to the back room and unload the truck. John started to walk to the back room. On the way, the store manager stopped him and asked him to clean the meat department.

   Explain what you would do if you were John.

2. Marcia asked her dad if she could go to her friend's house. He said, "I don't care." As Marcia was going out the back door, her mother said, "Remember, your dad told you to help him clean the garage."

   Explain what you would do if you were Marcia.

3. Mr. Wolfe said Rhonda could draw when she finished the assignment. Later, when Mr. Wolfe was walking around the room, he said, "Rhonda, you know you're not supposed to draw in class."

   Explain what you would do if you were Rhonda.

4. Charlie's friend Jim said he would give Charlie a lunch ticket. Later, when Charlie asked Jim for the lunch ticket, Jim said, "I didn't say I'd give you a lunch ticket."

   Explain what you would do if you were Charlie.

Name:_____

CONTRADICTION QUESTIONS

DIRECTIONS: Answer the questions about dealing with contradictions.

1. Explain the two types of contradictions.

2. Why is it important to remain calm when you are telling someone about a contradiction?

3. Describe a situation in which a teen-ager has to handle a contradiction at school.

4. Describe a situation in which you would have to deal with a contradiction on the job.

DEALING WITH CONTRADICTIONS

1. Define the social skill of dealing with contradictions and tell the two types of contradictions.

   (definition) _____

   _____

   (#1) _____

   (#2) _____

2. Explain why it's important to handle contradictory messages in an appropriate manner.

   _____

   _____

   _____

3. Describe a situation when you might need to handle a contradiction on the job. Tell what could happen if you handled the contradiction in a bad way.

   _____

   _____

   _____

4. Compare two-people contradictions with a one-person contradiction. Tell one way they are the same and one way they are different.

   (same) _____

   _____

   (different) _____

   _____

5. Write a story about a boy/girl who constantly has to deal with contradictory messages from his/her parents. Describe how you think he/she would be feeling.

   _____

   _____

   _____

6. Evaluate yourself on the social skill of dealing with contradictions. Place X's on the lines where you feel you are now. Then, explain why you placed your X's where you did.

   I handle contradictory   I don't handle
   messages appropriately.   contradictory messages
                   appropriately.

   (reason)_____

   _____

   I never give contradictory   I always give contradictory
   messages.   messages.

   (reason)_____

   _____

SKILL HOMEWORK ACTIVITY

_____
(Due Date)

Dear Parent or Guardian of: _____

This week we are learning about the social communication skill:

BEING HONEST

This social skill is very important in interpersonal relationships.

The students have learned that they should be honest so that people trust them. It is sometimes difficult to be honest (e.g., when you're afraid of getting in trouble). The students have learned that they will usually get in less trouble if they tell the truth.

Before the due date, please complete one of the following activities with your son or daughter: (put a check mark by your choice)

_____ A. We acted out the role play situation listed below.

_____ B. I observed my son/daughter using this social skill in a real-life situation. (I have described the situation below.)

Description of real-life observation:

Role play situation:

YOU FORGOT TO PICK UP THE MEDICINE YOUR FATHER ASKED YOU TO GET. YOU KNOW HE IS GOING TO BE VERY UPSET. BE HONEST AND TELL HIM THE TRUTH.

- -

Please circle the word below which best describes how your son or daughter did while using this social skill in either the role play or real-life situation.

NEEDS MORE HELP   GOOD   EXCELLENT

It is important for you to reinforce your child's use of this social skill at home in a positive way. Encourage and praise your child when you see the skill appropriately used. Remind him/her to use the social skill when necessary.

Thank you for your assistance.

Sincerely,

* *

PARENT/GUARDIAN SIGNATURE: _____

Name:_____

Being Honest

Being honest means *telling people the truth*. It is important to be truthful with people so that they can trust you.

DIRECTIONS: Read the scripts on this page and the following page and answer the questions after each script.

Script #1

Jesse: You should have seen it. Those guys said I have the best bike around. Each of them wanted to buy it from me. They said I was the best stunt rider they had ever seen.

Karen: Oh, that's pretty neat.

Jesse: I've won several bike competitions. I'm number one in the state. I've got all kinds of trophies.

Karen: I'd really like to see your trophies. Can we see them?

Jesse: Well, uh, how about some other time? I think today is the day my mother dusts them.

Mark: (walking up) Hi, what are you guys doing?

Karen: Jesse was just telling me about all of the bike competitions he's won and how good he is.

Jesse: (looking uncomfortable) Well, I-I didn't really mean I had won that many competitions.

Mark: (laughing) What are you talking about? You haven't won any! Why don't you quit lying to people? Let's go, Karen; Jesse's got to practice for his bike competition.

(Karen and Mark laugh as they walk away).

Questions

1. Do you think Jesse was telling the truth? Explain why or why not.

2. How did Mark act toward Jesse?

3. How do you think Karen felt about Jesse when she was walking away?

Script #2

Mrs. Klein is standing outside of her classroom. As she looks into the classroom, she sees a student, Ron, hit another boy in the class. Mrs. Klein talks with Ron.

Mrs. Klein: Ron, what just happened in the room?

Ron: What? What do you mean? I didn't do anything.

Mrs. Klein: Ron, I saw what happened. I saw you hit Mark.

Ron: I didn't hit anyone. I didn't hit Mark.

Mrs. Klein: (getting upset) Ron, I looked into the classroom and I saw you hit Mark. I want to know why you hit him.

Ron: I didn't hit him. I was just sitting here doing my work.

Mrs. Klein: Ron, I am going to give you two detentions. One is for hitting Mark and the second detention is for not being honest with me.

Questions

1. Why do you think Ron didn't tell the truth?

2. Why do you think Mrs. Klein was upset?

3. Did Ron make things worse by not telling the truth? Explain why or why not.

4. Do you think Mrs. Klein will believe Ron the next time he tells her something? Explain why or why not.

Name:_____

Hard to be Honest

It is often difficult to tell people the truth when you have done something wrong. It is important, however, to take responsibility for your actions and to be honest. Usually, when you tell the truth, you get in less trouble than if you lie about something.

DIRECTIONS: Read each situation. Write the consequence you think the person should receive.

1. Mary's parents asked her why she came home an hour past her curfew. Mary said she didn't feel like leaving the party so she stayed longer than she should have.

   What consequence should Mary receive? Tell why.

2. Mary's parents asked her why she came home an hour past her curfew. Mary said that Mr. Tartin was late picking them up from the party. Mary's mother called Mr. Tartin and found out that he had not even given Mary a ride home.

   What consequence should Mary receive? Tell why.

3. Michael accidently broke his mother's favorite statue. He told his mother about it and said he was very sorry.

   What consequence should Michael receive? Tell why.

4. Michael accidently broke his mother's favorite statue. He told his mother that his little sister broke it. His mother found out the truth later that day.

   What consequence should Michael receive? Tell why.

5. Tara copied her assignment from Linda. Tara's teacher asked her if she had copied the assignment. Tara said, "No." Tara's teacher found out the truth.

   What consequence should Tara receive? Tell why.

6. Tara copied her assignment from Linda. Tara's teacher asked her if she had copied the assignment. Tara said, "Yes, because I didn't have time to do it."

   What consequence should Tara receive? Tell why.

The Girl Who Lost Credibility

DIRECTIONS: Read the following story and answer the questions that follow it.

Mr. Markus taught ninth grade English. He enjoyed all of the students in his class. He was concerned, however, about one student named Melissa. Mr. Markus had caught Melissa telling several lies. For example, one time he saw Melissa push another student. When Mr. Markus asked Melissa about it, she denied doing it. Another time, Mr. Markus saw Melissa take another student's pen. When he asked Melissa to give the pen back, she said it was her pen and she had been using it all day long. She said, "I didn't take this pen from anyone." Mr. Markus made her give the pen back, but she still insisted that it was her pen. There were several other times when Melissa told Mr. Markus something and he knew she was lying.

Now Mr. Markus was faced with a new problem. He had just finished talking with Melissa. She had accused one of the other students of taking money from her. Mr. Markus wanted to believe Melissa. She seemed to be telling the truth this time. But he remembered all of the other times Melissa had lied to him.

QUESTIONS

1. What would you do if you were Mr. Markus?

2. Why is it difficult to believe someone like Melissa?

3. What does *losing your credibility* mean?

4. Why is it difficult to get people to believe you when they no longer trust you?

5. Do you know anyone like Melissa? How do you feel when you're with a person like Melissa?

Name:_____

Being Honest Questions

DIRECTIONS: Answer the questions below.

1. Explain what can happen to someone who often lies.

2. Why is it important for people to trust one another?

3. Why do people not like someone who is always exaggerating and making up stories?

4. Tell three reasons why people don't tell the truth.

5. Explain why people usually feel better when they tell the truth (even if it means they get in trouble).

6. Tell about a time when you were not honest. Tell how you felt.

7. Tell about a time when you were honest. Tell how you felt.

8. Is it ever all right not to be honest? Why or why not?

EDUCATOR PAGE: DO NOT DUPLICATE FOR STUDENTS

Purpose:

The purpose of this lesson is to teach students that being *too* honest can sometimes cause problems. The students will learn what being *tactful* means.

Educator Instructions:

1. Discuss being *too* honest with your students. The questions below can be a guideline for that discussion.

2. Have your students complete the activity below.

Discussion:

1. Read the following situation to students:

   One of your friends asks how you think he looks. His face is broken out with acne very badly. You say . . .

2. Have students tell how they would respond to the above situation.

3. Discuss how being *too* honest can sometimes hurt people's feelings.

4. Have one of the students look up the word *tactful* in the dictionary.

5. Discuss what being *tactful* means.

6. Have the students brainstorm a list of situations when they should be tactful rather than too honest.

Activity:

1. Tell students to make up a poem or write the lyrics to a song about being tactful.

2. Have the students read what they have written, the following day in class.

Name:_____

BEING HONEST - BEING HONEST - BEING HONEST

1. Define *being honest.*

   _____

2. Explain why it is very important to be honest with people.

   _____

   _____

   _____

   _____

3. Describe a situation when you would need to be honest with each of the following people.

   (friend) _____

   _____

   (parent) _____

   _____

   (teacher) _____

   _____

4. Compare being honest and being tactful. Tell one similarity and one difference.

   (similarity) _____

   _____

   (difference) _____

   _____

5. Write a short story about a person who was not honest, and include some of the problems the person faced because of not being honest.

   _____

   _____

   _____

   _____

6. Read the following situation. Answer the question that follows.

   It was Friday night. Nancy's brother, Tim, told her he was going to a party. Nancy knew that her parents would be upset if they knew about it. Nancy heard her brother tell his parents that he was going to a movie. Nancy's mother asked Nancy if she was going to the movie with Tim. Nancy said "No."

   Later that night, when Tim was late coming home, Nancy's dad asked her if she knew which movie Tim had gone to see. Nancy said she didn't know which movie he had gone to.

   Do you think Nancy was being honest with her parents? Give reasons for your answer.

   _____

   _____

   _____

   _____

SKILL HOMEWORK ACTIVITY

_____
(Due Date)

Dear Parent or Guardian of: _____

This week we are learning about the social communication skill:

BEING OPTIMISTIC

This social skill is very important in interpersonal relationships.

The students have learned that an "optimistic" person is one who expects good things to happen and tends to look at the positive side of things.

They have learned that a "pessimistic" person is one who expects bad things to happen and tends to look at the negative side of things.

They have discussed the idea that optimistic people tend to enjoy life more and seem to have more friends.

Before the due date, please complete one of the following activities with your son or daughter: (put a check mark by your choice)

_____ A. We acted out the role play situation listed below.

_____ B. I observed my son/daughter using this social skill in a real-life situation. (I have described the situation below.)

Description of real-life observation:

Role play situation:

PRETEND THAT YOU HAVE A BIG TEST COMING UP IN HISTORY. DEMONSTRATE HOW YOU COULD MAKE AN OPTIMISTIC COMMENT ABOUT THE TEST TO YOUR MOM OR DAD.

- -

Please circle the word below which best describes how your son or daughter did while using this social skill in either the role play or real-life situation.

NEEDS MORE HELP   GOOD   EXCELLENT

It is important for you to reinforce your child's use of this social skill at home in a positive way. Encourage and praise your child when you see the skill appropriately used. Remind him/her to use the social skill when necessary.

Thank you for your assistance.

Sincerely,

* *

PARENT/GUARDIAN SIGNATURE: _____

Guess What It Means

DIRECTIONS: Read the stories below about Optimistic Olly and Pessimistic Pete. Answer the questions at the end of each story.

Story #1

Optimistic Olly

Optimistic Olly woke up and saw that it was raining outside. He was supposed to go on an outing with the bike club after school that day. He had been looking forward to it all week. His mom came into his room to wake him up. She said, "Good morning, Olly. I see you're already awake. Sorry about the rain. I know your bike trip was scheduled for today." Olly said, "There's a good chance the rain will stop before school lets out. Besides, look at the bright side. If the bike trip is cancelled, then I'll have more time to study for that big U.S. History test I have tomorrow." Olly's mom said, "That's my Olly! Always looking at the bright side of things."

When Olly got to school, he saw that his friend Bruce was looking miserable, so he went to see what was wrong. Bruce explained that his girlfriend had broken up with him and was already going out with someone else. Olly said, "Look at it this way, Bruce: Now you'll have more time to be with the guys again. Besides, that new girl, Whitney, has a crush on you." Bruce said, "Olly, you're always so optimistic! I wish I could be more like you." Olly wasn't quite sure what the word *optimistic* meant. He decided to look it up during his first-hour study hall.

Questions

1. When Olly looked up the word *optimistic* in the dictionary, what do you think it said? (Circle the correct definition.)

   a. One who expects good things to happen; one who looks at the positive side of things

   b. One who expects bad things to happen; one who expects the worst and looks at the negative side of things

   c. One who enjoys bike riding; one who is very skilled at bike riding

2. Tell two things Olly was optimistic about in the story:

   a.

   b.

3. How could you tell that Olly was optimistic?

Name:_____

Story #2

Pessimistic Pete

Pessimistic Pete was in math class. The bell rang and class was over. The teacher reminded everyone that there was a test coming up next week. Pete said to the person sitting next to him, "Oh, great! Another test to fail." As Pete got up to leave the class, the teacher asked if she could talk to him. She said, "Pete, I know this unit has been a hard one for you. Do you have a study hall where you could work with the tutor before the test? Or, could you stay after school this week to work with me? I think that if you spend some time, you could pass this test." Pete shook his head and said, "Why should I bother studying? I'll just fail the test anyway." The teacher said, "Oh, Pete. Don't be so pessimistic. Why don't you give it a try?" Pete said, "No thanks!" and left the classroom.

As Pete walked into his next class with his friend Greg, he noticed that there was a substitute teacher. Pete said to Greg, "Oh no, not another substitute. He'll probably be awful." Greg said, "Have you ever had him before?" "No," said Pete. "Well then, how do you know he'll be awful?" asked Greg. Pete said, "I don't know. I just bet he's no good, that's all." Greg said, "Don't be so pessimistic! Maybe he'll be a good teacher." There was that word *pessimistic* again. Pete didn't know what it meant, but he decided he should look it up when he got a chance. Then he thought, "I probably won't understand the definition."

Questions

1. What do you think the word *pessimistic* means?

   a. Expecting good things to happen; looking at the positive side of things

   b. Expecting bad things to happen; looking at the negative side of things

   c. Being afraid of tests

2. Tell two things Pete was pessimistic about in the story:

   a.

   b.

3. How could you tell that Pete was pessimistic?

Don't Be Such a Pessimist!

A person who is an optimist (is optimistic) tends to look at the bright side of things. He tries to be positive and expects to be successful.

A person who is a pessimist (is pessimistic) tends to look at the bad side of things. He is negative and expects things to go wrong.

If you tell yourself things will probably go wrong, they usually do! If you tell yourself things will go well, then good things usually happen! It is important to try to be optimistic whenever you can.

Everything has a good side and a bad side to it. For example: Pretend that you go to a store to buy a radio that was advertised as being on sale. You find out that all of the radios have been sold. The bad part about this situation is that you can't get the radio you wanted. The good part about this situation is that you can save your money and maybe find a radio you like better another time.

Sometimes when bad things happen, it's difficult to look on the bright side. If you can get yourself to see the good side of things, you will feel better and be a happier person.

DIRECTIONS: For each of the situations below, write down what you think would be the good side of what happened.

1. Yesterday you tried on a pair of pants in a store. You really liked them. Today, when you go back to the store to buy them, you discover the pants have already been sold.

2. You have a lot of homework to do over the weekend, but you know you won't get to do it because you are going camping with your family. You have been looking forward to the camping trip for weeks. When you get home from school on Friday, your mom tells you that the camping trip has been cancelled.

3. Your teacher tells your class that you will be taking a unit test at the end of the week.

4. You agree to baby-sit for your neighbor and then find out that there is a big party you'd like to go to on the same night.

Name:_____

Looking on the Bright Side

DIRECTIONS: Change each of the following pessimistic statements into optimistic statements.

1. This glass of soda is half empty.

2. We have a substitute teacher today. I bet she'll be mean.

3. I've got a headache. I'll probably get sick and miss the school dance.

4. I've studied very hard for this test! I'll probably fail it.

5. I better not borrow your video. You know me; I'll probably break it.

6. I met a new kid at school today. He probably thought I was weird.

7. I can't wait for the picnic. Knowing my luck, it will rain and be cancelled.

8. I got a new job today. I usually mess things up, so I'll probably end up getting fired.

9. I got some new clothes for school. I bet everyone else has clothes that are better.

Name:_____

Answer These

1. Tell how you feel when you are around a person who is pessimistic and always expecting bad things to happen.

2. Think of someone you know who is pessimistic. Write down one pessimistic comment this person might make.

3. Tell how you feel when you are around a person who is optimistic and always expecting good things to happen.

4. Think of someone you know who is optimistic. Write down one optimistic comment this person might make.

5. Do you tend to be optimistic or pessimistic? Tell why.

6. Write down three bad things that have happened to you recently. Look on the bright side and tell something positive about each of the things you listed.

"Bad thing"	"Something positive"

7. Tell three good things that you expect to happen in the next week

   •

   •

   •

Name:_____

The Self-Talk Factor

If you want to be an optimistic person, not only is it important to talk positively to other people, but it is also important to talk positively to yourself. When you talk to yourself, it is called self-talk. **Self talk** is *all the thoughts you have about yourself and other people*. There are two different types of self-talk: positive self-talk and negative self-talk. **Positive self-talk** is *when you look on the bright side and think good things about yourself or other people*. **Negative self-talk** is *when you think bad things about yourself or other people*.

People give themselves THOUSANDS of self-talk messages everyday. Some people use mostly negative self-talk, and it makes them pessimistic. Some people use mostly positive self-talk, and it makes them optimistic.

DIRECTIONS: Rewrite each negative self-talk comment so it is a positive comment.
Rewrite each positive self-talk comment so it is a negative comment.

NEGATIVE SELF-TALK   POSITIVE SELF-TALK

Oh no, it's raining outside. Well, this will give me a chance to read my new book.

I should have known my date would get sick. She will probably never go out with me again.

Oh great. I said I would babysit tonight and now I find out there's a school dance. This will probably be the best dance all year.

I'm sorry I lost my job, but now I'll have more time for my friends and studying.

Name:_____

BEING OPTIMISTIC - BEING OPTIMISTIC - BEING OPTIMISTIC

1. Define the words *optimistic* and *pessimistic*.

   (optimistic) _____

   _____

   (pessimistic) _____

   _____

2. Tell two benefits of being optimistic.

   (1) _____

   (2) _____

3. Explain how being pessimistic can hurt you on the job.

   _____

   _____

4. List four characteristics of an optimistic person.

   (1) _____

   (2) _____

   (3) _____

   (4) _____

5. Pretend you are a teacher and you want your students to learn the difference between being optimistic and being pessimistic. Describe a game you could ask your students to play that would give them practice with this concept.

   _____

   _____

   _____

6. Do you tend to be more like Optimistic Olly or Pessimistic Pete?
   Explain your answer.

   _____

   _____

   _____

APPENDICES

Social Communication Skills Rating Scale

(Adult Form)

Name of student: _____ Grade: _____

Age: _____ Date rating scale completed: _____

Name of person completing rating scale: _____

Relationship with student (e.g., parent, case-
manager, regular education teacher): _____

_____

DIRECTIONS: Rate this student on how well he/she uses the following social skills. Circle:

1 - If the skill is NEVER used correctly.
2 - If the skill is SELDOM used correctly.
3 - If the skill is SOMETIMES used correctly.
4 - If the skill is OFTEN used correctly.
5 - If the skill is ALWAYS used correctly.

For example: A student who **usually** speaks too loudly would be rated as follows:

VOLUME - Speaks at a volume that is   1 ② 3 4 5
appropriate to the situation.

Please give examples/comments when appropriate (e.g., if you give a low rating for volume, you should explain if the student speaks too softly, or too loudly).

Social Communication Skill	Never	Seldom	Sometimes	Often	Always
A-1. EYE CONTACT - Looks at the person he/she is speaking with when appropriate.	1	2	3	4	5
A-2. MANNERS - Uses manners, such as saying "please" and "thank you" in social situations.	1	2	3	4	5
A-3. VOLUME - Speaks at a volume that is appropriate to the situation. (Speaks with a normal volume, softer volume, and louder volume when necessary.)	1	2	3	4	5
A-4. TIME AND PLACE - Chooses a good time and place before beginning a conversation with another person.	1	2	3	4	5

	Never	Seldom	Sometimes	Often	Always

A-5. TONE OF VOICE - Uses a tone of voice which is pleasant. Is not sarcastic or disrespectful.   1 2 3 4 5

A-6. GETTING TO THE POINT - Does not "beat around the bush." Brings up the main point of his/her conversations when appropriate.   1 2 3 4 5

A-7. STAYING ON TOPIC AND SWITCHING TOPICS - Sticks to the topic of conversation or prepares the listener for a topic shift.   1 2 3 4 5

A-8. LISTENING - Gives his/her full attention to a speaker in order to understand the meaning of the message.   1 2 3 4 5

A-9. STARTING AND ENDING A CONVERSATION - Takes the initiative to start a conversation. Begins with a greeting and name. Ends a conversation smoothly and with a farewell.   1 2 3 4 5

A-10. PROXIMITY - Stands at a proper distance (not too close and not too far) while talking to a person.   1 2 3 4 5

A-11. BODY LANGUAGE - Uses body language (expression of feelings with body parts) which is appropriate to the situation.   1 2 3 4 5

A-12. MAKING A GOOD IMPRESSION - His/her actions, appearance, and personal qualities make other people think favorably about him/her.   1 2 3 4 5

A-13. FORMAL/INFORMAL LANGUAGE - Talks in a more "traditional" way and uses the longer forms of words when speaking to people in respected positions. Talks in a more "relaxed" way, by using shorter forms of words and slang, when speaking to peers and adults he/she feels close to.   1 2 3 4 5

A-14. GIVING REASONS - Gives reasons which are specific and relevant when answering questions.   1 2 3 4 5

A-15. PLANNING WHAT TO SAY - Thinks about what he/she will say before speaking.   1 2 3 4 5

A-16. INTERRUPTING - Interrupts in an appropriate way and only when necessary.   1 2 3 4 5

A-17. GIVING A COMPLIMENT - Remembers to compliment others, and is honest when doing so.   1 2 3 4 5

A-18. ACCEPTING A COMPLIMENT - Accepts compliments by saying "thank you."   1 2 3 4 5

A-19. SAYING *THANK YOU* - Expresses appreciation when someone has done something nice.   1 2 3 4 5

SSS: SOCIAL SKILL STRATEGIES (Book A)

Never Seldom Sometimes Often Always

A-20. INTRODUCING YOURSELF - Introduces him/herself to a new person. Remembers to give his/her name when doing so.   1 2 3 4 5

A-21. INTRODUCING TWO PEOPLE TO EACH OTHER - Helps two people who do not know each other to learn each other's name. (Makes the introduction reciprocal. For example, "Steve, meet Beth. Beth, meet Steve.")   1 2 3 4 5

A-22. MAKING A REQUEST - Remembers to ask instead of demand when he/she wants something.   1 2 3 4 5

A-23. OFFERING HELP - Offers help to people in need. Remembers to ask first instead of just "taking over."   1 2 3 4 5

A-24. ASKING FOR HELP - Asks for help when needed, but attempts something on his/her own first.   1 2 3 4 5

A-25. ASKING PERMISSION - Asks for permission from authority figures.   1 2 3 4 5

A-26. ACCEPTING NO - Responds appropriately when told no by an authority figure.   1 2 3 4 5

A-27. MAKING AN APOLOGY - Says he/she is sorry when appropriate.   1 2 3 4 5

A-28. STATING AN OPINION - Does not try to pass his/her opinion off as a fact.   1 2 3 4 5

A-29. AGREEING/DISAGREEING - Disagrees without putting down the other person's idea/opinion. Doesn't get angry when someone disagrees with him/her.   1 2 3 4 5

A-30. CONVINCING OTHERS - Provides good reasons when trying to convince others.   1 2 3 4 5

A-31. GIVING INFORMATION - Is precise and easy to understand when giving information (e.g., explaining a problem, giving directions).   1 2 3 4 5

A-32. DEALING WITH CONTRADICTIONS - Knows when he/she is receiving messages which are unclear or opposite in meaning and asks for clarification.   1 2 3 4 5

A-33. BEING HONEST - Is honest and understands the consequences of losing someone's trust.   1 2 3 4 5

A-34. BEING OPTIMISTIC - Looks on the "bright side." Expects good things to happen. Has a positive attitude.   1 2 3 4 5

B-1. REPUTATION - Has a "good" reputation in the home, school, and community.   1 2 3 4 5

		Never Seldom Sometimes Often Always

B-2.   STARTING A FRIENDSHIP - Is able to start new friendships with   1 2 3 4 5
people based on common interests.

B-3.   MAINTAINING A FRIENDSHIP - Is able to treat a friend appropriately   1 2 3 4 5
in order to maintain the relationship.

B-4.   GIVING EMOTIONAL SUPPORT - Listens and provides encourage-   1 2 3 4 5
ment to a friend who is making a difficult decision, or who is feeling
depressed.

B-5.   GIVING ADVICE - Gives advice only when asked, and only in areas   1 2 3 4 5
he/she is competent in.

B-6.   IGNORING - Ignores disruptions and negative behaviors of other people.   1 2 3 4 5

B-7.   RESPONDING TO TEASING - Responds appropriately to "friendly"   1 2 3 4 5
teasing and ignores "unfriendly" teasing.

B-8.   PEER PRESSURE - Says *no* to negative peer pressure.   1 2 3 4 5

B-9.   JOINING IN - Joins into an activity or a conversation without disrupting   1 2 3 4 5
those involved.

B-10.   BEING LEFT OUT - Copes with being left out of an activity or   1 2 3 4 5
conversation.

B-11.   TATTLING - Does not tattle in front of his/her peers.   1 2 3 4 5

B-12.   BEING ASSERTIVE - Can make comments in a confident and firm way,   1 2 3 4 5
without making threats.

B-13.   MAKING A COMPLAINT - Makes a complaint to the correct person   1 2 3 4 5
in a nonaggressive manner.

B-14.   RECEIVING A COMPLAINT - Suggests a solution when he/she is   1 2 3 4 5
responsible for a complaint received.

B-15.   GIVING CONSTRUCTIVE CRITICISM - Is specific about behaviors   1 2 3 4 5
he/she would like to see improved without making personal insults.

B-16.   ACCEPTING CONSTRUCTIVE CRITICISM - Accepts constructive   1 2 3 4 5
criticism without getting defensive.

B-17.   MAKING AN ACCUSATION - Seeks proof before accusing someone.   1 2 3 4 5

B-18.   DEALING WITH A FALSE ACCUSATION - When falsely accused,   1 2 3 4 5
he/she offers proof and/or offers another explanation without getting
angry.

SSS: SOCIAL SKILL STRATEGIES (Book A)

	Never Seldom Sometimes Often Always

B-19. COMPROMISING/NEGOTIATING - Meets a person "half-way" when working to solve a problem. 1 2 3 4 5

B-20. ACCEPTING CONSEQUENCES - Accepts negative consequences of his/her behavior. 1 2 3 4 5

B-21. EXPRESSING FEELINGS - Expresses his/her feelings instead of holding them inside. 1 2 3 4 5

B-22. DEALING WITH ANGER - Expresses his/her anger without acting impulsively. 1 2 3 4 5

B-23. DEALING WITH EMBARRASSMENT - Reacts appropriately when something makes him/her feel uncomfortable/self-conscious. 1 2 3 4 5

B-24. COPING WITH FEAR - Takes steps to reduce unrealistic fears. 1 2 3 4 5

B-25. DEALING WITH HUMOR - Enjoys "safe" humor and avoids "unsafe" humor (i.e., humor that hurts or upsets others). 1 2 3 4 5

B-26. DEALING WITH FAILURE - Deals with failure appropriately and does not let it get him/her "down." 1 2 3 4 5

B-27. EXPRESSING AFFECTION - Lets other people know about his/her positive feelings in an appropriate way. 1 2 3 4 5

B-28. DEALING WITH DISAPPOINTMENT - Handles disappointment without getting impulsive. 1 2 3 4 5

B-29. UNDERSTANDING THE FEELINGS OF OTHERS - Is perceptive to the way other people are feeling. 1 2 3 4 5

Write down the five social skills you believe this student needs to work on improving the most.

1.

2.

3.

4.

5.

SSS: SOCIAL SKILL STRATEGIES (Book A)

STUDENT SOCIAL SKILL SUMMARY FORM

STUDENT'S NAME:	Identified as Being Problematic	Demonstrated Comprehension of Skill in Class	Demonstrated Correct Use of Skill in Class	Reported/Observed Use of Skill Outside of Class	GRADE: _____ YEAR: _____	Identified as Being Problematic	Demonstrated Comprehension of Skill in Class	Demonstrated Correct Use of Skill in Class	Reported/Observed Use of Skill Outside of Class
A-1. Eye Contact					B-1. Reputation				
A-2. Manners					B-2. Starting A Friendship				
A-3. Volume					B-3. Maintaining a Friendship				
A-4. Time And Place					B-4. Giving Emotional Support				
A-5. Tone Of Voice					B-5. Giving Advice				
A-6. Getting To The Point					B-6. Ignoring				
A-7. Staying On Topic And Switching Topics					B-7. Responding To Teasing				
A-8. Listening					B-8. Peer Pressure				
A-9. Starting, Maintaining, And Ending A Conversation					B-9. Joining In				
A-10. Proximity					B-10. Being Left Out				
A-11. Body Language					B-11. Tattling				
A-12. Making A Good Impression					B-12. Being Assertive				
A-13. Formal/Informal Language					B-13. Making A Complaint				
A-14. Giving Reasons					B-14. Receiving A Complaint				
A-15. Planning What To Say					B-15. Giving Constructive Criticism				
A-16. Interrupting					B-16. Accepting Constructive Criticism				
A-17. Giving A Compliment					B-17. Making An Accusation				
A-18. Accepting A Compliment					B-18. Dealing With A False Accusation				
A-19. Saying Thank You					B-19. Compromising/Negotiating				
A-20. Introducing Yourself					B-20. Accepting Consequences				
A-21. Introducing Two People To Each Other					B-21 Expressing Feelings				
A-22. Making A Request					B-22. Dealing With Anger				
A-23. Offering Help					B-23. Dealing With Embarrassment				
A-24. Asking For Help					B-24. Coping With Fear				
A-25. Asking Permission					B-25. Dealing With Humor				
A-26. Accepting NO					B-26. Dealing With Failure				
A-27. Making An Apology					B-27. Expressing Affection				
A-28. Stating An Opinion					B-28. Dealing With Disappointment				
A-29. Agreeing/Disagreeing					B-29. Understanding The Feelings Of Others				
A-30. Convincing Others					NOTES:				
A-31. Giving Information									
A-32. Dealing With Contradictions									
A-33. Being Honest									
A-34. Being Optimistic									

SSS: SOCIAL SKILL STRATEGIES (Book A)

Social Communication Skills Rating Scale

(Student Form)

Name: _____ Grade:_____

Age:_____   Date: _____

_____

DIRECTIONS: Rate yourself on how well you use the following social skills. Please be honest.

Circle:

1 - If you NEVER use the skill correctly.
2 - If you SELDOM use the skill correctly.
3 - If you SOMETIMES use the skill correctly.
4 - If you OFTEN use the skill correctly.
5 - If you ALWAYS use the skill correctly.

For example: If you **usually** speak in a volume which is too loud, you would rate yourself on skill number three in this way:

A-3. VOLUME - I use correct volume.   1 ② 3   4   5

Please give examples/comments when necessary (e.g., If you give yourself a low rating of "1" or "2" on volume, you should explain if you speak too softly or too loudly).

_____

Social Communication Skill

Rating

Never Seldom Sometimes Often Always

A-1. EYE CONTACT - I am good at looking at a person during a   1 2 3 4 5
conversation.

A-2. MANNERS - I use good manners (e.g., saying "please" and "thank   1 2 3 4 5
you," and using good table manners).

A-3. VOLUME - I use correct volume.   1 2 3 4 5

A-4. TIME AND PLACE - I choose a good time and place to talk to   1 2 3 4 5
someone.

		Never Seldom Sometimes Often Always

A-5. TONE OF VOICE - I use a pleasant tone of voice. I do not sound sarcastic or "snotty." 1 2 3 4 5

A-6. GETTING TO THE POINT - I bring up the main point of my conversation at the correct time. I do not "beat around the bush" or "put off" saying something. 1 2 3 4 5

A-7. STAYING ON TOPIC AND SWITCHING TOPICS - My comments deal with the main topic when I have a conversation. I warn the listener before I switch topics. 1 2 3 4 5

A-8. LISTENING - When someone is talking to me, I give that person my full attention, so I can understand him/her. 1 2 3 4 5

A-9. STARTING AND ENDING A CONVERSATION - I feel comfortable starting conversations. I begin with a greeting and name. I end conversations smoothly and I say "good-bye." 1 2 3 4 5

A-10. PROXIMITY - I stand at a good distance while talking to a person. I don't stand too close or too far away. 1 2 3 4 5

A-11. BODY LANGUAGE - I know which body actions and facial expressions to use to show my feelings. 1 2 3 4 5

A-12. MAKING A GOOD IMPRESSION - I try to make a good impression by how I look and by what I say and do. 1 2 3 4 5

A-13. FORMAL/INFORMAL LANGUAGE - When I speak to people in respected positions, I talk in a more "traditional" way. I use longer forms of words (e.g., "Thank you very much."). When I speak to people my own age or adults I feel close to, I talk in a more "relaxed" way. I use shorter forms of words and slang (e.g., "Thanks a lot."). 1 2 3 4 5

A-14. GIVING REASONS - When someone asks me to explain something, I give reasons that are specific and relevant. 1 2 3 4 5

A-15. PLANNING WHAT TO SAY - I think about what I am going to say before I speak, so it comes out sounding right. 1 2 3 4 5

A-16. INTERRUPTING - I only interrupt people when it is necessary. I interrupt in a good way. 1 2 3 4 5

A-17. GIVING A COMPLIMENT - I give people compliments about the way they look, the things they have, and what they say and do. 1 2 3 4 5

A-18. ACCEPTING A COMPLIMENT - When someone gives me a compliment, I say "Thank you." 1 2 3 4 5

SSS: SOCIAL SKILL STRATEGIES (Book A)

	Never	Seldom	Sometimes	Often	Always

A-19. SAYING *THANK YOU* - I thank people when they do something nice for me.　　1 2 3 4 5

A-20. INTRODUCING YOURSELF - I introduce myself to people I don't know. I remember to tell my full name.　　1 2 3 4 5

A-21. INTRODUCING TWO PEOPLE TO EACH OTHER - I introduce two people when they do not know each other. (For example, "Steve, meet Beth. Beth, meet Steve.")　　1 2 3 4 5

A-22. MAKING A REQUEST - When I want something, I ask for it in a polite way. I do not demand it.　　1 2 3 4 5

A-23. OFFERING HELP - I offer help to people in need. I ask first, instead of just "taking over."　　1 2 3 4 5

A-24. ASKING FOR HELP - I try things on my own first. If I can't do something, then I ask for help.　　1 2 3 4 5

A-25. ASKING PERMISSION - I ask for permission from authority figures whenever I should.　　1 2 3 4 5

A-26. ACCEPTING *NO* - When I am told that I can't do something, I can accept it in a calm way.　　1 2 3 4 5

A-27. MAKING AN APOLOGY - I say "I am sorry" when I have done something wrong.　　1 2 3 4 5

A-28. STATING AN OPINION - When I say something that is just my opinion and can't be proven as a fact, I remember to begin with "I think . . ." or "In my opinion . . ."　　1 2 3 4 5

A-29. AGREEING/DISAGREEING - When I disagree with someone, I do not put down his idea or opinion. I do not get angry when someone disagrees with me.　　1 2 3 4 5

A-30. CONVINCING OTHERS - I give good reasons when I try to convince someone to believe the same way I do.　　1 2 3 4 5

A-31. GIVING INFORMATION - I express myself clearly when I give information (e.g., give directions, explain a problem).　　1 2 3 4 5

A-32. DEALING WITH CONTRADICTIONS - When someone contradicts himself (says something that is unclear and opposite in meaning), I ask what he means.　　1 2 3 4 5

A-33. BEING HONEST - I am honest, even when I have done something wrong. I don't want to lose people's trust in me.　　1 2 3 4 5

		Never Seldom Sometimes Often Always

A-34. BEING OPTIMISTIC - I try to have a positive attitude. I expect good things to happen. I look on the "bright side" when something goes wrong.   1 2 3 4 5

B-1. REPUTATION - I have a "good" reputation at home, at school, and in the community.   1 2 3 4 5

B-2. STARTING A FRIENDSHIP - I am good at starting new friendships with people.   1 2 3 4 5

B-3. MAINTAINING A FRIENDSHIP - I keep my friends because I treat them well.   1 2 3 4 5

B-4. GIVING EMOTIONAL SUPPORT - When one of my friends is feeling depressed or is having a problem, I listen and give encouragement.   1 2 3 4 5

B-5. GIVING ADVICE - I only give advice when someone asks me for it. I avoid giving advice about things I don't know much about.   1 2 3 4 5

B-6. IGNORING - I am able to ignore disruptions. I ignore kids when they try to get my attention in a negative way.   1 2 3 4 5

B-7. RESPONDING TO TEASING - I laugh when people tease me in a nice way. I ignore people when they tease me in a mean way. (I don't let them get me upset.)   1 2 3 4 5

B-8. PEER PRESSURE - I say *no* when kids try to pressure me into doing things I don't feel comfortable doing.   1 2 3 4 5

B-9. JOINING IN - I join conversations and activities after they have already begun, in a way that is not a disruption.   1 2 3 4 5

B-10. BEING LEFT OUT - When I am left out of an activity or a conversation, I try to determine if it happened by mistake or on purpose.   1 2 3 4 5

B-11. TATTLING - I am not a "tattletale."   1 2 3 4 5

B-12. BEING ASSERTIVE - When someone goes against my rights, I tell the person how I feel and what I want. I do not make threats and get aggressive.   1 2 3 4 5

B-13. MAKING A COMPLAINT - When I complain to a person about something he is doing wrong, I correct the person without getting angry/upset.   1 2 3 4 5

SSS: SOCIAL SKILL STRATEGIES (Book A)

B-14. RECEIVING A COMPLAINT - When someone complains to me and I know I am responsible, I apologize and offer a solution.   1 2 3 4 5

B-15. GIVING CONSTRUCTIVE CRITICISM - When I criticize someone, I tell exactly what I think should be improved. I do not personally insult the person. I try to say something positive about the person first.   1 2 3 4 5

B-16. ACCEPTING CONSTRUCTIVE CRITICISM - I can handle it when someone tells me I need to improve on something. I don't get defensive.   1 2 3 4 5

B-17. MAKING AN ACCUSATION - I make sure I have proof, before I accuse someone of doing something wrong.   1 2 3 4 5

B-18. DEALING WITH A FALSE ACCUSATION - When someone accuses me of doing something and he is wrong, I stay calm. I offer proof that I am innocent or try to offer another explanation.   1 2 3 4 5

B-19. COMPROMISING/NEGOTIATING - I am willing to give in a little to help solve a disagreement. I don't always have to have things my way.   1 2 3 4 5

B-20. ACCEPTING CONSEQUENCES - When I know I have done something wrong, I am willing to pay the consequences.   1 2 3 4 5

B-21. EXPRESSING FEELINGS - I talk about my feelings. I do not hold them all inside.   1 2 3 4 5

B-22. DEALING WITH ANGER - When I get angry, I can control myself. I don't lose control.   1 2 3 4 5

B-23. DEALING WITH EMBARRASSMENT - I handle myself well when I get embarrassed. I don't fall apart.   1 2 3 4 5

B-24. COPING WITH FEAR - When I am afraid of something, I don't let it get the best of me. I face my fears and try to reduce them.   1 2 3 4 5

B-25. DEALING WITH HUMOR - I only use humor that is "friendly" and will not upset or hurt anyone. I avoid "unfriendly" humor.   1 2 3 4 5

B-26. DEALING WITH FAILURE - I don't let myself get "down" when I fail at something. I just try to do better the next time.   1 2 3 4 5

B-27. EXPRESSING AFFECTION - I let other people know that I have   1 2 3 4 5
positive feelings about them in an appropriate way.

B-28. DEALING WITH DISAPPOINTMENT - When I am disappointed   1 2 3 4 5
because someone or something lets me down, I stay in control.

B-29. UNDERSTANDING THE FEELINGS OF OTHERS - I am   1 2 3 4 5
sensitive to the way other people are feeling.

Write down the three social skills you think you should work on the most.

1.

2.

3.

CLASS SUMMARY FORM
BOOK A

(Mark the social skills which are problematic for each student.)

STUDENTS' NAMES / SOCIAL SKILLS										
A-1. Eye Contact										
A-2. Manners										
A-3. Volume										
A-4. Time And Place										
A-5. Tone Of Voice										
A-6. Getting To The Point										
A-7. Staying On Topic And Switching Topics										
A-8. Listening										
A-9. Starting, Maintaining, And Ending A Conversation										
A-10. Proximity										
A-11. Body Language										
A-12. Making A Good Impression										
A-13. Formal/Informal Language										
A-14. Giving Reasons										
A-15. Planning What To Say										
A-16. Interrupting										
A-17. Giving A Compliment										
A-18. Accepting A Compliment										
A-19. Saying Thank You										
A-20. Introducing Yourself										
A-21. Introducing Two People To Each Other										
A-22. Making A Request										
A-23. Offering Help										
A-24. Asking For Help										
A-25. Asking Permission										
A-26. Accepting NO										
A-27. Making An Apology										
A-28. Stating An Opinion										
A-29. Agreeing/Disagreeing										
A-30. Convincing Others										
A-31. Giving Information										
A-32. Dealing With Contradictions										
A-33. Being Honest										
A-34. Being Optimistic										

SSS: SOCIAL SKILL STRATEGIES (Book A)

CLASS SUMMARY FORM
BOOK B

(Mark the social skills which are problematic for each student.)

STUDENTS' NAMES SOCIAL SKILLS									
B-1. Reputation									
B-2. Starting A Friendship									
B-3. Maintaining A Friendship									
B-4. Giving Emotional Support									
B-5. Giving Advice									
B-6. Ignoring									
B-7. Responding To Teasing									
B-8. Peer Pressure									
B-9. Joining In									
B-10. Being Left Out									
B-11. Tattling									
B-12. Being Assertive									
B-13. Making A Complaint									
B-14. Receiving A Complaint									
B-15. Giving Constructive Criticism									
B-16. Accepting Constructive Criticism									
B-17. Making An Accusation									
B-18. Dealing With A False Accusation									
B-19. Compromising/Negotiating									
B-20. Accepting Consequences									
B-21. Expressing Feelings									
B-22. Dealing With Anger									
B-23. Dealing With Embarrassment									
B-24. Coping With Fear									
B-25. Dealing With Humor									
B-26. Dealing With Failure									
B-27. Expressing Affection									
B-28. Dealing With Disappointment									
B-29. Understanding The Feelings Of Others									

Dear_____:

As you know, your child will be participating in a social skills class. The purpose of the class is to teach children social skills which will help them to get along better with people and to feel better about themselves. A list of social skills taught during the class is attached.

Each social skill taught is broken down into small steps to make it easier to learn. For example, the social skill of "Asking For Help" is divided into the following skill steps:

1. Try to do it on your own first.

    If you can't,
2. Ask for help (explain yourself clearly).
3. Pay attention when the person helps you.
4. Thank the person for helping you.

Your child will have several homework activities during each social skill unit. One assignment, entitled the **SKILL HOMEWORK ACTIVITY**, should be completed together by you and your child. The activity sheet includes information about how the social skill was taught in class. You are asked either to complete a given role play situation with your child or to describe a real-life situation in which you have observed your child using the skill.

The major goal of the class is to get students to transfer what they learn in class to other settings (e.g., other classes, home, and the community). You can assist your son/daughter in becoming more socially appropriate in other environments by completing the **SKILL HOMEWORK ACTIVITY** with your child. You can also help your child by giving praise when you observe him/her using a social skill appropriately (e.g., "John, you really did a good job of asking for help.").

I look forward to working together with you to improve your child's skills for getting along with others. If you would like further information about the class, please contact me at any time. In addition, if you have any questions, concerns, or suggestions, I will be glad to discuss these with you.

Sincerely,

Dear_____:

As you know, many students have a difficult time getting along with their peers and/or adults. Some are too aggressive, while others are extremely withdrawn. These students lack the social skills necessary to get along with people.

We assume that all students have learned appropriate social skills in their early years. Many have not, and thus need to have these skills taught directly to them. Research has indicated that students can learn social skills through modeling, role playing, and other activities. Therefore, instruction in appropriate social skills will be provided through my social skills class.

The following student(s) will be participating in the social skills class which meets

_____:

Since you have contact with the above mentioned student(s), I would like to provide you with some information about social skill instruction. A list of the social skills taught in the class is attached. Throughout the school year, you will receive further information about specific social skills as they are taught.

A major goal of the class is to get students to transfer what they learn in class to other settings (e.g., other classes, home, and community). You can assist the students to transfer their use of social skills by positively reinforcing them when you observe correct use of a skill (e.g., "You accepted your consequence in a mature manner.").

I look forward to working together with you to improve our students' skills for getting along with others. If you would like further information about the class, please contact me at any time. In addition, if you have any questions, concerns, or suggestions, I will be glad to discuss these with you.

Sincerely,

Independent Activity #1   Name:_____

DIRECTIONS: Work on your own to complete the activities on this page. Do both activities. You will earn extra credit points from your teacher for:
- working without asking for help
- working without distracting other students
- working and ignoring other students

ACTIVITY A   How Social Are You?

1. Get a large piece of construction paper.
2. Write your name in large letters across the page. Use stencils if you wish.
3. Draw a large oval on the paper.
4. Think of ten words that describe what you are like when you are around other people. Here is a list of words to help you, but you may think of words on your own.

shy	out-going	bashful	passive
loud	aggressive	assertive	a good listener
funny	serious	a complainer	talkative
friendly	honest	a liar	exciting
boring	scared	a tattler	a troublemaker
a bully	a leader	concerned	quiet
helpful	humorous	caring	a know-it-all

5. Look in a magazine or newspaper to find the ten words you have chosen. You may have to cut out individual letters to make the words.
6. Glue the words inside the oval.
7. Decorate the paper using markers.
8. Write your full name on the back of the paper.

ACTIVITY B   Getting Social

1. Get a piece of lined paper.
2. Write a 7-8 sentence paragraph about how you think this class can help you (or is helping you) get more friends and get along better with people.
3. Remember to indent, use good punctuation/capitalization, and write in complete sentences.
4. Proofread your paragraph when you are finished.

IF YOU FINISH BEFORE CLASS IS OVER, FIND SOMETHING TO DO QUIETLY!

285   SSS: Social Skill Strategies (Book A)

DIRECTIONS: Work on your own to complete the activities on this page. Do both activities. You will earn extra credit points from your teacher for:
- working without asking for help
- working without distracting other students
- working and ignoring other students

ACTIVITY A Communicating!

1. Get a piece of lined paper.
2. Make a list of 30 situations when you communicate with other people. Here are some examples: when you talk to your teacher
   when you tell someone you're sorry
   when you ask your brother for something
3. Write your situations on the lined paper.
4. Make sure your name is on the paper.

ACTIVITY B Positive Poster

1. Get a large piece of construction paper and a piece of typing paper.
2. Think up a positive saying or choose one from below.
3. Design a "positive poster." Use pencil and draw a sketch of your poster on a piece of typing paper. Put your saying on the paper. Add things such as a rainbow, a sun, flowers, a tree, a butterfly, clouds, stars, etc. These items will add interest to the poster.
4. After you have drawn your design on typing paper, use your pencil to draw it on the larger piece of construction paper.
5. Color your poster with magic markers.
6. Put your name on the back of your poster.
7. Turn in both your sketch and your poster to the teacher at the end of the class.

POSITIVE SAYINGS

You are responsible for your day!
Have a good day!
I feel happy around you!
Friends are forever!
You are human, you have dignity!
May your accomplishments be many!
People like you make the world much brighter!
Communicate! Try it, you'll like it!
I like you just the way you are!
Friendship keeps hearts in touch!
Friends are always in our hearts!
Life is outstanding!
Tell your face you're happy!
People make the world go 'round!
There's no problem so great it cannot be solved!

Keep smiling!
You're the greatest!
Today's your lucky day!
Friends are special!
You're so special!
May life bring you joy!
You brighten my day!
Friends mean so much!
You're the best!
You're lookin' good!
Today is a great day!
Everyone is important!
You can do it!
It's a super day!

IF YOU FINISH BEFORE CLASS IS OVER, FIND SOMETHING TO DO QUIETLY!

DIRECTIONS: Work on your own to complete the activities on this page and the next. Do both activities. You will earn extra credit points from your teacher for:
- working without asking for help
- working without distracting other students
- working and ignoring other students

ACTIVITY A   **Find the Social Words**

Complete the following word search puzzle, which is filled with "social skill" words. The words you need to find are listed below for you. The words run vertically ↓ or horizontally → with the puzzle. Leave out the spaces when you are looking for phrases. Systematically search through each row of letters to find the words.

```
D I S A P P O I N T M E N T T E A T H J O P R Q S T
C N G Q A E R E A A D M I L B E I N G L E F T O U T
O T R S E A R E D N E G O T I A T E T I F R E I D O
N R B O D Y L A N G U A G E E G U G R S U I A O P F
T O M E I N B O P E G U A G E R D I S T B O S B O F
R D T H S E A T R R W E A D R E W A N E K L I Q W E
A U B O A C C U S A T I O N E E I K F N F O N C E R
D C B E G M Y O U R S M A C C I E P T I A C G G R I
I E L F R I E N D S H I P E I N O P O N Q W E R E N
C B E I E N G C O M O F F E R G C O M G G I V G I G
T M A N E N E C O M P L I M E N T E R S L I S T E H
I E W X I M I J K O C O M P L A I N T Q U A R S M E
O T H R N E N I M C O M A G G R O F H F E O F F A L
N T E A G S T E A M I K L O P F R I U E F R E I N P
S A C C E P T I N G N O L E R O V E M R S T U V N H
A Z C A R T E A S N G C O P T O N E O F V O I C E Q
N L C O M P R O M I S E D O G T E A R S A T E L R B
G I V I N G R E A S O N S F R E D W R I T E N S S S
```

FIND THESE WORDS AND PHRASES:

		introduce	contradictions
manners	compliment	friendship	negotiate
tone of voice	offering help	teasing	anger
listening	accepting NO	being left out	humor
body language	agreeing	complaint	disappointment
giving reasons	disagreeing	accusation	compromise

ACTIVITY B   **TV Social Skills**

1. Think of one of your favorite TV characters.
2. Write down the character's name, and the title of the show he/she appears in.
3. List three social skills the character has. Then write a sentence for each, explaining why he/she is good at the skills.
4. List three social skills the character lacks. Then write a sentence for each, explaining why he/she is not good at the skill.
5. Look at the list of social skills in your journal if you need help thinking of different skills.

IF YOU FINISH BEFORE CLASS IS OVER, FIND SOMETHING TO DO QUIETLY!

DIRECTIONS: Work on your own to complete the activities on this page. Do both
activities. You will earn extra credit points from your teacher for:
- working without asking for help
- working without distracting other students
- working and ignoring other students

ACTIVITY A   Picture/Emotion

1. Get some magazines, to cut pictures from, and five pieces of typing paper.
2. Choose 5 feelings from this list:

happy	relaxed
angry	sorry
tired	excited
scared	confused
bashful	embarrassed

3. For each feeling word, find a picture of a person in a magazine who looks like he/she
   is expressing that feeling.
4. Cut out the picture and glue it to a piece of typing paper.
5. Write the feeling word under the picture. Describe the main cue you used to decide
   how the person in the picture was feeling (e.g., TIRED - the person was yawning).
6. Do the same for the other four feeling words you chose.
7. Staple the five pieces of typing paper together to make a booklet.

ACTIVITY B   School and Social Skills

1. Get a piece of lined paper.
2. Make a list of ten situations in school when you would have to use social skills.
   Here are some examples:
   - I have to control my temper when someone makes fun of me at lunch.
   - I should compliment my friend when she gets an "A" on a test.
   - I have to listen to the teacher when he's giving a lecture.
3. Use a complete sentence when you write down each situation.
4. Make sure your name is on the paper.

**IF YOU FINISH BEFORE CLASS IS OVER, FIND SOMETHING TO DO
QUIETLY!**

DIRECTIONS: Work on your own to complete the activities on this page and the next. Do both activities. You will earn extra credit points from your teacher for:
- working without asking for help
- working without distracting other students
- working and ignoring other students

ACTIVITY A   **A Story**

1. Choose one of the topics below.
2. Write a story about the topic you choose. The story should be 1-2 pages long.
3. Write neatly and use good punctuation/capitalization. Write in complete sentences and give your story a title.

Topics: Write a story about . . .

- a teen-ager who has a hard time resisting peer pressure.
- a teen-ager who is very bashful and doesn't have conversations with people.
- a teen-ager who is really well-liked and has many friends.
- a teen-ager who does something wrong and has to apologize for it.
- a teen-ager who uses good manners.
- a teen-ager who doesn't know how to make friends.
- a teen-ager who gets accused of something she didn't do.
- a teen-ager who doesn't know how to express his anger.
- a teen-ager who is good at resisting peer pressure.
- a teen-ager who is good at listening.

ACTIVITY B   **You Are a Star**

1. Read the directions on the attached "I'm a Star" page.
2. Complete the page.

IF YOU FINISH BEFORE CLASS IS OVER, FIND SOMETHING TO DO QUIETLY!

Name:_____

You are a Star!

DIRECTIONS: You are a STAR! There are many good things about you. In each star below, write something that's good about yourself.

I'm . . .

I'm good at . . .

I'm . . .

I'm . . .

I have . . .

SSS: Social Skill Strategies (Book A)

Independent Activity #6   Name:_____

DIRECTIONS: Work on your own to complete the activities on this page and the
next. Do both activities. You will earn extra credit points from your
teacher for:
  • working without asking for help
  • working without distracting other students
  • working and ignoring other students

ACTIVITY A   **Social Word Search**

Complete the following word search puzzle, which is filled with "social skill" words.
The words you need to find are listed below for you. The words run vertically ↓ and
horizontally → within the puzzle. Leave out the spaces when you are looking for phrases.
Systematically search through each row of letters to find the words.

```
I M C O N S T R U C T I V E C R I T I C I S M P E E
N B O M E I N F O R M A T I O N A P S O A P R E E M
F I N U M M A R P E A P I J I O F R L P I M S E F O
O R S E A R S T I F O R N A L E T O P I C Y O R F T
R W E T I M E A N D P L A C E P E X S C M I N P O I
M Z Q C E R E B I F X E W L K H N I G M V V U R R O
A D U E R A W C O F O I F W V U A M R A T F I E M N
L R E Q U E S T N A S T F S S E R I I V E P R S A A
L S N T U V O R E N B R A S S E R T I V E F L S L L
A P C R M I S S I O N A I R E A T Y O C K H I U L S
N P E R M I S S I O N A L N O U J L A S J P O R A U
G W S E R F R E A M I N U T I N T E R R U P T E N P
U I N P E R R U P V L O R R E Y E C O N T A C T G P
A O P T I M I S T I C C E E O I U T H A N K Y O U O
G P T I E M I S T L C B E F E E L I N G S A S T A R
E M B A R R A S S M E N T E L L I R G Z A R T E G T
J X N O B G R L A Z P M I C H U K E Y Q F T D V E W
```

FIND THESE WORDS AND PHRASES:

			consequences
eye contact	interrupt	optimistic	embarrassment
time and place	thank you	emotional support	failure
topic	request	peer pressure	feelings
proximity	permission	assertive	informal language
formal language	opinion	constructive criticism	information

ACTIVITY B   # Analyze Someone You Know

1. Think of a person you know well (e.g., a family member, teacher, friend).
2. Write down the person's name on a piece of paper. Tell the person's role in your life (e.g., parent, teacher, friend, brother, sister).
3. List three social skills the person is good at. Then write a sentence for each, explaining why he/she is good at that skill.
4. List three social skills you think the person lacks. Then write a sentence for each, explaining why he/she isn't good at that skill.
5. Be honest! The person you choose will not see your list.
6. Look at the list of social skills in your journal if you need help thinking of different skills.

IF YOU FINISH BEFORE CLASS IS OVER, FIND SOMETHING TO DO QUIETLY!

DIRECTIONS: Work on your own to complete the activities on this page. Do both activities. You will earn extra credit points from your teacher for:
- working without asking for help
- working without distracting other students
- working and ignoring other students

ACTIVITY A   **How Great I Am . . .**

1. Get a lined piece of paper.
2. Write a paragraph about all of your good qualities. Tell all of the nice things you can think of about yourself.
3. Your paragraph should be at least 7-8 sentences long.
4. Make sure your name is on your paper.

ACTIVITY B   **My Collage**

1. Get a large piece of construction paper.
2. Get magazines and newspapers you can cut from.
3. Make a collage on construction paper that represents YOU. Find pictures/words that show things you like to do. Find pictures/words that represent what your personality is like. You can put anything on the collage that is about you.
4. If you would like, you can draw the pictures rather than cutting them from a magazine.
5. Make sure your name is somewhere on the front of the collage.

IF YOU FINISH BEFORE CLASS IS OVER, FIND SOMETHING TO DO QUIETLY!

SSS: Social Skill Strategies (Book A)

DIRECTIONS: Work on your own to complete the activities on this page. Do both activities. You will earn extra credit points from your teacher for:
- working without asking for help
- working without distracting other students
- working and ignoring other students

ACTIVITY A **The People You Know**

Write the names of seven people you know in the left hand column of the table below. Think of a compliment you could give to each person about a social skill they are good at. Write the compliments in the column on the right. An example has been provided. Look at your list of social skills in your journal if you need ideas.

EXAMPLE

NAME	COMPLIMENT
➡ *Bill (my dad)*	*Dad, you are really good at listening.*

ACTIVITY B **Hand It To Yourself**

1. Draw an outline of each of your hands on a piece of typing paper.
2. Write different social skills you are good at, inside each finger on the left hand. (There will be five skills in all.)
3. Write different social skills you need to improve on, inside each finger on the right hand. (There will be five skills in all.)

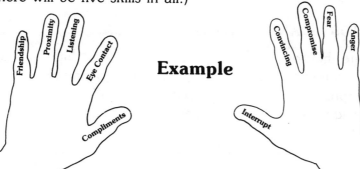

Example

IF YOU FINISH BEFORE CLASS IS OVER, FIND SOMETHING TO DO QUIETLY!

295   SSS: Social Skill Strategies (Book A)

DIRECTIONS: Work on your own to complete the activities on this page and the next. Do both activities. You will earn extra credit points from your teacher for:
- working without asking for help
- working without distracting other students
- working and ignoring other students

ACTIVITY A   # Where Are the Social Words?

Complete the following word search puzzle, which is filled with "social skill" words. The words you need to find are listed below for you. The words run vertically ↓ and horizontally→within the puzzle. Leave out the spaces when you are looking for phrases. Systematically search through each row of letters to find the words.

```
O V T X U S U R F P W U X A  A G A E C C O H C T S A
A G E T T I N G T O T H E P O I N T V O L U M E X A
C O N V I N C E C R S L Y O N U P L A N N I N G A F
A O A D I Y Q F O F V I C L T I C R Q V E E A L R F
P D K M A I H O V R A G B O K I O G H E L P D L B E
P I F N C G E I Q I A H L G N G L D O R B J F E M C
R M J E F P H O N E S T Y I U N D E R S T A N D N T
E P A K J B F C E N V M J Z K O G P E A H G L P C I
C R L D M H I O A D V I C E N R G R A T I T U D E O
I E K F E A R L P L H G D O F I X J O I N I N G I N
A S E G U M E N K Y O L P B Q N R J Q O T F R Q P L
T S B I L D C A G Q J I M R H G A E I N M C R O D I
I I O S I N T R O D U C E S F C O M P L I M E N T O
O O I R Q K B E A T I N G A R O U N D T H E B U S H
N N S B O P I E X P R E S S I N G F E E L I N G S N
```

FIND THESE WORDS AND PHRASES:

volume	getting to the point	planning	ignoring	appreciation
fear	beating around the bush	compliment	joining in	gratitude
help	good impression	introduce	affection	convince
advice	expressing feelings	apologize	understand	honesty
friendly	conversation			

ACTIVITY B # Design a Social Skill Poster

1. Pick one social skill listed in your journal to create a poster.
2. Write the name of the skill at the top of a piece of construction paper.
3. Create your poster by doing one or more of the following:
   • Draw a person who is using the skill correctly.
   • Draw a person who is using the skill incorrectly.
   • Write the skill steps or important tips for the skill.
   • Find pictures from magazines of people who are using the skill.
   • Draw a cartoon about the skill.
4. Put your name on the back of the poster when it is complete.

IF YOU FINISH BEFORE CLASS IS OVER, FIND SOMETHING TO DO QUIETLY!

Independent Activity #10   Name:_____

DIRECTIONS: Work on your own to complete the activities on this page. Do both
activities. You will earn extra credit points from your teacher for:
- working without asking for help
- working without distracting other students
- working and ignoring other students

ACTIVITY A   Write a Story About . . .

1. Choose one of the topics below.
2. Write a story about the topic you choose. The story should be 1-2 pages long.
3. Write neatly and use good punctuation/capitalization. Write in complete sentences
   and give your story a title.

   Topics: Write a story about . . .
   - a teen-ager who has a difficult time looking at people while talking.
   - a teen-ager who always seems to choose a bad time and place to talk.
   - a teen-ager who has a problem with switching topics.
   - a teen-ager who is good at offering help to others.
   - a teen-ager who is good at introducing himself to new people.
   - a teen-ager who has a problem because he holds all his feelings inside.
   - a teen-ager who is a poor sport when he loses.
   - a teen-ager who gives advice appropriately.
   - a teen-ager who has a habit of spreading rumors.
   - a teen-ager who remembers to think about the consequences of his actions.

ACTIVITY B   Facial Expressions

Each of these face outlines has a feeling word written below it. Draw the mouth, eyes,
eyebrows, nose, and forehead inside each outline, so that the facial expression represents
the feeling word. If you need help, look through books and magazines to find people
who look like they have the feelings listed below.

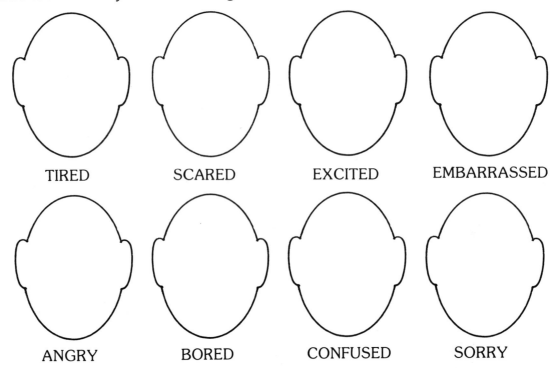

| TIRED | SCARED | EXCITED | EMBARRASSED |
| ANGRY | BORED | CONFUSED | SORRY |

SSS: Social Skill Strategies (Book A)

Pair Practice Record

Name:_____

Skills to Practice

_____ (Skill)	**Date**												
	Initials												
_____ (Skill)	**Date**												
	Initials												
_____ (Skill)	**Date**												
	Initials												
_____ (Skill)	**Date**												
	Initials												

SSS: SOCIAL SKILL STRATEGIES (Book A)

QUESTION REVIEW

A-1. EYE CONTACT

1. What does *having good eye contact* mean? (Looking at the person you are talking to or listening to)

2. What is the tip to remember for having good eye contact? (Look at the person you are talking to or listening to, most of the time.)

3. When Alex gave his book report, he looked at either his notes, or at the floor. What social skill does Alex need to improve on? (Eye contact)

4. Complete this sentence: When you have good eye contact, you let the person you are talking to know that . . .

5. Tell about a time when it would be difficult to have good eye contact.

6. What might a person think about you if you do not have good eye contact?

A-2. MANNERS

1. What does *having good manners* mean? (Speaking and acting politely)

2. Tell an important tip to remember about using good manners when speaking. (Use words such as *excuse me*, *please*, and *thank you*.)

3. When Beth asked her mom for some money, she did not say *please*. After her mom gave her some, she did not say *thank you*. What social skill does Beth need to improve on? (Manners)

4. Why is it important to have good manners in the way you speak and act?

5. Name three good table manners.

6. Complete the following sentence: It is very important to have good manners when you . . .

A-3. VOLUME

1. Define the social skill of volume. (Speaking in a voice that can be heard easily, neither too loudly nor too softly)

2. Explain the important tip to remember about speaking with a good volume. (Ask yourself whether you are in a situation where you should talk with a normal volume, a soft volume, or a loud volume.)

3. Craig is a waiter at a restaurant. When he takes people's orders, they say things like, "What? I can't hear you." and "What did you say?" What social skill does Craig need to improve on? (Volume)

4. Tell about a situation when you would need to talk more loudly than normal.

5. Tell about a time when you would need to talk more softly than normal when you are out in the community.

6. Tell a reason why someone may have a habit of talking too softly.

A-4. TIME AND PLACE

1. Define the social skill of time and place. (Choosing a good time to talk to a person, and the best location to talk to that person)

2. Tell about the important tip to remember for the social skill of time and place. (Before you begin a conversation, ask yourself: Is this the best time and is this the right place?)

3. Denise asked her boss if she could have the weekend off, while her boss was busy helping a customer. Her boss got irritated. What social skill should Denise work on improving? (Choosing the right time and place)

4. Complete this sentence: The best time and place to talk to your friends during school is . . .

5. Tell what may happen if you ask someone to do a favor for you but you ask them at a bad time.

6. Tell one good time and place and one bad time and place to ask your mom or dad for some money.

A-5. TONE OF VOICE

1. Define the social skill of tone of voice. (Showing your feelings by the way your voice sounds)

2. Tell the important tip to remember about tone of voice. (How you say something is just as important as what you say.)

3. When Ed found out that his friend's bike was stolen, he said, "I'm sorry that happened," in a happy voice. What social skill does Ed need to work on improving? (Tone of voice)

4. Tell three words that can describe a person's tone of voice.

5. Complete this sentence: If you apologize for doing something wrong, but use a "snotty" tone of voice, then . . .

6. Think of a time when it would be important to use a sincere tone of voice.

A-6. GETTING TO THE POINT

1. What does *getting to the point* mean? (Talking about the main reason for your conversation, without delay)

2. Tell the important tip to remember for getting to the point. (Do not put off or delay the main reason for your conversation. Do not "beat around the bush.")

3. Fran called a boy she liked, to see if he wanted to go to a movie. She said, "I bet you want to know why I called. Well, I was wondering, you see, I want to know, well, it's okay if you say no . . ." What social skill does Fran need to work on improving? (Getting to the point)

4. Tell a situation when it would be difficult to get straight to the point in a conversation.

5. Explain why someone might get impatient if you "beat around the bush."

6. Tell about a situation when you would not want to blurt something out right away, but instead you would want to bring it up gradually.

A-7. STAYING ON TOPIC AND SWITCHING TOPICS

1. Define the social skill of staying on topic and switching topics. (Not changing to a different topic when you are talking to someone, unless you warn your listener of the topic shift first)

2. Tell the important tip to remember for staying on topic and the important tip to remember for switching topics. (Staying on topic - What you say should deal with the main topic of the conversation. Switching topics - Let the listener know in advance that you are going to talk about a different topic.)

3. Gilda was talking to her friends. She was confusing because she talked about her weekend, her favorite teacher, and her new bike, without warning her listeners that she was going to talk about something different. What social skill does Gilda need to improve on? (Staying on topic/switching topics)

4. Tell two different things you can say to warn your listener that you are about to switch topics.

5. Explain why it is bad to switch topics without giving advance warning.

6. Make a comment that would be on the topic of education.

A-8. LISTENING

1. Define "good" listening. (Giving your full attention to a speaker so you can understand the meaning of the message)

2. Name six ways to be a good listener. (1. Give the speaker good eye contact. 2. Lean forward slightly to show interest. 3. Nod your head and give the speaker feedback to show you understand. 4. Ask questions that deal with the speaker's topic. 5. Give the speaker your full attention. 6. Let the speaker finish before you talk.)

3. Hal was thinking about his girlfriend when his teacher was giving directions for the assignment. He got an "F" on his assignment because he didn't follow the directions. What social skill does Hal need to improve on? (Listening)

4. Which of the following communication skills should people devote the most time to - speaking, reading, listening, or writing? (Listening)

5. Think of a situation at home, at school, and in the community when it would be important to be a good listener.

6. Tell a consequence of not being a good listener with your friends.

A-9. STARTING, MAINTAINING, AND ENDING A CONVERSATION

1. Define the social skill of starting and ending a conversation. (Knowing how to begin and how to end in an appropriate way when you are talking to someone)

2. Tell the important tips to remember for beginning and ending a conversation. (Begin with a greeting, a name, and small talk. End with a farewell.)

3. Janet walked up to a salesclerk and asked, "How do I get to the theater?" After the salesclerk finished giving directions, Janet left without saying good-bye. Which social skill should Janet improve on? (Starting and ending a conversation.)

4. Define small talk and tell *why* it is important when beginning a conversation. (Light/casual talk or chitchat; it helps people ease into a conversation)

5. Think of a comment you can make to let your listener know you need to end your conversation.

6. Tell a word that can be used as a greeting and a word that can be used as a farewell.

A-10. PROXIMITY

1. Define *proximity*. (The distance between you and another person)

2. Tell the important tip to remember about promixity. (Usually, you stand an arm's length away from someone.)

3. When Ken talks to people, he stands so close that it makes them feel uncomfortable. What social skill does Ken need to work on? (Proximity)

4. How might a person feel if you stand too close during a conversation?

5. How might a person feel if you stand too far away during a conversation?

6. Complete the following sentence: It is important to stand about an arm's length away when talking to someone because . . .

A-11. BODY LANGUAGE

1. Define *body language*. (Emotions/feelings that are expressed with the body)

2. Tell the important tip to remember about other people's body language. (Look for clues about how another person is feeling by paying attention to his/her body language.)

3. Lanore's best friend, Ann, was angry. The expression on Ann's face and her body posture showed her anger. Lanore didn't even recognize that Ann was angry. What social skill does Lanore need to work on improving? (Body language)

4. Tell the important tip to remember about your own body language. (Be certain to think about your body language so that it expresses the emotions/feelings that you want it to.)

5. List three different body parts that can express feelings. Describe how they would look for sorrow and for excitement.

6. What would you think if a person said she was fine, but her body language looked very sad?

A-12. MAKING A GOOD IMPRESSION

1. What does *making a good impression* mean? (Causing other people to think favorably about you)

2. List the three important tips to remember for making a good impression. (You make a good impression by what you say, what you do, and how you look.)

3. When Marty met his girlfriend's parents for the first time, he didn't put on clean clothes. He wasn't very careful about the way he acted or the things he said. Her parents didn't think very favorably of him. What social skill does Marty need to improve on? (Making a good impression)

4. Name a situation when it would be important to make a good impression.

5. You want to make a good impression with your teacher the first day of class. List three things you could do or say.

6. Sometimes, your first impression of a person you just met can be incorrect. Explain why.

A-13. FORMAL/INFORMAL LANGUAGE

1. Define *formal* and *informal language.* (Formal - Speaking in a more "traditional" way when you are with people in respected positions; Informal - Speaking in a "relaxed" way when you are with peers, or adults that you feel close to)

2. Describe the important tips to remember for using formal and informal language. (Formal - Use the longer forms of words. Informal - Use the shorter forms of words and slang.)

3. When Natalie met the governor, she said, "Hey! Nice to meet ya. I'm Natalie. What's up?" What social skill does Natalie need to work on improving? (Formal/informal language)

4. List one person you should use formal language with, and one person you should use informal language with.

5. Give an example of something you could say that would be formal.

6. Tell why it is inappropriate to use formal language with your friends.

A-14. GIVING REASONS

1. Tell what *giving reasons* means. (Giving information that will help someone understand what you want, why you did something, or why you believe something)

2. Describe the important tips to remember for giving reasons. (Make certain the reasons you give are relevant and specific.)

3. When Coach Brandt asked Olly why he wasn't at swim practice yesterday, Olly said, "Because my sister is on the track team." What social skill does Olly need to improve on? (Giving reasons)

4. Complete the following sentence: Giving relevant and specific reasons helps when . . .

5. Give three good reasons why it is important to take notes in class.

6. Describe a situation when you may need to give a reason.

A-15. PLANNING WHAT TO SAY

1. Define the social skill of planning what to say. (Thinking about what you will say before you say it)

2. Name two ways you can plan what to say. (Think about what to say in your head, or write down what you want to say.)

3. Polly raised her hand in class to answer a question. When the teacher called on her, Polly started to think about what she wanted to say. What social skill does Polly need to work on improving? (Planning what to say)

4. Tell what might happen if you don't think about what you want to say before you have an interview for a job.

5. Think of a time when it would be important to plan what to say in advance.

6. Complete the following sentence: When you are going to have an important conversation, it is a good idea to plan what you want to say so that . . .

A-16. INTERRUPTING

1. Define *interrupting*. (Breaking into a conversation that two or more people are having, to deliver a message or make a comment)

2. List the skill steps for interrupting in a good way. (1. Get the person's attention. 2. Apologize for interrupting, 3. Give the reasons for interrupting.)

3. Quinton's mom was talking to her secretary. Quinton broke into the conversation and asked, "What are we going to have for supper?" What social skill does Quinton need to improve? (Interrupting)

4. Think of a situation when it *would* be appropriate to interrupt and a situation when it *would not* be appropriate to interrupt.

5. Explain how the word GAG can help you remember the skill steps for interrupting.

6. True or False? A person should learn *never* to interrupt two people who are having a conversation. (False)

A-17. GIVING A COMPLIMENT

1. Tell what *giving a compliment* means. (Saying something positive about another person)

2. Explain the important tip to remember about giving a compliment. (Use a sincere tone of voice when giving a compliment, so it is not mistaken as sarcasm.)

3. Roxanne never makes positive comments about other people. What social skill does she need to improve on? (Giving a compliment)

4. Describe the difference between an "inside" compliment, and an "outside" compliment.

5. Give an example of an "outside" compliment that you could give to your teacher.

6. Say an "inside" compliment that you could give to your friend.

A-18. ACCEPTING A COMPLIMENT

1. What does *accepting a compliment* mean? (Accepting a positive comment that someone makes about you or one of your accomplishments)

2. Tell the important tip to remember for accepting a compliment. (Say *thank you.*)

3. Scott's boss said to him, "I really like the way you dress for work. You always look so clean and professional." Scott said "Really? I think I look terrible!" What social skill does Scott need to improve? (Accepting a compliment)

4. Explain why it might be difficult for someone to say *thank you* after receiving a compliment.

5. Give an example of a good way and a bad way to accept the following compliment: "You really look good in this picture."

6. True or false? If you just say *thank you* when someone compliments you, it means you are stuck-up. (False)

A-19. SAYING *THANK YOU*

1. Tell what *saying thank you* means. (Expressing your appreciation to someone who has done something nice)

2. List the three skill steps for saying *thank you*. (1. Decide if the person has done something nice. 2. Thank the person. 3. Tell what you are thanking the person for.)

3. Tami had a costume party to go to. Her dad made a costume for her to wear. She never expressed her appreciation. What social skill should Tami improve on? (Saying *thank you*)

4. List three things that you appreciate and would want to say *thank you* for.

5. Complete the following sentence: If you don't say *thank you*, then . . .

6. Describe a situation when you would want to thank your brother/sister.

A-20. INTRODUCING YOURSELF

1. Define the social skill of introducing yourself. (Telling someone your name when you meet for the first time)

2. Give the three skill steps for introducing yourself. (1. Walk up to the person. 2. Greet the person and say your name. 3. Make small talk.)

3. When Valerie met Tom for the first time, she forgot to tell him what her name was. What social skill does Valerie need to improve on? (Introducing yourself)

4. Give an example of how you could introduce yourself using formal language.

5. What can you do if you introduce yourself to someone and the person doesn't introduce himself back?

6. Think of a time when you may need to introduce yourself when you are out in the community.

A-21. INTRODUCING TWO PEOPLE TO EACH OTHER

1. Tell what *introducing two people to each other* means. (Helping two people who do not know each other to learn each other's name)

2. Describe the three skill steps for introducing two people to each other. (1. Decide if the introduction should be formal or informal. 2. Make the introduction two-way. 3. Say something that will help the people get a conversation started.)

3. William and his sister Beth were shopping at the mall. A friend of William's, from school, stopped to talk to him. Beth did not know William's friend. William did not do anything to help them learn each other's name. What social skill does William need to improve on? (Introducing two people to each other)

4. Tell what you would say to introduce your father to Mr. Luedke, your English teacher. (Use all three skill steps.)

5. Tell what you would say to introduce your friend Aldo to another friend named Carol. (Use all three skill steps.)

6. Why is it important to say something that will help to get a conversation going when you introduce two people to each other?

A-22. MAKING A REQUEST

1. What does *making a request* mean? (Asking someone to do something)

2. Tell the important tip to remember about making a request. (Ask in a polite way, instead of telling or demanding what you want.)

3. Abby wanted a sharper pair of scissors. She found her teacher and said, "I can't cut with these. You gotta give me a better pair of scissors!" What social skill does Abby need to improve on? (Making a request)

4. Change the following demand into a polite request: "You have to sign this sheet before I leave."

5. Explain why it is important to choose a good time and place when you make a request.

6. True or false? If you make a request in a polite way and you choose a good time and place to make it, you will always get what you want. (False)

A-23. OFFERING HELP

1. Define the social skill of offering help. (Offering your assistance to someone who is in need)

2. Explain the important tip to remember about offering help. (Ask first instead of just taking over.)

3. Ben is a good cook. He notices that his younger brother is making cookies and is having some trouble. Ben says, "Here, let me do that for you." What social skill does Ben need to improve on? (Offering help)

4. Think of a situation when you may want to offer help to someone at school.

5. Give an example of how to ask if someone wants your help.

6. Complete this sentence: If you want to help someone . . .

A-24. ASKING FOR HELP

1. Tell what *asking for help* means. (Letting someone know you are having difficulties and asking that person for assistance)

2. List the four skill steps for asking for help. (1. Try to do it on your own first. 2. Ask for help. 3. Pay attention when the person helps you. 4. Thank the person for helping you.)

3. Conney was having trouble with her assignment. She did not seek any assistance because she didn't want to admit that she didn't understand something. What social skill should Conney improve? (Asking for help)

4. Complete the following sentence: It is not good to ask for help too much and not try anything on your own first, because . . .

5. Why is it important to pay attention when you ask for help and get it?

6. Think of a time when you would ask for help *without* trying it on your own first.

A-25. ASKING PERMISSION

1. Tell what *asking permission* means. (Asking to be allowed to participate in a desired activity)

2. Tell the three skill steps for asking permission. (1. Decide if it is necessary to ask permission to do what you want to do. 2. Decide whom you should ask for permission. 3. Choose a good time and place to ask.)

3. Duane works at a car wash. He decided to go skiing over the weekend, so he didn't show up for work. What social skill does Duane need to work on improving? (Asking permission)

4. Name three authority figures you may need to ask for permission.

5. Give an example of a time when you would need to ask permission at home.

6. If you get impulsive when told NO after asking for permission, the person may be more likely to say NO the next time you ask too. Why?

A-26. ACCEPTING *NO*

1. Define the social skill of accepting NO. (Going along with the decision in a mature way, when someone says NO to something you want)

2. Tell the five skill steps for accepting NO. (1. Decide if the NO is coming from an authority figure. 2. Stay calm. 3. Think about the consequences of not following the decision. 4. Respond by saying "O.K." or don't say anything at all. 5. Follow the authority's decision.)

3. When Elaine is told that she can't do something she wants to do, she either makes faces, has a temper tantrum, talks back, or starts to beg. What social skill does Elaine need to work on improving? (Accepting NO)

4. Tell the acrostic (funny sentence) you learned to help remember the skill steps of accepting NO and explain how it works. (All Cops Can Run Fast.)

5. Tell three things which may help you to stay calm when someone says NO.

6. True or false? Even your parents and teachers have authority figures from whom they must accept NO. (True).

A-27. MAKING AN APOLOGY

1. Tell what *making an apology* means. (Saying you are sorry)

2. Describe the four skill steps for making an apology. (1. Choose a good time and place to apologize. 2. Say you are sorry in a sincere way. 3. Tell what you are sorry about. 4. Offer a solution, if necessary.)

3. When Fernando does something wrong or makes a mistake, he has a difficult time telling someone that he regrets what he has done. What social skill should Fernando improve on? (Making an apology)

4. Explain why a person may be the type who apologizes too much and says he is sorry even when he hasn't done anything wrong.

5. Explain what a fake apology is, and why someone might make one.

6. Complete the following sentence: Everyone needs to make an apology now and then because . . .

A-28. STATING AN OPINION

1. What does *stating an opinion* mean? (Telling what you believe, in a way that recognizes that someone else may believe differently)

2. Tell the important tip to remember for stating an opinion. (When you state an opinion, begin with a phrase such as, "In my opinion . . ." "Personally, I think . . ." or "I feel that . . . .")

3. Gail was shopping with her friend David. David picked out a shirt to try on that Gail didn't like. Gail said, "Everyone knows that style is ugly." What social skill does Gail need to improve on? (Stating an opinion)

4. Explain the difference between a fact and an opinion.

5. State your opinion about which fast food restaurant has the best French fries. (Remember to begin with an opinion phrase.)

6. Complete the following sentence: It is bad to try to pass off your opinion as a fact because . . .

A-29. AGREEING/DISAGREEING

1. Tell what *agreeing* and *disagreeing* means. (Agreeing - Having the same opinion as another person; Disagreeing - Having a different opinion than someone else)

2. Describe the five skill steps for agreeing/disagreeing. (1. Listen carefully to the other person's idea or opinion. 2. Decide if you agree or disagree. 3. Use a nice tone of voice. 4. Tell the person you agree or disagree. 5. Explain your reason.)

3. Hal's friend said, "I love to read. How about you?" Hal said, "Don't be stupid! I think reading is a waste of time." What social skill does Hal need to improve on? (Agreeing/Disagreeing)

4. Complete the following sentence: When you disagree with someone, you should not put down the other person or use an angry tone because . . .

5. What could you say to let someone know you agree with him/her?

6. Tell one thing parents and teen-agers typically disagree about and why.

A-30. CONVINCING OTHERS

1. Define the social skill of convincing others. (Trying to persuade someone to believe as you do)

2. Tell the four skill steps for convincing others. (1. Plan what you are going to say. 2. Choose a good time and place. 3. Give good reasons. 4. Stay calm when talking to the person.)

3. Janine asked her parents to increase her allowance. They said, "If you can persuade us, we will think about it." Janine said, "I want more allowance because I just do." What social skill does Janine need to work on improving? (Convincing others)

4. Give an example of a time when you may need to try and convince your teacher of something.

5. Tell three things you could tell an interviewer to help convince that person to hire you.

6. Tell something advertisers do to try and convince you to buy their product.

A-31. GIVING INFORMATION

1. What does *giving information* mean? (Providing knowledge about something)

2. List the five tips to remember for giving information. (1. Give the information in order. 2. Use specific names and words. 3. Give enough information to be understood. 4. Include only relevant information. 5. Check with your listener to see if you're being understood.)

3. Keith was a witness to a crime. He was asked to give the facts about what he saw to the police. He told his story out of order, and used general words that were not very specific. What social skill does Keith need to improve on? (Giving information)

4. Think of a time when you may need to give information to your boss.

5. Complete the following sentence: When you give information to someone, it is important to use specific words and names so that . . .

6. What can you say to check with your listener to see if he understands you?

A-32. DEALING WITH CONTRADICTIONS

1. Tell what it means when someone gives two contradictory messages. (Giving messages that are unclear because they are opposite in meaning)

2. Tell the two skill steps for dealing with a contradiction. (1. Point out the contradiction using a good tone. 2. Ask what was really meant.)

3. First, Linda's teacher said the assignment was due on Wednesday and then the teacher said it was due on Thursday. Linda didn't ask which day the teacher really meant. What social skill does Linda need to improve on? (Dealing with contradictions)

4. Tell the difference between a one-person and a two-person contradiction.

5. Give an example of two contradictory messages.

6. Why is it important to remain calm when you point out a contradiction?

A-33. BEING HONEST

1. Tell what *being honest* means. (Telling the truth)

2. Tell the important tip to remember about being honest. (Being honest is important if you want people to trust you.)

3. Mike skipped school, but didn't want to admit to his mom what he had done. He told her he was at school all day. What social skill does Mike need to improve on? (Being honest)

4. What does *losing your credibility* mean?

5. Give two reasons why you think a person lies.

6. True or false? Usually, when you tell the truth, you get in less trouble than if you lie about something and get caught. (True)

A-34. BEING OPTIMISTIC

1. Tell what it means to be optimistic. (Being a positive person)

2. Tell the two important tips to remember about being optimistic. (Expect good things to happen in life and look for the positive side of things.)

3. Nancy decided not to go skiing because she thought it would be too cold and she would probably have a bad time. What social skill should Nancy improve on? (Being optimistic)

4. Tell a word that means the opposite of being optimistic.

5. Give an example of a situation that has a good and a bad side to it.

6. Tell why it is difficult to spend a lot of time with a pessimistic person.

┌─────────────────────────────────────┐
│ **POSITIVE COMMENTS**   │
│   │
│ • **I am a good person.**   │
│   │
│ • **I am a friendly person.**   │
│   │
│ • **When I use my social skills,** │
│   **I get along better with people.** │
└─────────────────────────────────────┘

Personal Page

Date:_____

Today's class was about the social skill of_____

_____

I will be able to use what I learned today during_____

_____

_____

Today, class was _____

_____

_____

━━━

Date:_____

Today's class was about the social skill of_____

_____

I will be able to use what I learned today during_____

_____

Today, class was _____

_____

_____

ATTENDANCE AND DAILY PARTICIPATION POINTS

Date:_____

Students' Names	Attendance (50%)	60%	70%	80%	90%	100%	Total Participation

Comments:

SSS: SOCIAL SKILL STRATEGIES (Book A)

Role Play Critique Sheet

Name of person doing role play: _____

Name of person completing this sheet: _____

---

1. List two positive things you saw in this role play situation.

   •

   •

2. Did the person use all the skill steps (or tips) correctly?   YES   NO
   If not, what skill steps did the person forget to do or have problems with?

3. What did the partner do to help in the role play situation?

4. Could this role play situation really happen?   YES   NO
   Explain your answer.

SSS: Social Skill Strategies (Book A)

Student Evaluation Form

Name of Social Skill Unit: _____

	Strongly Agree	Agree	Undecided	Disagree	Strongly Disagree
I understand the skill steps of this social skill.	1	2	3	4	5
It was helpful to role play in class.	1	2	3	4	5
I practiced this social skill enough in class.	1	2	3	4	5
The activity pages were helpful.	1	2	3	4	5
Reading the scripts helped me to understand the skill better.	1	2	3	4	5
The filmstrips/videos (if any) were helpful.	1	2	3	4	5
I know when I should use this social skill.	1	2	3	4	5
I will be able to use this skill correctly outside of class.	1	2	3	4	5
This unit was interesting.	1	2	3	4	5

I liked this unit because _____

_____

_____

The thing I liked least about this unit was_____

_____

If I were the teacher, I would include a section in this unit about _____

_____

_____

_____

An interesting thing for students to do in this unit would be_____

_____

_____

Student Name: *John D.*

Date

A = Acceptable
U = Unacceptable
NA = Not Applicable

	Reading (M-F)	Math (M-F)	History (M-F)	English (M-F)	Social Skills (T-Th)	Physical Education (M-F)	Science (M-W-F)	Drafting (M-S)	At home		
Goal #1: Used a tone of voice appropriate to the situation (was not sarcastic).	A U	A U	A U	A U	A U	A U	A U	A U	A U		
Goal #2: Made a good impression based on his actions and appearance.	A U NA	A U NA	A U NA	A U NA	A U NA	A U NA	A U NA	A U NA	A U NA		
Goal #3: Remembered to ask/request instead of demand/tell when he wanted something.	A U NA	A U NA	A U NA	A U NA	A U NA	A U NA	A U NA	A U NA	A U NA		
SIGNATURE & COMMENTS:											
NEXT ASSIGNMENT:											
WHEN DUE:											

PARENT/GUARDIAN SIGNATURE:

SSS: SOCIAL SKILL STRATEGIES (Book A)

COOPERATIVE LEARNING ASPECTS

The following eighteen aspects should be considered when planning a cooperative learning lesson (Johnson and Johnson, 1984). Cooperative learning is discussed in Chapter One, pages 4-5 and Chapter Two, page 24.

THE TEACHER'S ROLE IN COOPERATION

Objectives

Specifying Academic and Collaborative Objectives. These need to be specified before the lesson begins.

Decisions

Deciding on the Size of the Group. Once the objectives are clear, the teacher must decide which size of learning group is optimal. Cooperative learning groups tend to range in size from two to six.

Assigning Students to Groups. Questions asked include the following: Homogeneous or heterogeneous in ability? Non-task-oriented and task-oriented students together or separated? Should students select the group or teacher assign? How long should groups stay together?

Arranging the Room. This will be a symbolic message of what is appropriate behavior, and can facilitate the learning groups within the classroom. Members should sit in a circle and be close enough to communicate without disrupting the other learning groups.

Planning Materials. Teachers may wish to distribute materials in carefully planned ways to communicate that the assignment is to be a joint effort.

Assigning Roles. Cooperative interdependence may also be arranged through the assignment of complementary and interconnected roles to group members.

Task, Goal Structure, Learning Activity

Explaining the Academic Task. Several aspects should be considered: Setting the task so that students are clear about assignment; explaining the objectives of the lesson and relating the concepts; defining relevant concepts, explaining procedures, and giving examples; and asking specific questions to check students' understanding of the assignment.

Structuring Positive Goal Interdependence. Communicate to students that they have a group goal and must work collaboratively.

Structuring Individual Accountability. A learning group is not truly cooperative if individual members let others do all the work. In order to ensure that all members learn and that groups know which members to provide with encouragement and help, teachers will need to assess frequently the level of performance of each group member.

Cooperative Learning Aspects (Con't)

Structuring Intergroup Cooperation. Positive outcomes found within a cooperative learning group can be extended throughout a whole class by structuring intergroup cooperation other than through tournament format.

Explaining Criteria for Success. Evaluation within cooperatively structured lessons needs to be based on criteria established for acceptable work. At the beginning of the lesson, teachers should clearly explain the criteria by which the students' work will be evaluated.

Specifying Desired Behaviors. Teachers need to define *cooperation* operationally by specifying the behaviors that are appropriate and desirable within the learning groups.

Monitoring and Intervening

Monitoring Students' Behavior. Much of the teacher's time after the groups start working should be spent in observing group members in order to see what problems they are having in completing the assignment and in working collaboratively.

Providing Task Assistance. In monitoring the groups as they work, teachers will wish to clarify instructions, review important procedures and strategies for completing the assignment, answer questions, and teach task skills as necessary.

Intervening to Teach Collaborative Skills. While monitoring the learning groups, teachers sometimes find students without the necessary collaborative skills and groups with problems in collaborating. In these cases, the teacher may intervene to suggest more effective procedures for working together and more effective behaviors for students to engage in.

Providing Closure to the Lesson. To reinforce student learning, teachers may wish to summarize the major points in the lesson, ask students to recall ideas or give samples, and answer any final questions they may have.

Evaluating and Processing

Evaluating the Quality and Quantity of Students' Learning. Whatever the product of the lesson, student learning needs to be evaluated by a criteria-referenced system. Group members should also receive feedback on how effectively they collaborated.

Assessing How Well the Group Functioned. Even if class time is limited, some time should be spent talking about how well the groups functioned today, what things were done well, and what things could be improved.

Reprinted with permission